Making the Cut

BY

CYNTHIA JOHNSON MACKAY, MD

Improved Edition – 2nd Print

TABLE OF CONTENTS

Part Three: Looking Inward: Physician, Heal Thyself

Development Editor: Dr Ian Hough, PhD

Front cover image by Artist: Amanda J Waldron (Pandasart Studio)

Editor-in-Chief: Andrew Waldron

Proofreader: Amanda J Waldron

2nd printing edition 2024

Publisher

Authorit Services Ltd.

Scotland, UK

PROLOGUE

I have dedicated my life to healing sick eyes. After retiring from practice, I threw myself into a crusade to tell the truth about LASIK. financing, and co-authoring a book, "The Unsightly Truth of Laser Vision Correction: LASIK Makes Healthy Eyes Sick" written with Dr Morris Waxler (former head of the FDA committee that approved LASIK), Paula Cofer (one of millions of LASIK-damaged patients) and Ed Boshnick (optometrist), and a movie, "Broken Eyes". The book is now published, and the movie was released, in April 2024.

Dr Cynthia J MacKay, MD

I was born on September 20, 1942. My parents, Helena Edey Johnson, and Francis Edgar Johnson Jr., named me Cynthia Noel Johnson.

When I was nine years old, in 1951, I was walking down Holland Road in Far Hills, New Jersey with my German nurse, my seven-year-old sister Lynn, and my three-year-old brother Frank, when I saw a dead turtle lying on the side of the road. It had been struck by a car, and its shell was split wide open.

I could not believe what was packed inside that small body—foamy pink sacs, gleaming yellow loops, and a glistening purple bag. The colors were so vivid I can see them today. Everybody else moved away fast. Not I. I could have looked at that turtle for da. I always wondered how bodies worked. How do we move? Breathe? Think? There, before my eyes, was the answer—the secret to life itself.

I wanted to learn the name of everything inside that turtle, how it works, and how it can be fixed if it gets broken. I didn't realize it then, but after that day I wanted to be a surgeon when I grew up.

I didn't think seriously about becoming a surgeon until I was in my late twenties, because I was focused on marrying the perfect man and having two perfect children. When I finally turned my attention to medical school, several questions jumped into my mind.

Did I have the guts to cut into a human body? What skills do surgeons need? How would I control my fear when I was in the Operating Room?

Would I face extra challenges because I am a woman? Would my privileged childhood help me or hold me back?

I tried to find a book that would answer my questions. This book does not exist. So, I wrote it. I hope the reader will learn how surgeons do what they do, what type of person thrives as a surgeon, what life was like as a woman in a man's world in the 1970s, 80s, and 90s, how a woman can succeed despite overwhelming odds, and how a mother can combine family life with a demanding profession.

PART ONE: THE MAKING OF A SURGEON

The first part of this book describes the pluses and minuses of a childhood that had a remarkable amount of privilege, but almost no parental attention. I dreamed of becoming a surgeon, but this career did not seem possible for a girl who grew up in the 1940s and 50s and was raised in Far Hills, New Jersey. I was a driven perfectionist who had no friends, trying to win the approval of my parents. This relentless perfectionism paid off when Ito got into the operating room.

CHAPTER ONE
Johnsons Get the Job Done

My first memory is my nurse putting me into my crib for a nap. I remember scraps of sunlight flickering through the trees outside and dappling the floor. I am four years old. I do not go to sleep. I start to pick off my hated ivy-covered wallpaper, scrap by scrap. I work diligently—you might say obsessively. I am determined to succeed.

My mother and father have never come, and never will come, to my bedroom. They will never get to admire that steadily expanding patch of white plaster. I never complete the job only because they move me to another bedroom.

I was a serious little girl. My idea of fun was to take on a seemingly hopeless task and work single-mindedly to make it happen. I had no interest in things other girls enjoy, such as dolls, shopping, clothes, cooking. It is not easy for sober, businesslike girls like me to make friends.

I dreamed of being a doctor, but the odds were stacked against me because I was a girl, and I grew up in the 1940s and 50s. Ninety-five percent of doctors, and ninety-eight percent of surgeons, were male at this time. The only female doctor I knew was my aunt, who had a part-time psychiatry practice.

Another problem was that I grew up in Far Hills, New Jersey, an enclave for the super-rich. My hometown was a world of business and art. It was not a world of science and medicine.

A serious career, especially a career in medicine, was not considered appropriate for a girl from Far Hills. My destiny was clear—debutante, wife, mother. Nobody told me I could be anything else. Nobody asked me what I wanted to do with my life. Nobody took me seriously.

I only began to realize how different Far Hills was from the rest of the world when I saw a magazine cover with the title: "The Twelve Richest People in New Jersey." Looking up at me were the faces of eleven of our neighbors. The only person I did not recognize was Doris Duke.

My upbringing made me believe marriage would solve all my problems. Once I had a man to take care of me, all would be well. My ticket to financial security would be my socially acceptable, successful husband. My mission in life was to catch a perfect man.

You don't believe me? This comes from a letter I wrote when I was a nineteen-year-old college student to the man who became my husband: *"I am getting an education I do not deserve. What use will a lot of biological knowledge be to me when I am a homemaker and a mother? Am I justified in staying in college when all this education will just go dead in me?"*

A girl whose ambition is to become the decorative appendage of a man, and get her identity through her husband, is not a good bet to become a surgeon.

I had unconsciously absorbed the belief that women were second-class citizens, but I had no idea how inferior we really were. Here are some facts about women in the 1940s and 50s: We could not open a bank account, practice law, serve on a jury, or attend most Ivy League colleges. We could not draw up contracts and wills or buy or sell property in most states. We could not own a credit card unless our husband gave his approval …in writing. We earned fifty-nine cents for every dollar earned by a man who did the same job.

A woman's looks, not her brains, were what counted in many jobs. Airline stewardesses had to be young, thin, attractive, single and female. They were fired when they turned thirty-two and earlier if they married or became pregnant. They were also let go if they failed a weight check. The upper limit for a 5-foot 5-inches woman was 129 pounds. This should give you an idea of the environment and time in which I grew up.

Our house in Far Hills was two houses in one. Lynn, Frank, and I lived in the back of the house with our German cook, Tina, and a succession of dismal nurses. We rarely went into the large, lavishly decorated rooms in the front of the house, where our parents gave their black-tie dinner parties. On those terrifying occasions, a butler and maid were hired to supplement our cook, Tina.

One of my Johnson cousins told me my house looked strange to her because she could not figure out where we all hung out together. The truth was that we children hung out with the cook and nurse, and our parents hung out with their rich friends.

My mother and father were far-off, glittering stars. I caught brief glimpses of them—a flash of blue-green silk, a whiff of French perfume—as they swept past me on the way to their formal dinner parties.

I rarely spoke to my parents. When I started to talk, I spoke with the heavy German accent of my nurse. My mother told me that I saw the moon one day and said: *"Zee, der Mond!"* This made an impression on her—at least, she noticed it—but it never occurred to her she should talk to me more.

Twenty-two Johnsons lived in Far Hills when I was young. They included me (the first-born, disappointingly a girl; my parents hoped for a boy), and my two siblings: my younger sister Lynn (another girl, another disappointment), my even younger brother, Francis Edgar Johnson, the Third (at last, the long-awaited son, the boy wonder who can do no wrong, now we can stop). Then there was my charismatic artist mother Helena Edey Johnson, my shy businessman father Francis Edgar Johnson Junior, three Johnson uncles and aunts, nine Johnson cousins, my ebullient grandfather Francis Edgar Johnson Senior, and my introverted grandmother, Elga Horn Johnson.

Social life in Far Hills revolved around the Essex Fox Hunt. The Essex was one of the best hunts in the U. S. because the rich people there, including my family, owned thousands of acres of open, rolling fields, and, by long-standing tradition, they kept their land open to the hunters. When I started to ride my horse cross-country, I realized almost every fence in Far Hills had jumps through it—usually those tent-shaped wooden ones called "chicken coops"—so the hunters could get through easily.

I and the other twenty-one Johnsons ended up in Far Hills because Grandpa was crazy about fox hunting. This sport had everything he loved—danger, excitement, and social status. He was born, raised, and started his married life, in modest, quiet Orange, New Jersey, but once he started to hunt with the Essex he quickly decided to move to intoxicating, flashy Far Hills.

The top layer of Far Hills society did not welcome Grandpa at first, but nothing stopped this confident, forceful man. His brain spewed out ideas, night, and day. The winning grin that lit up his broad face pulled everybody into his orbit. He was as restless as a cat in heat, always impatient to move on to something new.

In 1927, he bought several hundred acres of gently rolling land, and built a mighty stone house with the best view in Far Hills. He added stables for several dozen horses. He moved to Far Hills with his wife and their four sons in 1931, right in the middle of the Great Depression. Now that is optimism.

The Douglas Dillon and Charles Engelhard houses are bigger, but Grandpa's house has presence, crouched on a hilltop where you can see it for miles. I think that is why the Essex Fox Hounds gave Grandpa the honor of hosting the biggest hunt meet of the year on Thanksgiving Day.

When I asked my father about his childhood, he refused to talk about it. I eventually learned from my Uncle Coddy, number three of the four sons, about my father's early days in Far Hills, and, most important, his relationship with his father. Then I began to understand him better.

The discrete signs in front of the long driveways going to the Far Hills manor houses never state the owner's name or the street number, they say the name of the house. Grandpa named his big new house *"Ellistan"* after a famous racehorse buried on his land. I believe Grandpa chose this name because it put his neighbors on notice that he was just as horse crazy as they were.

Pictured: Grandpa Johnson on his Irish hunter, Boswell.

My grandfather didn't wait around for his neighbors to notice him. Coddy told me when a new family moved to Far Hills, Grandpa was at their door the next day, telling them they would be in trouble if they did not come over soon to swim in his pool. At the end of every day, including the day he died, he said: "This has been the best day of my life."

The only problem with Grandpa's unfailing optimism was it allowed no room for failure, or for feelings like sadness, pain, or fear.

A key part of Grandpa's plan to make it to the top of the Far Hills social ladder was to fox hunt religiously and make sure his four sons hunted. Even more important, he made his Bo play the ultimate high society sport—polo, which is so expensive that it is called the "sport of kings".

There are four players on an outdoor polo team, four sons, perfect. There are four to six chukkers (periods) in each game, and a fresh horse is needed for each chukker. This meant the boys needed at least sixteen— probably more like twenty-four—polo ponies. Polo was the perfect way to put Grandpa's neighbors on notice that he had plenty of money.

Coddy told me our neighbors were even more impressed when Grandpa bought a chunk of land in nearby Burnt Mills with some of his rich friends and built the *Burnt Mills Polo Club.* and proceeded to invent a device to water the fields. Burnt Mills is in action to this day.

Coddy also told me about the day Tommy Hitchcock, the best polo player in the world at that time, invited Grandpa's youngest son, Bobby, to play on his team in the US Open Polo Championship in Long Island. There was one problem—number two son Ben's wedding reception was scheduled that same day in Manhattan.

Tommy solved that problem by flying his seaplane to a dock in the East River, grabbing sixteen-year-old Bobby, and flying him to Long Island. Bobby wriggled out of his white tie outfit and into his polo clothes in mid-air. A waiting limousine whisked them to the polo grounds. They won the championship, and the Johnson family zoomed to the top of the Far Hills social ladder.

I always wondered how Grandpa made his money. Uncle Coddy told me it was through fox hunting. Grandpa struck up a conversation with Morris W. Kellogg in 1909 while they were fox hunting together. Morris was putting together the *M. W. Kellogg Company*, a giant international firm that built oil refineries and chemical plants. He took a shine to my charismatic, effervescent grandfather. He asked Grandpa to join him. Grandpa was Morris's right-hand man at Kellogg for forty years.

Grandpa knew how to negotiate a deal better than anybody, according to my cousin Rick. His father, my Uncle Ben, the number two son, played so much polo at Princeton he almost flunked out. Grandpa jumped into his chauffeur-driven limousine, roared down to Princeton, and talked his way into the office of the Head of the Chemistry Department. He proposed a deal to this eminent professor—develop a method to turn coal into gas, let his son Ben figure out the details, and the Kellogg Company would fund it.

This turned out to be a *win-win* for everybody. Ben got an exciting topic for his thesis, so he worked hard and graduated with honors. The professor got the credit for inventing an important new technique. The Kellogg Company, which owned the patent for the process, got to build the world's first coal gasification plant in South Africa. South Africa won because it had plenty of coal but no gas, and it was worried the world would put sanctions on its gas imports to protest apartheid. The world won because now everybody knew how to gasify coal.

Grandpa thought big. He had no trouble figuring out how to spend the money he made at Kellogg.

A giant house. Dozens of servants. Acres of fields dotted with cows, and a colossal bull to service them. A big pen full of turkeys. Dozens of chickens scratching in a dusty yard. Scores of pigs up to their bellies in mud, and a smoke house, to turn the pigs into bacon. A big orchard of apple, pear, and peach trees. A woodworking shop, where his clever Johnson hands made surprisingly good furniture. A dairy, complete with a dairyman, where sweet-smelling milk churned around in shining steel vats the size of bathtubs.

He even had a gas pump, which impressed one of my boyfriends when he ran out of gas in front of Grandpa's driveway one night while he was driving me home.

My grandfather was a confident, commanding extrovert. Grandma was a shy, short introvert. She had a cloud of hair, dyed purple, and yellow buck teeth. She panicked at parties, and she shuddered at the thought of travel. She wanted to stay home and knit sweaters for her twelve grandchildren.

The last straw for Grandma was the bash Grandpa threw for their 50th wedding anniversary in 1958. She marched up to her bedroom, and she never came down again. Grandpa became the hottest "bachelor" in Far Hills, as wealthy widows fought for his company at their dinner parties and bridge games.

All my memories of my grandmother are of her sitting in bed with a cigarette in her hand. I could not take my eyes off that cigarette as the ash got longer and longer. Would it tumble onto her bed and set it on fire? Unfortunately, it never did. She always flicked it off at the last possible moment with a practiced, casual flip of her wrist.

Grandma had all her meals in bed from then on. After breakfast, she went into her dressing room, rubbed a pink circle of rouge on each cheek, selected one of her lace-trimmed silk bed jackets, and went straight back to bed, where she watched soap operas on TV for the rest of the day. She usually was glad to see me when I visited, but I got a frosty reception if I arrived during one of her favorite shows.

Today, it would be unthinkable for a healthy woman in her sixties or seventies to "take to her bed", but it was considered perfectly acceptable—indeed, rather refined—in those days. I know of at least three other Far Hills dowagers who took to their beds. So did Morris Kellogg's wife, Marie. This says a lot about the role of women at that time.

I think Marie Kellogg and Grandma knew just what they were doing when they "took to their beds." Their forceful husbands always got their own way. This was the way these women took control of their lives.

Grandma handed over her agency to her husband in all other matters. She had no influence over the iron control Grandpa had over their four boys. Only one woman was able to say *no* to Grandpa. She was not Grandma. She was certainly not me. She was my mother.

One fall day, when I was eight or nine, I heard a horn outside. I ran to the window. Two to three dozen white-black-tan fox hounds, tails waving gaily like flags, followed by a huntsman in a green coat, two or three whips (assistants to the huntsman), and, finally, forty riders in red or black coats on a variety of giant black, chestnut, and grey horses were thundering down our driveway. The sun glinted off the huntsman's horn, the metal bits on the horses, and the silver handles of the riding crops. The Essex Fox Hounds had arrived.

Pictured: The Essex Fox Hounds meet at Ellistan on Thanksgiving Day, 1959. Buster Chadwell, the huntsman, and his hounds are front and center. My father is walking with his hands in his pockets to the right.

When my mother saw the horses were trampling our grass, she jumped up. I could tell she was angry. She grabbed her coat. She had her hand on the doorknob when my father yelled: "STOP!" My antennae shot up. My reserved, introverted father—he had inherited Grandma's shyness—always took his orders from my brash, confident mother. I expected she would ignore him, but, to my surprise, her hand dropped. He was talking to her in the hall in a serious tone of voice I had never heard before. I strained to hear, but he was too far away.

I puzzled over this incident for years—seemingly so trivial, but obviously so important to my father. My father sounded so… terrified. Why? My mother almost did something very …dangerous. What was it, and why did I remember it so well?

Even at that young age, I knew that kicking the Essex Fox Hounds off your land was not a good idea in a community where the social life revolved around the fox hunt and would provide months of gossip for our neighbors. I now think my father was worried about only *one* neighbor— his father. Grandpa would have been hopping mad if he found out his eldest son, the one who bore his name, turned away his beloved Essex

Fox Hounds. I think I remember this incident because it showed me how frightened my father was of his father.

The fact that my father refused to tell me anything about his childhood made me wild with curiosity. I eventually scraped together scraps of evidence that explained his grumpiness, his silence, and his unexpected explosive rage.

One clue was hiding in plain sight. Everybody in my family called the four Johnson brothers "the boys", even when they were grandparents. Grandpa must have been a tough act to follow. He was away most of the time, traveling around the world on Kellogg Company business. When he was home, he barked out orders—not a good way to give his sons self-confidence.

When he was ninety years old, my cousin Beverly asked her father, my Uncle Bobby, if he felt Grandpa's love when he was a child. Bobby replied: "My father loved us, but he never showed it."

Another clue popped up the day I discovered a curious open porch while I was exploring the third floor of Ellistan. The windows had no glass, only rotting screens. Four rust-covered iron beds were lined up against one wall. The only sign of life was a dry leaf scuttling across the floor. It reminded me of an army barracks or a prison. Who slept there, and why?

Years later, Uncle Coddy told me the inside story of that strange porch. Grandpa made his four boys sleep out on that porch …twelve months a year. I could not believe my ears. Really? All through the freezing winters of northern New Jersey?

Grandpa must have believed sleeping on that porch would toughen his boys up and prepare them for life. This belief was in the air back then. He was a big fan of President Theodore Roosevelt, and TR was an enthusiastic proponent of trial by nature.

When I asked Uncle Bobby about that porch, he said he piled six or seven blankets on top of him in the winter, but the icy wind roared right up through the mattress. My father told me he often saw a foot of snow on his blanket when he woke up. I concluded that sleeping on that porch was not pleasant.

My father and uncle spoke as if they had no choice but to sleep outdoors all winter long in sub-zero temperatures. I think of those four boys, shivering in their freezing beds, teeth chattering, and I ask myself why did they obey their father? Why didn't they just sneak back into the house?

I put the sleeping porch together with the panic my father showed when my mother tried to kick the Essex Fox Hounds off our land. I throw in the fact that Grandpa must have had extra high standards for my father because he was the oldest son. I realize my father could never do enough to please his father. Grandpa was the one who taught him fathers should be strict and disapproving.

I am a generation away from Grandpa, just far enough so he could be my inspiration instead of the slave driver he was to his boys. Watching him in action gave me optimism and ambition. He was proof that anything is possible. He also taught me a lot about marketing.

Like many things in life, the rigid discipline Grandpa imposed on my father by, among other things, making him sleep on that open porch was both a blessing and a curse. On the plus side, it made him into a principled, dogged, indefatigable, uncomplaining worker. On the minus side, it made him passive, frustrated, and angry.

My father craved routine. He was most comfortable when he was in one of his ruts—golfing, playing the piano, chopping brush, watching football—where he felt safe and in control. That is where my dynamic mother came in. Her emotional, irrational side lit him up and kicked him out of his ruts.

My father orbited around Grandpa when he was a child. When he chose a wife, he unconsciously replicated the relationship he had with his father. He picked a strong, ambitious woman so he could play a role that was familiar to him. He went into orbit around my mother.

Like father, like daughter. I spent my childhood orbiting around my mother. This type of intimacy was familiar to me, so I unconsciously chose a strong, ambitious man, Malcolm MacKay, to be my husband.

My father's way of dealing with his feelings was to clamp a lid on them, tighter and tighter, until he just had to let off steam. Then, he would suddenly and unpredictably explode and lash his children with the same anger his father had used on him.

I never knew what would set my father off. I had no idea his anger came from inside his head, and I was not the cause. I thought it was my fault.

I coped with my father's anger by launching a life-long quest to be perfect. I was determined to be what I thought he wanted me to be. I became a workaholic, a teacher's pet. I was the skinny girl with thick glasses in the front row at Far Hills Country Day School, my hand always up, wondering why I didn't have any friends.

I was on a different wavelength from the other children. I was driven and serious. I almost never laughed. I didn't like circuses and amusement parks. I thought clowns were grotesque. I never joined in the games of the other girls. When the boys found out I would burst into tears when they said something mean, I became their favorite amusement.

Don't take my word for it. Listen to the comments from my third-grade teachers. "Cynthia tends to withdraw." "She is much happier watching the other children." "She is not interested in group activities." "She is very serious while working." "She is a sincere student whose desire to be a perfectionist causes her to work too slowly."

Like many things in life, being a perfectionist is both a blessing and a curse. On the plus side, perfectionists have strong work ethics, so we perform well in the workplace when we become adults. We are persistent, and persistence is one of the best predictors of success in life. The ideal surgeon is an obsessive-compulsive perfectionist.

On the negative side, perfectionist children do not know how to have fun. We do not enjoy activities where the only purpose is amusement. We can never allow ourselves to just let go and be a kid. If we do something frivolous, we feel guilty.

Far Hills Country Day School was not a good fit for a withdrawn, shy perfectionist. The students, not the teachers, were in control. During one class, the boys sat behind me and flicked my legs with their belts. Another day, a gang of boys dragged Lynn and me into the bushes and pulled down our underpants. My mother told me I often came home from school with a ripped dress and tear-stained cheeks.

My aunt Helen, Ben's wife, realized that Far Hills was a rough school, so she sent her sons to a school in Bernardsville. The thought of moving her children to a different school never crossed my mother's mind. All her friends sent their children to Far Hills Country Day, and the Bernardsville school was an inconvenient ten minutes further away.

The tradition in my family was: never make a fuss, never show your feelings, and solve all your problems by yourself. My parents expected their children to be perpetually happy. We were not allowed to have problems. If I complained—for example, about the bullies at school—my words sank like a stone, and the atmosphere turned frosty.

This makes for a successful adult—but at a price. When I was many years older, I found out there is a downside to enforced cheerfulness. It threw me into a harrowing downward spiral of pain that almost killed me.

After the four Johnson brothers graduated from college, there was no question what they would do next—all four of them went to work for the Kellogg Company. When they got engaged to be married, Grandpa made sure they did not escape Far Hills by offering each a house and thirty acres of land.

There was one catch to Grandpa's offer. If a boy did not want a house on Grandpa's land in Far Hills, he did not get a house. These houses were not gifts. Grandpa kept ownership of them, so the boys could not sell them and move away.

All four boys accepted. Grandpa built four smaller houses around Ellistan. Four obedient planets swung into orbit around Grandpa.

I always wondered why the house Grandpa built for my father is bigger and grander than my uncles' houses. Our house has the same glorious view as Ellistan—across a meadow where "Queen Ann's Lace" explodes into a white froth in the spring, over the Essex Fox Hounds kennels, over the valley carved out by the sleepy, brown Raritan River, to the horse farm owned by the King of Morocco. A well-known architect, Wallace Heath, designed it. The other boys got smaller houses, designed by Grandpa, with views of the woods.

Why did we get the best house? The answer became clear when I was old enough to notice how Grandpa behaved around my mother. He never concealed who were his favorites. I eventually realized that he was madly in love with her. He often wondered aloud how his modest, shy oldest son managed to capture this beauty.

My mother radiated sex appeal, glamour, and animal magnetism. She was catnip to men. She had thirty-one proposals of marriage. When she was in her sixties and seventies, I saw the men turn and look at her when she walked into a room with that cool self-confidence of hers.

Grandpa saw himself in my mother. She was the only one in the family who was as self-confident and hard driving as he was. She built a successful career in Far Hills as a portrait artist. Our neighbors fought to have their children painted by Helena Edey (she used her family name for portraits). When I went into a house in Far Hills, my mother's portraits looked down on me. Grandpa relished pointing out her portraits on his neighbors' walls.

It was obvious to me—and, I am sure, to everybody else in my family—my mother had Grandpa wrapped around her little finger. He could not say *no* to her.

I watched as he gave her a mink coat, a *Buick*, and an oak tree. He made furniture for her in his woodworking shop, including a drum table, two stands holding framed Japanese silk prints, and half-a-dozen side tables. She asked for a desk with a secret drawer, and he spent months making her one.

Then she asked for a studio, and he built her one the size of an airplane hangar. He designed it to her exact specifications—all the light came from one large window on the north wall. It was clear to everybody in the family that considerable benefits came to people who pleased Grandpa.

The smell of turpentine always takes me back to my mother's studio, where the ceiling reached to the sky, and she presided like a queen over tables covered with pastels and oils in all colors of the rainbow.

Grandpa's presents drove my three aunts wild with jealousy. My mother could have made her sisters-in-law into her friends, but, as she often told me, she never did care much for women.

It wasn't until I was middle-aged that I learned from Uncle Coddy about the role the Kellogg Company played in winning World War Two. You can read all about it in Arthur Herman's book, "Freedom's Forge", which explains how the War was won, not on the battlefield, but by companies in the US, including the Kellogg Company.

My three uncles served in the Navy during the War. Grandpa commissioned my mother to paint portraits of all three of them in their uniforms, and he hung them prominently in the Ellistan living room. There was no portrait of my father. I always wondered why. I couldn't imagine why he wasn't up on the wall, too, decked out in a sexy uniform.

I finally learned from Coddy—long after my father died, sadly—that my father tried to sign up, but the Navy refused to take him. He was much more valuable on the home front because he was the head of the Kellogg division that made *toluene*, the key ingredient in TNT. I wish that father of mine had told his scientifically minded daughter about toluene, but he refused to boast.

Kellogg had another wartime project that was even more important than making toluene. It set up a front company called *Kellex* to carry it out because it did not want anybody to know what the company did or that it was associated with Kellogg.

The Kellex project was top secret. Grandpa and his four boys were among a handful of people who knew about it. Even Vice President Harry Truman knew nothing about the Manhattan Project until President Franklin Roosevelt died.

Kellex designed and built the gaseous diffusion plant in Oak Ridge, Tennessee that separated Uranium 235 from Uranium 238, which went into the atomic bomb *Little Boy*, which destroyed Hiroshima on August 6, 1945. Little Boy, in addition to saving millions of American and Japanese lives, almost certainly saved the lives of Ben and Bobby, who were scheduled to participate in the invasion of Japan.

Coddy was on leave in Nantucket when he heard the bomb had exploded. He felt a wave of relief. Nobody knew the thing would work, until it did.

And there you have the best of the sleeping porch discipline—it creates hard-working, determined men with lots of "can-do" spirit. *Johnsons get the job done.*

After the war was over and the boys were home safe, twenty Johnsons trooped up to Ellistan every Sunday for lunch. After lunch, we went upstairs to visit Grandma in bed, decked out in one of her silk bed jackets. Then we went outside to play touch football. Girls were allowed to play, but we almost never carried the ball.

A video of Sunday lunch at Ellistan would begin by panning down the great table, surrounded by twenty-two chattering Johnsons. Candles flickered. Silver flashed. Furniture gleamed. The sideboard groaned.

The camera would catch one of my uncles, head thrown back, letting out a laugh that rattled the windows. It would pick up a yelp from one of the half dozen family dogs milling around underneath the table. It would include a brief shot of the fox-hunting scenes on the wall. It would linger on Grandpa at the head of the table—our benevolent dictator, beaming with approval as he surveyed his loyal subjects.

The final shot would focus out the French doors, past the giant elms, and over the wide lawn. The fade-out would show a dozen horses flicking their tails and tossing their manes in the great front field.

The camera would skip one Johnson—a skinny, intense, serious, bookish girl with ugly pink glasses: the oldest granddaughter. I would be trying to fade into the woodwork, listening but not speaking. I would be the only Johnson without a smile on my face.

I always felt out of place amid that festive din. The other Johnsons were awash with cheerfulness. I was awash with worry. I felt more comfortable with the servants in the kitchen than with my own family in the dining room. I could sense the jealousies and rivalries that lay underneath all that light-hearted banter. The camera would not pick up that everybody at that table was jockeying to please Grandpa.

Christmas at Ellistan
Greetings from The Johnsons
danny wann
1953

Pictured: Christmas in the living room at Ellistan, 1953. My family is in the back row in front of my two grandparents. Lynn is kneeling. I am standing at the far right. My mother's portraits of Uncle Ben Johnson (center) and Uncle Bobby Johnson (to the right) in their naval uniforms hang on the walls.

Then someone started to sing. We all joined in, taking different parts. Music comes as easily as breathing to Johnsons. Singing always lifted my blue mood. We sang "You Are My Sunshine" and "Oralee" and "The Old Oaken Bucket That Hung in the Well".

Everybody else stopped singing when the four boys began to sing together in close harmony. I closed my eyes. Every hair on the back of my neck stood up. I shivered with delight as those deep, resonant male voices gave out one melting chord after the other.

I forgot for a while the quest of my life—to figure out how to please my mother, father, and grandfather, to do something, anything, that would make them notice me, but what? The task seemed impossible, and this made me chronically anxious.

The enemy I have fought all my life is family expectations I thought I could never live up to. This ran through my nightmares and eventually drove me to a therapist.

CHAPTER TWO

Armstrong Energy

We lived in Far Hills in fall, winter, and spring. We moved to Edgartown, Martha's Vineyard, for two months in the summer, to spend time with my mother's family, the Edey-Armstrongs. (My mother's mother was Marion Armstrong, and she married Alfred Edey.)

The Johnson family produced optimistic, dependable, solid workers who made a good living but did not have visions of glory. The Edey-Armstrong family bred people who set the world on fire—artists, writers, politicians, and intellectuals—who created works that lived after them.

My mother told me so many stories about her grandfather, David Maitland Armstrong (*DMA* to keep things simple), that I thought of him as my friend, though he died long before I was born. DMA was a well-known stained-glass window designer whose windows blaze across the eastern US. Every DMA window explodes with energy. He used up to five different layers of glass to create his deep, glowing colors, so they are a nightmare for restorers.

DMA knew everybody who was anybody in the nineteenth-century US art world. Whenever I visit the Metropolitan Museum of Art in New York, I remember he was one of the founders. He was also a founding member of the Tile Club, whose other members included Winslow Homer, William Merritt Chase, John LaFarge, Louis Comfort Tiffany, Augustus Saint Gaudens, Charles McKim, and Stanford White. Saint Gaudens slept in DMA's studio when he first moved to New York.

My great-grandfather and his artist friends were at the epicenter of a fizzing mass of creativity called the *Beaux-Arts* generation. His memoir, *Day Before Yesterday*, has been a gold mine for historians. He contributed so much to the arts that France awarded him its Legion of Honor.

DMA had six children. Four of them were artists and writers, including my grandmother, Marion Armstrong Edey. Granny Edey's books of poetry include *Do Not Awake Me* and *The Unicorn*. Her witty memoir, *Early in the Morning*, describes growing up with her eccentric Armstrong family on the Hudson River. Sales surged when the Book of the Month Club chose it as one of their selections.

The Armstrong creativity kept on going for generations. My mother, of course, was a portrait painter. Her brother, Maitland Armstrong Edey, my uncle Mait, was a writer and editor at *Time-Life*. Mait wrote dozens of books about nature and anthropology. He was co-author of the popular book *Lucy*, about early man and the implications of the discovery of an ancient skeleton—who happened to be a woman.

Our bookshelves sagged with books written by my relatives. Books, books, books. Just looking at them gave me a headache. They murmured to me: *Make something of your life before we are passed down to future generations.* I thought I would never be able to live up to this famous family of mine.

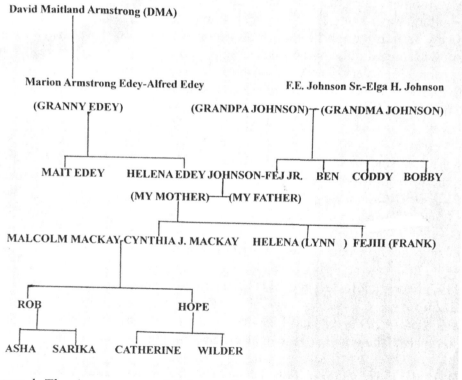

Pictured: The Armstrong and Johnson Family Tree.

26

My mother told me so many glowing tales about her Armstrong relatives that I thought they were all famous. It was not until I was well into middle age that I found out there was a flip side to the Armstrong family.

Armstrongs come in two flavors. The ones my mother described with such pride were the success stories. However, there were other Armstrongs she never mentioned who were hopeless drunks. Their main talent was to squander family money.

I never understood why some Armstrongs rocketed to the stars while others crashed and burned on take-off until I read Kay Redfield Jamieson's book *Touched with Fire*. Jamieson draws an excellent picture of manic depression, a hereditary mental disease. Jamieson knows whereof she speaks. She is herself a manic depressive.

I tore through the book, exclaiming out loud, reading, and rereading it. I realized manic depression is the price all creative families, including the Armstrongs, pay for their imagination and drive, and that most of my mother's family had this disease. Ninety percent of artists have manic depression, according to Jamieson.

Manic depression runs through my Armstrong family tree like a great underground root, popping up generation after generation. Manic depression produced the diplomats and drunkards, money-makers and money-takers, geniuses, and madmen.

Different Armstrongs inherited different degrees of mania. A moderate dose of manic energy spurred some on to greatness. A bigger dose destroyed the failures. Their minds simply burned up like overheated machinery, despite copious amounts of alcohol employed in a futile effort to cool them down.

High intelligence and creativity go hand in hand with manic depression. Gifted, brilliant children are at increased risk of manic depression when they become adults. Today, manic depression is often called *bipolar disorder*.

People with manic depression suffer from extreme shifts in mood. They alternate between highs, called *mania*, and lows, called *depression*. James Parker, a staff writer at *The Atlantic* who is manic depressive, has written:

"If you are not enjoying me right now, be patient. I'm like a London bus. There will be another me along in a minute".

When they are in a manic phase, manic depressives have inexhaustible energy, limitless creativity, unshakable optimism, and mind-blowing productivity. Life is too much fun to sleep. They spend exuberantly. Jamieson bought a collection of stuffed foxes during one of her manic phases.

As night follows day, depression follows mania. Manic depressives inevitably run down like broken clocks. They feel hopeless and worthless. They cannot think. They cannot move. Sometimes, they commit suicide.

A prime example of an artistic family with manic depression is Ernest Hemingway's family. Five members of the Hemingway family in the last four generations have committed suicide, including Ernest Hemingway himself, his father, two of his siblings, and his granddaughter.

Today, we have medications to treat manic depression. *Lithium* was the first one discovered.

From the time I was a small child, I would tackle seemingly impossible tasks and then work like a maniac to make them happen. Think, wallpaper. My mother liked to tell me I had inherited "Armstrong energy".

The question was whether my Armstrong energy, drive, and creativity was balanced by enough Johnson stability to allow me to function in the world. The answer turned out to be: "Just barely".

My mother and father were remarkably hands-off as parents. When I went to Treetops Camp, the summer I was ten years old, I didn't miss my parents, I missed our new kittens. Inattentive parents often produce children who lack self-confidence. I am living proof one consistent, supportive person can lessen the damage from neglectful parents. My mother's mother, Granny Edey, more than made up for my parents' lack of interest.

Pictured: A great love affair—Granny Edey and me in 1943.

Granny was thin as a whippet. She had a bundle of Armstrong energy. Her interest in fashion was zero. Her clothes were simple and mannish, and she wore them until she had to throw them out.

She was a woman of strong opinions, which she did not hesitate to share. Her values were clear, and she held them with passionate intensity. She championed the poor, the unjustly accused, and the environment. She had a wicked, dry, understated sense of humor.

She prided herself on her frugality. She bought a Ford sedan in 1939, and she drove it until she died eighteen years later. Then, my parents drove it for another eighteen years. She spent serious money on only a few things—trips to far-away jungles to add to her life list of birds she had seen in person, and a cook/housekeeper.

My father's and mother's families had such different values it made my head spin. Johnsons value business; Armstrongs value art. Johnsons are extroverts; Armstrongs, introverts. Johnsons want to enjoy life in the here and now. Armstrongs devote themselves to projects that will live on after they die.

Grandpa Johnson took a keen interest in the success of all his grandchildren. He studied my report card carefully and rewarded me for every *A*. Granny Edey had no interest in reading my report cards. She wanted to know about my inner world, the life of my mind, what books I was reading, and what I was thinking and feeling. She made me believe that these things are important.

Ellistan was all opulence, luxury, and comfort. My toes disappeared in the thick pile of the carpets. The seats of the upholstered armchairs were so soft it took an effort to get out of them.

Granny's Edgartown Eel Pond house was all Puritan restraint. Granny did not approve of what she called "bought furniture". She inherited most of her dark, warped, ancient, and uncomfortable tables and chairs from her Armstrong family. The few rugs on her floors were thin and threadbare. On the walls she had bird prints with severe black frames, and a British Tudor butter mold riddled with wormholes. A stuffed pheasant, shot by her brother Noel, glared from the top of her desk.

Dessert at Ellistan was always piles of cakes, pies, and cookies served with mountains of ice cream. Granny believed sugar was bad for children, so she served us something like stewed prunes for dessert. After the meal was over, she took down a jar of peppermints and offered me just one. These clever bonbons were mostly air. They dissolved instantly on my tongue, leaving behind a faint taste of minty sweetness.

Granny and I spent most of our time in Edgartown on her screen porch, looking across a field of beach plums, bayberry bushes, and beach grass, over Eel Pond, over the sailboats flying in outer Edgartown Harbor, to the dun-colored cliffs of Chappaquiddick Island.

She hung a black concave mirror called a *Claude Lorraine* glass on the back wall of her porch. The name comes from a seventeenth-century French artist, Claude Lorraine, who painted his eerily beautiful landscapes by looking backward into such a glass. This glass miniaturized the view and made the colors vivid and intense, as an artist might see them.

The tiny world floating inside Granny's glass seemed charmed, surreal, like the worlds I saw in my dreams. It summed up everything Armstrong—unique, of use only to artists, something you could not buy in a store.

In Far Hills, I had no protection from the judgment of adults. I spent my days straining forward like a dog on a leash, eyes bulging, paws scrabbling, panting to please them.

Edgartown gave me approval and peace. Granny loved me just the way I was, so I didn't have to struggle. She told me I was smart and special, so I believed I was smart and special. When I was with her, I became the person I was meant to be—my best and most complete self.

The wild beauty of the Island brought me more peace. Peace drifted in as the soft sea breeze sighed through pine boughs. It floated up with the spicy scent of bayberry bushes baking in the hot Island sun. It flooded into my brain when I looked at the deep turquoise sky, that bottomless *lapis lazuli* I have seen only on an island.

It rolled in with the thick Island fog that spangled my eyebrows and eyelashes with gleaming droplets. I could hear it in the mournful foghorns, the melancholy wail of the wheeling gulls, and the merry calls of songbirds—especially the Bob Whites, comical little brown-and-white quail that scurried briskly around the Eel Pond meadow all summer long, piping the same question over and over: "Bob- WHITE"?

Edgartown was a sleepy fishing village in those days. The streets were crushed white shells. The shops carried useful stuff—food, hardware, newspapers, fishing tackle, and marine equipment.

Granny listened to everything I said with unfailing interest. She took my opinions seriously. She infected me with her passion for books. When I spent the night with her at Eel Pond, she woke me at dawn to go birdwatching. I do not remember enjoying our early morning excursions to mosquito-infested swamps, but she taught me to let nature speak to me, and this has been my solace during difficult times.

Granny was a passionate supporter of civil rights. One day, she drove me to Oak Bluffs, then and now the premier African American summer resort in the US. As she pointed to the people lying on the beach she said:

"Black people are wonderful, fine people, just as good as white people. Promise me you will always respect them." As we drove away, I asked her: "Granny, are you a Black person?"

Granny has inspired me to speak up against wrong. Thanks to her, I launched a campaign to get an incompetent doctor out of a hospital (see Chapter Ten) and an unqualified surgeon out of the eye OR (see Chapter Sixteen). I am one of a handful of ophthalmologists willing to tell the truth about LASIK, a cosmetic eye operation that has left many patients blind, and others in unbearable, untreatable pain (see Chapter Eighteen).

I thought Granny would always be waiting for me in the Eel Pond house, and I would have many happy summers with her. In fact, I only had ten. Ten was enough to make a difference.

Granny's husband, Alfred Edey, died when my mother was seventeen. This was the defining tragedy of my mother's life. She never talked about her father. She could only cry when I asked about him. She kept his photograph near her until the day she died. It shows a handsome, rugged man with a good-natured twinkle in his eyes.

My mother spent her teens and twenties searching for a man to replace her father. She ran through boyfriends at a rapid clip. She collected thirty-one proposals of marriage before my father took her off the market when she was thirty.

When I started to have boyfriends, she started to tell me, in detail, about her own boyfriends. She made it clear she had many more boyfriends, of far higher quality, than I had. To this day, I can recite, in order, the names of her rejected suitors and the plusses and minuses of each.

My mother was a romance addict. She was happiest when a man was chasing her, calling her night and day, and showering her with presents. She lost interest after he proposed marriage. She craved courtship and illusion, not the humdrum affection of everyday married life—until my father came along.

Success for her was attracting the attention and admiration of men. She switched on like a light bulb in the presence of a man. Young, or old, tall, or short, handsome, or plain, she was crazy about all of them. She would cross and re-cross her flawless legs, which, she often reminded me, won the Legs Contest one year at Yale University. Then she would lean forward so her bountiful breasts came into full view and fix her prey with a challenging gaze. One look into those sapphire eyes, and he would be a goner.

Whoa! Let's take a closer look at that Yale Legs Contest. Presumably, this involved a group of women exposing their legs (in short shorts? Bathing suits?) to a bunch of dudes who took a careful (close?) look to pick a winner. The winner was so proud she frequently mentioned it to her daughter.

I haven't told my granddaughters about the Yale Legs Contest. They would be appalled. They refuse to be objectified by the male gaze. They do not shave their underarms or legs because they believe altering their bodies to please a man is degrading. They wouldn't go near a Legs Contest unless they were attending a protest rally against it.

From the time she was small, it was obvious my mother had inherited the Armstrong artistic talent. She started to draw as soon as she could hold a pencil. Her brain was filled with colors and designs.

Colors spoke to my mother. She saw everything as a painting. She felt physically ill when she was in a room that was painted a color she hated, for example, the bleak grey of my living room in Brooklyn Heights when I was an adult. All her clothes had to be green, blue, or greenish blue. Even our car was greenish blue.

Nobody knew as many names for colors as my mother. The names melt like chocolates in my mouth. *Burnt Umber. Ochre. Teal. Turquoise. Ultramarine. Cerulean Blue. Burnt Sienna.*

I always knew art was my mother's number one priority. Her brother, Mait, was number two. Her children were a distant third.

My mother felt compelled to create art. She did not have a choice in the matter. She did not feel fully alive unless she was painting. She needed to paint the way other people need food and water.

She sat in the back of the classroom at the Brearley School in New York, sketching her friends and making quick portraits of her teachers, filling her lesson books with drawing after drawing. Her teachers despaired of teaching her anything.

Granny sent her away to St. Timothy's School, an all-girl boarding school in Maryland, when she was fifteen. She was miserable at St. Tim's—no men, and many rules. Her life picked up when she came back to New York to live with her mother. She never had to sew a hem or clean a dish. She went to house parties in Maine, Long Island, and Newport on the weekends. Her most demanding task each day was deciding which of her numerous suitors to have dinner with.

She was accepted at Vassar but decided to study at New York's Art Students League. She quickly developed a bold, colorful painting style. She had a knack for getting a likeness, and she began to get commissions for portraits.

My mother thought rules were for ordinary, boring people. Special people—most especially, free spirits like artists—were exempt. One of her pranks was to go on a painting trip to Mexico with a female artist friend in the 1930s, which was shocking behavior for two single women at that time.

You probably assume she would not find any suitable suitors in the wilds of Mexico. You would be wrong. I don't know how she pulled it off, but somehow, she managed to attract the attention of a six-foot three-inch hunk, a five-time Olympic gold medal swimmer and actor called Johnny Weismuller, who was on location in Mexico shooting one of his *Tarzan* movies. She quickly added him to her list of conquests. I have a photograph of the two of them on a beach. Johnny has written on the back: "Never forget me!"

Johnny was not one of her thirty-one marriage proposals. Maybe he was too busy practicing his Tarzan yells.

My mother got away with murder with men. One day, a policeman stopped her for speeding. She rolled down her window and gazed up at him with those dazzling blue eyes. She apologized in her most sultry voice as she started to toy with a button on his coat.

The policeman's face flamed red. How could he give a ticket to this ravishing temptress? He stammered out a warning instead. Suddenly, she realized that his button had come off in her hand. She rolled up her window, blew him a kiss, and drove off with that button clenched in her fist.

I bet she kept that button. It was a testament to her power over men. I looked everywhere in the house for it after she died, but it was nowhere to be found.

When my father met my mother, he fell for her with every cell in his body. Loving her gave his life meaning. He often said that marrying her was his life's greatest achievement. He took his orders from Grandpa when he was young. When he met this electric force of nature, it was her turn to take over.

My father persuaded my mother to marry him when her thirty other suitors failed because he was the only man who could give her the single-minded devotion that died with her father. She accepted his proposal. It was number thirty-one.

My mother and father were married in Edgartown's tiny Episcopal Church in June 1941. They had a small reception at Granny's Eel Pond house afterwards.

They look as handsome as movie stars in their wedding photographs. My father looks so proud and happy I would think he has just won the Nobel Prize.

Pictured: My mother and father on their wedding day, with their parents.

It is not so easy for me to tell what my mother is thinking. She has on that special smile she used for photographs. She carefully worked it out in a mirror so it would show just the right number of teeth—enough to look happy but not enough to look like she was grinning. My father called it her "pussy smile". Her pussy smile has more teeth than usual, so I think she is happy, too.

In another photograph, Granny Edey, the mother of the bride, and Grandma Johnson, the mother of the groom, sit side by side on a bench. The photographer probably told them to sit there and smile. These two very different women do not look at each other. They give me the strong impression they both want to escape.

Pictured: My grandmothers at my parents' wedding, Edgartown, June 1941. Grandma Johnson, left, is wearing an expensive pearl necklace with a matching bracelet. Granny Edey, right, has a simple black watch.

They are wearing such different outfits it looks as if they are planning to attend entirely different parties. Grandma looks as if she is going to a reception at the White House. Her ample curves show off to advantage in her chic, obviously expensive silk dress. Wow, that dress has serious décolletage. A stylish hat, smothered in flowers and set at a rakish angle, is perched on her head. Around her neck is a triple strand of unquestionably flawless pearls, and around her wrist is the matching bracelet. On her feet are impressively high heels with fashionable bows and open toes. I would fall flat on my face if I tried to take one step in Grandma's shoes.

Granny Edey is a study in understated simplicity. Her plain polka-dotted dress has a high neck and long sleeves. It is the kind of dress that one of Grandma Johnson's maids might wear to church on Sunday. It looks elegant on her rail-thin figure. She has low-heeled white sandals on her feet. She could probably climb a mountain in them. A simple straw hat with a discrete brim sits on her head. Her only piece of jewelry is a watch with a black strap.

That opulent corsage perched on Granny's shoulder strikes a discordant note. It is not her style. My mother must have pinned it on to make her look fancy. I can almost see Granny's fingers twitch. I'm certain she ripped it off the minute the picture-taking was over.

Granny Edey looks happy and relieved. She has been lobbying for my simple, decent father from the moment they met. Grandma Johnson's expression is ambivalent. This new super-star daughter-in-law could be trouble.

Anybody looking at this picture-perfect bride and groom would think they would live happily ever after. I know that after her prince took her off to his castle in Far Hills, my mother realized marriage was not what she thought it would be.

CHAPTER THREE
Searching For Approval from My Parents

My parents somehow came to believe that training their children for life was not their responsibility. They thought we would magically grow into perfect adults without any input from them. They had no idea what to do with us, so they avoided us.

My parents were not evil; they were clueless. They didn't let themselves see anything they didn't want to see. They didn't want us to bother them with our feelings or problems. They pawned us off on nurses. They made me into a watchful, anxious child and, later, a resentful adult.

The definition of a good father when I was young was a man who put food on the table. My father left the house every weekday morning while I was still snoozing in bed to commute to New York City, two and a half hours in and two and a half hours out, to work at the Kellogg Company. He traveled via the Peapack–Gladstone train, the Hudson tubes, and two different subway lines.

The train seats were covered with woven straw coated with shellac, as hard as the floor, and so slippery I slid from side to side if the train hit a curve. There was no air conditioning, and the heat was intermittent in winter. The engine was coal fired, so cinders and smoke flew in if somebody opened a window.

The most exciting part of the day for Lynn and me was the moment our father came home from work. We dragged our small chairs to the top of the stairs and waited, breathless, freshly bathed, and dressed in nightgowns washed and ironed by our nurse. We had eaten hours earlier in the kitchen with the nurse and cook.

Finally, the door opened. We flew down, squealing with excitement, and jumped into his arms. I closed my eyes and breathed the sooty smell of father-just-home-from-work mixed with *Eau du Portugal* hair tonic. He gave us one perfunctory hug each. Then, our nurse took us off to bed.

Our father gulped down two stiff drinks. My mother dressed for dinner in a long, formal gown. They ate, by candlelight, a dinner prepared by our German cook, Tina Steinlein. My father, taciturn and exhausted, was not a dazzling conversationalist. He fell asleep after dinner the minute he sat down on the living room couch.

The weekends were worse. We never got a hug on weekends. My father had retired from polo and fox hunting by then, so he played golf, chopped brush, or watched television on Saturday and Sunday while my mother worked in her studio. In the evening, they went out to black-tie dinner parties.

My mother had lived in a bubble until she married my father. She had vague, unrealistic assumptions about marriage. This was not the life she expected. She missed her mother, her brother, her boyfriends, the excitement of New York, the art. She knew nobody in Far Hills. My shy, exhausted father was not the romantic husband she dreamed of.

My mother was the type of woman often portrayed in novels—gorgeous, mercurial, irresistible to men, taught mainly ornamental skills, and sheltered from reality. Think of Daisy in F. Scott Fitzgerald's novel, "The Great Gatsby".

She saw herself as an artist. She did not see herself as somebody who could look after others but as somebody who needed other people to look after her. She couldn't handle pressure—but *I* could. Taking care of my mother made me into a person who loves to nurture others, and this has served me well in life.

She coped with her disappointment in her marriage by pouring herself into the two things that reliably made her happy—art, and men. She painted portraits and taught a painting class. She also did an impressive amount of recreational flirting with men. No matter how many men admired her, she always wanted more. She had no energy left for her children.

She was pregnant with me six months after her wedding. Her tear-stained letters to her mother tell me she hated being pregnant. She complains about her bulging breasts and fat stomach. Her much-admired figure, a source of great pride, was ruined.

The woman who much preferred men to women delivered… me, a girl, on September 20, 1942. What a letdown. She often told me what Grandpa Johnson said when she brought me home: "So the best you could do was a girl!" She did not think that was funny. I suspect she was thinking along the same lines herself.

Unhappy mother, unhappy daughter.

My sister Lynn arrived two years later. I am certain this was another disappointment for my mother. It was a nasty shock for me. My thick German accent was proof my parents did not spend much time with me before Lynn arrived. Now, they were paying more attention to this pink blob than I thought was necessary.

I tried to turn the spotlight back where it belonged—on me. I began by throwing temper tantrums. They backfired. They made my mother even less inclined to spend time with me.

One day, while I was sitting on the toilet, I had a brilliant idea for a sure-fire way to get my mother's attention. I leaned back and, like an angry cat, I sent a stream of urine splattering on the bathroom floor. The scene of this odious crime was not my own bathroom but the sacred guest bathroom downstairs, the one my mother had painted with leaping figures of graceful female ballet dancers with swirling white skirts and flowers in their hair.

That got attention, all right, but not the kind I expected. My mother didn't clean up my pee; my nurse did, and she gave me the walloping of my life.

My mother did not have the energy to cope with this unsatisfying mess of a daughter. She spent even more time in her studio and even less time with me. I suspect she was depressed at that time because she was, after all, an Armstrong.

I am older now. I look down from a great height, like some all-seeing eagle, at my unhappy family as we lash out at each other, injuring the people we love, and I feel compassion for all of us. Everybody was frustrated, lonely, and sad. We all wanted to be loved and cherished. We all craved respect, appreciation, and tenderness.

My life improved when the blob grew up into an agreeable little sister. Our parents were disinterested ghosts floating high above our lives like benign balloons. They didn't care what we did if we didn't get into trouble or disrupt their comfortable lives. Lynn and I had almost no parental supervision, so we bonded for life. We like to say that we brought each other up.

We lived far out in the country, where amusement opportunities were few. Our mother was barricaded implacably in her studio. Our father was never around. Our wretched nurse was replaced by another wretched nurse, and then that nurse was replaced by another one who was even worse.

My absent parents made me into a self-starter. I knew nothing would happen unless I made it happen. Necessity made me creative. I invented games, and Lynn followed along, much in awe of my dazzling talents.

My games invariably featured me in the starring role, with Lynn playing my loyal sidekick. One of my games was "Mither and Fither Ribbit." I played a mother rabbit who gave birth to many rabbit babies (our stuffed animals played important supporting roles in this game). Lynn was a father rabbit who sat around guarding us.

Another favorite game featured a book of paintings I stole from our mother's studio. I turned a page, and we each pointed to a character we wanted to be. One Fragonard painting showed an elegant lady dressed in billows of pink silk soaring on a swing while a man lurks in the bushes below and a cupid statue gazes suggestively down on them.

I was quicker than my sister, so I always pounced on the lady. Lynn protested that she did not want to be the man. I generously allowed her to be the lady's pink slipper, which she had kicked into the air so her admirer could catch it.

My quest to be The Best never let go, even when I was playing imaginary games with my little sister.

To escape our chilly house, I began to walk Lynn up to Ellistan. First stop: the front door. This imposing slab of carved wood looks as if it has no doorknob, but I know how to grab the heavy ornate knocker in the center and wrench it clockwise. The door swings open, and we stumble into the great dim hall. We lower our voices. Always, a feeling of awe.

The thick stone walls and green slate floor keep the hall cool, even on the hottest days. Our eyes wander over antique tapestries that depict scenes from ancient Rome and massive medieval chairs, benches, and chests

(Grandpa made one of his famous deals on the contents of an Austrian castle).

Stop number two: the dining room. We swipe a handful of thin square chocolate mints wrapped in translucent paper with gold letters from white shell-shaped porcelain bowls adorned with delicate porcelain lace.

Next stop: the great lawn. All is serene except for a faint murmur from the cherub fountain presiding over the round reflecting pool. The great elms reach to the sky, immutable sentinels. The brilliant grass stretches for acres without a single weed, thanks to a small army of gardeners that pull each one out by hand.

Our last stop is the animals. We filch apples from the orchard, and offer them properly, palms flat, to the horses. We stroke their velvet muzzles and giggle as their hairy mouths delicately slobber up the apple. We breathe in the heady stable smell—the sharp reek of urine, the earthy odor of manure, and the spicy scent of leather tack rubbed with saddle soap.

We filch ears of corn from the crib and fling them to the pigs. This creates a delightful explosion of mud and an eruption of ear-shattering squeals. We gobble at the turkeys, and they gobble right back. We gaze into the profound brown eyes of the cows and watch as they steadily shove their cud, right to left. We duck as the massive bull roars and shakes its head and hurls spittle at us. I scrutinize its purple basketball-size testicles with unflagging interest.

I'm rarely satisfied with where I am and what I am doing. I have a compulsion to move on, go higher, deeper, and longer. It is as if I have a need to prove myself, to show the world I am worthy. After many Ellistan visits, we even get bored by the menacing mountain of bull muscle. The next time, I turn down the hill instead of up. We pay a call on the Essex Fox Hounds.

Our first visit is an unqualified success. One hound sees us and begins to howl out the news, a deep baying that echoes through the woods. In a flash, the whole pack is crammed up against the fence, a churning mass of white-brown-black bodies, barking furiously, tails thrashing, shoving each other aside, fighting for the privilege of sniffing and licking our fingers. We made their day. How gratifying.

The next time we go down to visit the fox hounds, after we have enjoyed a satisfactory amount of canine worship, I take Lynn to the field where antique horses, hound food on the hoof, live out their final days. Several of these giants have lined up to greet us, their coats matted with mud. They study us with ancient, clouded eyes. Lynn's head barely comes up to their bellies.

No bridle? No saddle? Neither of us knows how to ride? No problem. *Johnsons get the job done.* I tug twine from a hay bale, fashion it into a bridle, and shove Lynn onto one of those boney backs. The huge hulk of a horse snorts and jumps back. Somehow, Lynn hangs on. I suddenly realized that it is a long way to the ground, and those hooves are the size of her head.

And there you see the plusses and minuses of this older sister. She is determined, imaginative, and bold, but she can be appallingly casual in dangerous situations. Today, I am shocked by how stupid and risky this caper was, but part of me applauds her daring and creativity.

One day, when I was six and Lynn was almost four, my father rushed into the nursery. That was strange. He had never set foot there before. I had never seen him so excited. This man of few words was yelling, over and over: "You have a brother!"

My mother seemed delighted to have Frank. At last, a son. Lynn and I watched in amazement as she kissed, snuggled, giggled, and tickled him—things she never did with us. Photographs of Lynn and me as children show us with our nurse. Photographs of Frank show him sitting on our mother's lap.

Pictured left to right: Me at age six, Frank (newborn) and Lynn aged four. I was put in charge of my younger siblings when I was eleven years old.

I was my father's favorite, which made my mother jealous. Frank was my mother's favorite, which made my father jealous. My mother told me that our brother said to our father one day: "She's mine."

"No, she's not. She's *mine.*" replied our father.

Lynn remembers childhood as cowering in a bunker while bullets whizzed over her head.

I can understand why men were attracted to my mother. She was an artist and an Armstrong, so she was governed by strong and changeable moods. She was warm one minute and cool the next—a tease. They could not figure her out, and this made her irresistible.

A mercurial woman is exciting if you are a man, but she is not easy if she is your mother. I could never predict how my mother would behave. Would she stalk angrily away and ignore me, or would she talk to me?

My mother was very distractable. She focused on whatever caught her attention, so she sometimes forgot she had children.

One day in Edgartown, my family went over to Uncle Mait's house. I wandered off to a bedroom, where I discovered a chest of comics. I was instantly absorbed. After a while, I began to realize the house was surprisingly quiet. I went downstairs. Nobody was there.

I looked out the window at the driveway, squinting at the bright Island sun. All the cars were gone. Everybody was at the beach. My mother took Lynn and Frank, but she forgot about me and left me behind.

I lay down on the living room rug. I curled up in a ball. I thought what a bad, bad girl I was. I never thought what a hare-brained idiot my mother was. Children don't think that way.

I spent my childhood searching for crumbs of approval from my mother. I watched this elusive ice queen closely, trying to figure out how I could please her. I tried to woo her, summon her back, get her to focus her blissful attention on me.

I never complained. I kept an eager smile on my face. I made a big effort to amuse her friends, especially Uncle Mait, hoping they would speak well of me. Nobody would have guessed the neat, polite little girl, who was such a good student, was seething with anxiety inside.

My mother was so unpredictable I spent my childhood on edge, never able to trust her, always bracing myself for rejection. I couldn't withdraw from our relationship because she was my mother. I was too anxious to please her to protest, and my protests would not have changed her anyway.

Ambivalent relationships that contain a mixture of positive and negative feelings, like the one I had with my mother, are not healthy. They make blood pressure and heart rate go up.

My mother's maternal instincts finally emerged when I got sick. Then, I had straightforward, temporary needs she could understand and meet. She descended on me, a goddess from Olympus, and focused on me a glow of love so intense I melted with happiness.

She made me "milk toast" with her own hands—toast slathered with butter and sprinkled with cinnamon, floating in a bowl of hot milk. If I had a cough, she made me a "mist tent" out of a card table, a kettle, and a blanket.

I loved being sick, and I worked hard to prolong my illnesses. I faked coughs, stomach aches, and sore throats. I ran hot water over the thermometer to make my mother think I had a fever. One day, I ran the water too hot, and the bulb of the thermometer burst, sending tiny shiny beads of mercury scampering around the sink.

When I got well, my mother sent me right back to my nurse. My cousins had kind, loving nurses. My mother had a talent for finding creepy, sadistic ones.

One nurse put a rubber band around Frank's penis to stop him from wetting his bed at night.

One day, Lynn splashed water on the floor while she was playing with her rubber duck in the bath. When the nurse saw the water, she grabbed Lynn out of the bath, spanked her, and locked her in a closet, wet, naked, screaming, and shivering.

When the nurse let her out, Lynn ran to our mother to complain. Our mother was not sympathetic. She reminded Lynn that the nurse came with an excellent cook. Good cooks were impossible to find in the country. The cook stayed. So did the tyrannical nurse.

My mother, like all good artists, focused single-mindedly on her art. When clients came to her studio to sit for their portraits, or students came to her painting class, she blocked her children out of her mind.

I fell and hurt my knee one day. I pounded on the studio door, howling that I was cut and bleeding. No response. My mother often seemed surprised to see those vaguely familiar children running around her house when she came out of her studio.

When I try to call up my mother in my memory, she is as shifty and shape changing as a magician. I need to vanquish two rivals to get her attention—her studio, and her dressing room.

Beauty was my mother's passion. She created it in her paintings, swiftly laying down a network of strokes in pastel or oil until a shimmering picture appeared, as if by magic. In the evening, when she was preparing to go to a party, she disappeared into her dressing room and worked the same magic on herself.

When my mother was away from the house, I often sneaked into her dressing room, trying to discover who she was, like an archaeologist attempting to reconstruct the bustle and noise of a vanished civilization by studying its pottery shards.

One wall of her dressing room had three giant mirrors that ran from floor to ceiling. The left and right mirrors were cleverly concealed doors to her closet. When I pulled out these two side mirrors until they touched, I created a secret triangular mirror room where an army of *Cynthias* surrounded me. We became smaller and smaller as we disappeared into the green gloom.

Her dressing table was opposite the wall of mirrors. It had a white flounced skirt, and the top was made of a mirror. On top of the mirror top were several hand mirrors in different magnifications, plus an oval standing mirror surrounded by a circle of lights, like the mirrors actors use to put on make-up.

The mirror top held mysterious objects of great interest. There were small pots of eye shadow and rouge, and a round gold box of face powder with a pink powder puff inside. There were many tubes of lipstick with names like *Shocking Pink* and *Passionate Scarlet*. She had several small glass bottles sculpted into exotic shapes filled with French perfume, and a green leather box embossed with gold that glittered with jewelry.

I fingered these enigmatic objects. I sniffed every perfume bottle. I studied my enormous eye in the magnifying mirror. They seemed like the implements of a priest who was preparing to perform a sacred rite.

My mother would not allow anybody to watch her while she got dressed, including me, because, she said, it disturbed her concentration. My father waited patiently downstairs, playing the piano. The whole household waited, hushed.

After what seemed like hours, she finally emerged. It was always well worth the wait. She always pulled off another triumph. She floated downstairs with the confidence and carriage of a queen in one of her dramatic green-blue outfits, trailing scarves, and perfume. *Bravo*, I said to myself. *Bravo*, the other dinner guests would say to themselves.

My parents always stopped off in the kitchen before they left and looked in on their three children eating dinner with the cook and the nurse. They always said the same thing: "What a shame we must go to this stupid party. We would much rather stay home with you." I knew this was not true, but I smiled appreciatively anyway.

I can see my father as clearly as if he is bathed in a spotlight. He has a thick mat of curly fur on his barrel chest. Sprightly black hairs like coiled wires are sprinkled over his powerful arms and legs. There is a bald ring around the top of each calf where the garters that hold up his socks have rubbed the hair away.

The top of his head was bald by the time he graduated from Hotchkiss at age seventeen, despite the liberal application of bear grease, touted at that time to prevent hair loss. Around his shiny pate ran a rim of fine, silky hair, like a monk's tonsure. "Grass can't grow on a busy street," he said when the subject of hair came up.

My father was too shy to play with his children directly. He played the way babies play with each other—not interacting, just playing side by side, glancing at each other occasionally. His clever Johnson hands made toys for us in Grandpa's workshop, including a blue rocking horse and a marble roll, but he was not with us while we played with them.

When we were at the beach at Edgartown, he sat down and, without saying a word, began to dig. His giant hands methodically excavated great pits in the sand that were so deep the bottoms filled with seawater. When there was a heavy snowfall in Far Hills, he carved great caves in the snowbanks. They went so far back the light inside was blue. Then he sat back and waited for us to play with them.

I always knew my father loved me. My problem was to figure out how to connect to this reserved, silent man. My most reliable method was to get up early to watch him shave.

He began by putting a new blade in his safety razor. Then, he filled the sink with water. He always left a trickle running so the hairs would wash down the overflow drain. He worked up a lather with his brush, and made his chin disappear under a layer of thick white foam. He puffed out each cheek in turn as he made his chin reappear, stroke by stroke.

I kept my eyes glued to his hands as they moved surely and methodically. He was teaching me the importance of strict protocol and attention to detail. He never spoke to me during this sacred ritual, but I was with him, so I was happy.

My father never let me know his feelings through words. I had to guess what was on his mind by listening to him play the piano. He never took a piano lesson, he could not read one word of music, and he played every song in the key of *G*, but he could play any piece he heard by ear. He sat down at the piano one day and taught himself how to play.

I went to sleep listening to my father playing the piano, swinging through song after song—Cole Porter, George Gershwin, Noel Coward. This was his hymn of happiness, his way to show his joy in his family and home, like the purr of a cat or the Rhine maidens singing their delight in the Ring in Wagner's opera, *"Das Rheingold."* This lullaby was punctuated by an occasional hoot from a Peapack–Gladstone train across the valley, or a yelp from a hound in the kennel down the hill.

I knew my parents were not happy together. I never heard them laughing and joking. My mother was like an unhappy queen, and my father was like her long-suffering consort. He could not please her, no matter how hard he tried.

I survived by shoving the real world into the back of my mind and escaping into the world of books. I read my way through my childhood. Books were magic carpets that flew me away to happier worlds that felt more authentic and compelling than my physical world.

My favorite book was Walter Farley's *The Black Stallion*. Alec Ramsey, a boy of indeterminate age, is marooned on a deserted island with a wild black Arabian stallion after a shipwreck. Alec has learned in science class that a certain seaweed becomes edible when it is cooked. He uses this knowledge to save himself and the stallion from starvation.

This book told me what I needed to hear—that children who study hard and read books can make it in this world. Scientific knowledge saves lives. Nothing could be better than that.

Books were especially compelling because everything in the distance of my actual world was a blur. My teacher realized I could not read the blackboard. She told my parents I needed an eye exam. What a surprise— I was extremely near-sighted.

The day I went home with my first pair of glasses was a succession of miracles. The world was transformed from vague, fuzzy clouds into sharp-edged, recognizable objects. I always wondered why those tall poles were marching along the side of the road. Now I could see the telephone lines strung between them.

My mother chose pink frames for my glasses because, she said, they would be less noticeable. Those strange pink glasses inspired the boys at Far Hills Country Day School to bully me with greater gusto.

Around the time I got my glasses, I began to steal. Perhaps I felt a deep emptiness inside me I was trying to fill. Our *au pair* girl in Edgartown had a habit of leaving quarters on her bureau. I slipped one into my pocket one day. Nothing happened, so the next day, I took another one, then another. Again, nobody noticed. This made me bold.

When we got back to Far Hills, my mother took me to The Magic Shop, a store in nearby Oldwick, at Christmas time. I was entranced by a miniature wax *crèche*. The tiny baby Jesus was especially adorable. I deftly deposited him in my pocket.

That baby Jesus burned in my pocket like a lump of fiery coal. I was racked with guilt. I had sinned. I would roast in Hell. I woke up every night in a cold sweat. I begged my mother to take me back to the shop. I ran straight to the crèche. I took the little Jesus out of my pocket.

There was no redemption for me. The Jesus had melted into an unrecognizable grey lump coated with shreds of *Kleenex*. My career as a thief was over.

A few weeks later, I was awakened by the sound of somebody crying. I crept out into the hall. The house was dark except for a light shining out from under the door where our new nurse was sleeping. She was very young, fresh off the boat from Ireland, and bitterly homesick.

I hurried back to my room, grabbed a small glass animal, ran back, and handed it to her. She stopped crying. Even though she left the next day, I was suffused with happiness. I helped her. I was powerful and important.

The discovery that I can help myself by helping others has become such a large part of me that it sometimes turns up in my dreams. In one of them, I am with a boyfriend in his sparsely furnished, bleak midwestern house. He introduces me to his two sons, who are six and four. They are quiet and sad because their mother has left them.

These two pitiful boys begin to interest me much more than their father. I rub my hands with glee as I plan how I will make this wounded family happy again. I will begin by buying crayons so the boys can color in their stark black-and-white bedroom wallpaper.

CHAPTER FOUR

London, 1954-1957: I Get to Know My Parents

In 1954, when I was eleven, my father became head of the M. W. Kellogg offices in London. We said goodbye to our relatives in Far Hills and steamed off to England on the Queen Mary, the Cunard Line flagship.

Pictured: Helena and Frank Johnson and their three children on the Cunard line ship "Queen Mary" heading to London, 1954.

I don't remember what I expected to find in London—kings and queens riding around in gold carriages, perhaps. We could not believe how ravaged, dirty, and poor this great city was. We had no idea that London was in flames from German bombs only nine years earlier. We sat in the taxi without saying a word.

Everything was grey. The people had grey, pinched faces, and grey, shabby clothes, and they looked poor and hungry. They trudged stoically down grey streets lined with grey buildings pocked with shell-holes. Grey rain dripped steadily from the grey sky. It rained the day we arrived. It felt like it rained almost every day for the next four years.

Every street in London had bombed-out buildings, including the street where we lived. Whole blocks were nothing but rubble. One of the buildings near our townhouse had been a swimming pool. It was filled with rats, toxins, and feral cats.

We children immediately began to explore these captivating wrecks. My parents, cheerfully oblivious to danger as always, never knew where we were or what we were doing. I found out later that many of these ruins harbored unexploded bombs.

Most of the buildings in London, including ours, did not have central heating. It was so cold inside our house I could see my breath. The only heat came from fireplaces, one per room, where we burned lumps of coal the size of watermelons. The coal truck came once a month, and we children ran out to see the shiny black chunks rumble down into a bin under the sidewalk.

The word "smog"—a mixture of "smoke" and "fog"—was invented to describe the air in London while we were there during the 1950s. The coal smoke mixed with thick white fog from the Thames River to create smog. The air turned the color of caramel pudding when the smog was in. It reeked of sulfur and tar. It made our throats sore and our eyes red.

I could barely see a foot out of the windows when the smog came in. It was so thick it looked as if I could scoop it up with my hands. I watched its yellow fingers creep into the house through the crack under the front door. The silver turned black again an hour after it was polished. Tina, our cook, had to wash the leaves of the bay bushes in front of our house every week, or they would have died.

The smog was no joke. In 1952, two years before we arrived, a toxic smog sat over London for five days and killed at least four thousand people. The smog had killed all the songbirds in the city. In 1956, three years after we arrived, London passed laws to restrict the burning of coal. The smog went away, and birds began to sing in London again.

Lynn and I shared a bedroom. It was heated by an electric heater that hummed cheerfully when we turned it on. We crouched in front of its glowing orange coils at night, toasting our shins until we were warm enough to make a leap for our clammy beds.

Our bedroom window looked over a mews, a narrow cobblestone street designed for carriages and horses. Two older boys lived in the mews, and they could see into our lighted window at night. They jeered at us in Cockney accents as we changed into our nightgowns. I found this strangely exciting. I lingered in the window, which made them yell even louder, and I gloried my power over them. This was my first inkling of sexuality.

Meat, sugar, cheese, jams and jellies, butter, and sweets were rationed. The Brits ate six times as many potatoes during the 1950s as they do today. Our family's weekly allotment of butter in London was what we had once spread on a single piece of toast back in the US. The rationing had ended by the time we left London.

We had a choice of two vegetables in London—cabbage, or Brussels sprouts. The Brits boiled their vegetables, potatoes, and meat until they were mushy, grey, and tasteless. Desert was usually bread pudding with treacle, a golden syrup. Sandwiches were often made with *Marmite*, a salty yeast paste invented as a source of protein and B vitamins during the War. Even Granny served better meals than the ones we ate in London.

Lucky for us, our butcher, like all men, was helpless before my mother's charms. She soon had him madly in love with her. He often slipped us extra meat. She even seduced him out of a rasher of bacon one day, a treat I had not enjoyed since I left the United States. She also persuaded our British National Health Service doctor to make house calls by allowing him one kiss for each child he examined.

The toilet paper in our London house looked like the paper butchers use to wrap meat—stiff, waxed, shiny, and brown. I had to pull each square slowly and carefully from a metal box that was obviously designed to make the user frugal.

The toilet paper in our house was a luxury item compared to the squares cut from magazines and newspapers we used for toilet paper at our school. I could not decide which was worse - the newspaper, or the magazines. This was yet another reminder of the British hardships during the War.

Despite the cold, the non-absorbent toilet paper, the tasteless food, the constant rain, the rationing, and the smog, I quickly fell in love with London. London made me aware for the first time of the extraordinary privilege of my life back home. Far Hills was a well-tended playground for the rich where everything was in perfect repair. London was for real, and the Brits were coping with real problems with dignity and grace. I liked the real world in London better than the fantasy world back home.

London made me realize I did not fit into my parent's life of high society and lavish spending. I wanted challenges, not expensive leisure; a modest life, instead of a high-flying one of beautiful people in beautiful clothes. Even if I had a lot of money—which I eventually did—I had no interest in showing it off.

I admired the British discipline. Nobody dreamed of jumping the long lines for food, and nobody complained. It seemed the rule of law would always prevail in this strong, tough city.

In Far Hills, I had to be driven everywhere by adults. I grew wings in London. I could travel all around the big city by myself on those big red London Transport double-decker buses. I clamped roller skates with four prongs onto my shoes and rolled over the sidewalks—the smoothness of slate, the chatter of cement, the "*tic, tic*" of cracks.

I loved the buildings in London. They were black with soot, pitted with shell holes, and freezing inside, but they were majestic and dignified.

Pictured: The Johnson family in London, Trafalgar Square, 1956.

I loved the candy shop, the size of my clothes closet, that was around the corner from our house. I carefully placed my copper pennies on the counter—as big as cucumber slices, and so heavy they made holes in my pocket— and the little bent old lady handed me sweets in neon colors.

I enjoyed the street sellers who came to our street every week with their barrows and donkey carts. Each had his own unique cry. The ones I remember are "Rags and Bones!" and "Any old Papers, *Hup?*".

I resonated with the British values. Like Granny Edey, the Brits had just a few principles—order, discipline, and fair play. They celebrated their eccentrics. When we visited Bath, every house in one of the classic Georgian semicircles had a green door except for one. The owner, a cantankerous old lady, had painted her door red, as our guide pointed out with pride.

Americans like Grandpa could slap a stranger on the back, tell a few jokes, and become his friend. The British did not make friends as easily as Grandpa did, but they were unshakably loyal once they did. It took me a long time to make a friend in London, but once I found her I had her for life.

The British talked so fast they made me feel tongue-tied. They could chatter on politely about the weather for hours. They made an art of understatement. Noisy Americans stuck out. I began to see my fellow Americans as the British saw them—loud, boastful boors.

Lucky for me, my parents sent Lynn and me to a British school. *Queensgate,* a private all-girl day school, was a half hour away from our house by bus. My mother took us for an interview with the headmistress, Miss Johnson (no relation).

Miss Johnson was compact and stocky, with close-cropped salt-and-pepper hair. I tried not to stare at the jaunty black hairs that were scattered across her upper lip. She took a dim view of any school that was not British.

"Cynthia and Lynn must both go back a year," she said.

My mother sent Lynn to Far Hills Country Day School a year early because she wanted her out of the house after I went to school and was no longer around to amuse her. Holding Lynn back made sense, but—to my surprise—she fought for me to stay in my class. I realized she had paid enough attention to me to know I was a good student.

"If you insist on putting Cynthia back, I will send her to another school," my mother said.

Miss Johnson hesitated. Not many families in London could afford private school for their daughters right after WWII. She turned to me.

"A Swedish girl will join your grade." she said, in a patronizing tone of voice. "She will keep you company at the bottom of the class."

I drowned in the chaos at Far Hills Country Day School. I loved Queensgate School. It was strict and traditional, a perfect fit for a shy bookworm. The teachers expected our full attention, and they got it. I had to listen up and learn something. Best of all, there were no boys to terrorize me.

We had to memorize a poem every week at Queensgate. I remember most of them to this day. We had to learn the name every country, river, city, and mountain range in the world, and draw detailed maps of complicated historical events – such as the reunification of Italy and Germany. I began to think more creatively the more I memorized. The ability to memorize what I learned at Queensgate got me through medical school.

The Far Hills Country Day School students wrote with pencils. The Queensgate students wrote with steel nib pens. My pen was waiting for me in a ridge on top of my desk, near a glass inkwell. I had never even *seen* such a pen. After writing several compositions that resembled Jackson Pollack's drip paintings, I learned to dip the nib in carefully and meticulously wipe off excess ink before I began to write. Writing with that pen taught me to think ahead and move with precision and control— excellent training for the operating room.

We children learned to ride horses in England. We went riding every weekend, first in Hyde Park, and then in Richmond Park. Our parents sent us away to riding camp on vacations.

Pictured: In London, I am about to take Frank and Lynn to riding – all by myself.

I fell off my horse in Richmond Park one weekend. I did not let go of the reins, the horse dragged me, and I broke the little finger of my right hand. I went to my piano lesson the next week with my right fourth and fifth fingers in a splint. I expected my piano teacher, Mrs. Millner, to give me lots of sympathy and a nice long break from my lessons. Mrs. Millner took one look at my right hand and pulled out Paderewski's *Minuet in G.* The middle section has a trill that is played by the thumb and third finger of the right hand, which were not broken, while the left hand plays chords. She told me to learn the middle section by the following week. I did.

Mrs. Millner taught me how to make my hands do whatever I told them to do. She was with me every day I was in the operating room.

The Queensgate students learned their rank in class twice a year. This daunting ceremony took place in the auditorium. All the girls in the school filed in, by class, and sat down on the floor. Miss Johnson called out each girl's name. She began with the lowest-ranked girl in the lowest class and worked her way up. The students stood, one by one, as she favored them with a few crisp comments.

I fidgeted with anxiety as this intimidating ritual of public shaming dragged on at a leisurely pace. The process was so humiliating I thought the lower-ranked girls would burst into tears, but they didn't. The British developed stiff upper lips from an early age.

Finally, Miss Johnson came to our class. As she predicted, the Swedish girl, who barely spoke English, ranked last. She read name after name, but she did not read mine. Had she forgotten me? Finally, she looked up. She did not seem happy. "First in class: Cynthia Johnson."

Queensgate taught us science, which they called "Nature," every year. My other subjects paled in comparison. I was on fire to learn about the body since I saw that turtle. Now I learned those foamy pink sacs were lungs, the yellow loops were intestines, and the purple bag was the liver.

Our history course taught us British history, and only British history. Our textbook depicted everything that had anything to do with Britain with reverence. It barely mentioned other countries unless they impacted Britain. It frequently declared that Britain, only the size of Kansas, once ruled the largest empire in the world: one-quarter of the earth's surface.

The Queensgate students began to study history by learning about the ancient Druids in the lowest grades, then worked their way up to the present day. I was on the merry-go-round from King Henry the Seventh to Queen Anne.

I was taught at Far Hill Country Day School the American Revolution was the most important event in human history. Our British textbook skipped over it in one paragraph. It was called "the revolt of the colonies," and it was grouped with several other colonies that were also rebelling against Britain at that time. Patriotic myths are told by every country. This was not a happy story because Britain lost.

I fulfilled the dream of every bookworm in London—unlimited self-chosen books. *Harrod's*, the consummate British department store, had a children's library. I stopped off on my way home from school several times a week to pick up and return books.

Back in the US, girls my age were reading *Little Women* and *Little House on the Prairie*. I systematically chewed my way through the Rudyard Kipling books, the *Scarlet Pimpernel* series, the *Captain Horatio Hornblower* series, and every novel written by Jane Austen.

I was hopelessly addicted to J.R.R. Tolkien's trilogy, *Lord of the Rings*. I read each book at least fifteen times. I would check one of the books out of the library, read it, return it, and immediately check it out again. I memorized most of the poems and songs, including the ones in *Elvish*, a made-up language. I even made a few discrete corrections to the maps.

This anti-social bookworm found another anti-social bookworm in London. Elizabeth Snagge, now Lady Elizabeth Craig-Cooper, is sensible, cheerful, and intelligent. We became life-long friends. We spent most of our days reading. On rare days when the weather was fine, we lay beside each other under a tree in the park. We curled up together on a couch inside when it rained.

I basked in the warmth of Mr. and Mrs. Snagge's attention. Mr. Snagge teased me and plied me with lightly fermented cider. Mrs. Snagge listened to anything I said with unflagging interest. They were the parents I had dreamed of. This was the kind of family I had read about in books, the one I had imagined all my life, a family where children were appreciated. I wanted to become their child.

Throughout my life, I have found warm, generous people who filled in for my absent parents, and encouraged and supported me. I suspect I was giving off signals that I was eager for attention and affection and willing to work hard to get it. Granny Edey was my first mentor. Elizabeth's parents were my second.

London saved my parents' marriage. They seemed happy together for the first time during the four years we were there. They loved parties, and London was a four-year party for them. They were gregarious, socially adept, and good-looking, and they were not in any British social class, so they fit in everywhere and were accepted by everybody.

They escaped from the Ellistan compound, with its dependency and vying for Grandpa's favor. My father's commute was less than an hour. My mother didn't have a studio. Now, they had time for each other and even for their children.

They took trips to Switzerland to ski with friends. They went to romantic Capri, just the two of them. For the first time in my life, I heard them laughing and joking together. The anxiety that had gripped me all my life began to let go.

They even began to take their children along on some of their trips—Scotland, Cornwall, the Isle of Wight, the Cotswold's, and the Continent. Two distant gods turned into two interesting human beings. I gradually stopped worrying that something terrible was about to happen. At age eleven, I got to know my parents.

Did my mother continue flirting with men in London? Of course, she did. I remember the long, black, chauffeur-driven limousine that purred smoothly up to our house periodically and the famous diplomat inside who took her out to lunch.

Do I think lunch included any time in his bedroom? Not at all. She wanted romance, not sex. She told me years later when a man asked her to sleep with him, she saw my father's face in her mind's eye and refused. She was, in her own unique way, faithful to him.

I devised a new way to connect with my father in London—go along with him on his weekend runs. He ran long distances, mainly through the Parks—Hyde, Green, and St. James. I knew he would tolerate me only if I could keep up with him. I ran until my face was purple, my legs were shaking, and I was gasping for breath. He never told me he enjoyed having me along, but I was with him, so I was happy.

I think of that young girl struggling to keep up with her stone-faced father, and I try to understand why he never noticed how hard I was working. Why didn't he slow down his pace? Why didn't he stop occasionally and let me catch my breath? I remember that sleeping porch at Ellistan, and I know why. He raised me as *he* had been raised.

One day, my mother took me to a great grey building. We climbed dozens of steps, entered a big hall, and went into a large room. It was filled with paintings.

I stood with my mouth open, transfixed. Mysterious women with golden-brown skin were standing or lying in idyllic landscapes painted brilliant colors of scarlet, ochre, and blue. Their long, black hair cascaded over their bare shoulders. They had majestic, serene expressions. They looked savage and exciting and powerful, like mythical goddesses. I could not take my eyes off them.

My favorite painting showed two of these women standing side by side. The naked mahogany-colored breasts of one hovered over a basket filled with flamboyant red flowers. I bought a postcard of it. It was my bookmark for the rest of our time in London.

There was no better guide for my first art exhibit. My mother was confident, happy, alive, and completely herself. Every painting by Paul Gaugin was a religious experience for her. She studied them avidly, greedily, trying to figure out how he handled the hands, the dress, and the hair until the guard barked: "Please step back, madam."

She taught me the rules for a good painting: put dark colors against light, warm colors against cool, round shapes against square, and use strong diagonals. She taught me the primary colors: red, yellow, and blue. A painting had its greatest impact, she said, when a primary color is placed next to a mixture of the other two primaries, i.e., yellow against purple (Easter colors), red against green (Christmas colors), and blue against orange.

Before we left each room, she told me to pick my favorite painting and tell her why I liked it. To this day, I choose my favorite painting in each room at an art exhibit.

Children never get everything they want from their mother. My mother did not give me what most mothers give their children—reassurance, time, attention, and guidance. She never hugged me, tucked me into bed, helped me with my homework, brushed my hair, read stories to me, or taught me how to tie my shoelaces. She gave me what other mothers cannot give—the gift of understanding and enjoying art.

My mother could not give me my meat and potatoes, but she could give me dessert. She taught me how to enjoy the sweet treats of life. I eventually learned to get my meat and potatoes from other people.

Tina, our cook, came with us to London, but our nurse did not, so my mother made me into the nurse. She put me in full charge of my nine-year-old sister and five-year-old brother. I was a mini adult by the time I was eleven years old.

I recently read a letter my father wrote to Grandma Johnson from London. He describes to his mother how I put Frank to bed at night when Tina was off duty. He tells her I read my brother a story, gave him a bath, changed him, and tucked him in—all the motherly duties his wife, my mother, was not interested in.

 Like many eldest daughters, I was not cared for in the way I cared for others. My mother gave me a shocking amount of responsibility because I was the oldest. I thought it was my job to keep everybody in my family happy. I was wild for my mother's approval. She knew I would do anything for her. My life's goal was to make her happy. I did not protest. Indeed, I was grateful.

My relationship with my mother took an extraordinary turn in London. She made me into her mother. I became her closest confidant. We discussed her problems endlessly. She often complained about my father. It made me uncomfortable to hear her criticize my beloved father, but I put up with it.

When I focused on my mother's problems, I buried my own. I built walls around them. I refused to recognize they existed. This ability to wall off problems was a blessing when I became a surgeon and had to block out everything else in my life, from a sick child, to what to make for dinner, and concentrate single-mindedly on the eye I was fixing.

My mother conveniently convinced herself that Lynn and Frank would be perfectly safe if I was in charge. She often reminded me the London *bobbies* (policemen) do not carry guns. London was a safe city for adults, but it was not safe for unaccompanied children. Every creepy man in London was panting to run into us. My man-repellant pink glasses and frizzy hair kept me safe. The pedophiles were mostly interested in my beautiful, blond, nine-year-old sister.

One of my jobs as nurse was to take Lynn and Frank to school every morning. That was fun. We sailed along Knightsbridge on the top deck of a red six-wheeler London Transport double-decker bus, high above the cars, as if we were in our own flying chariot.

Another of my jobs was to take Lynn and Frank to our riding lessons in Richmond Park on Saturdays. That was not much fun. It was an hour's trip on the Underground, and we had to change to three different subway lines. I was riddled with anxiety most of the time.

On Sundays, my mother gave me some money and told me to take Lynn and Frank to the movies. One day, we were the only people in the dark theatre until a man came in. He kept changing his seat, slithering closer and closer to us. He finally sat down next to Lynn, and began to rub up and down against her, panting like a locomotive.

I grabbed Lynn and Frank, and we bolted for home. After my heart stopped pounding, I felt proud of myself. I had saved us. My mother would be impressed by my quick thinking, for sure. I waited modestly for her to praise me when we ran into the house.

My mother did not seem happy to see her three breathless, wide-eyed children trembling in the front hall. Her afternoon was ruined. "Why didn't you call an usher?" she snapped. She sounded cross. "You wasted three good tickets."

I felt as if she had slapped me in the face. I could not figure out what I had done wrong. How could I ever please this woman? To this day, a guaranteed way to make me upset is to criticize me for something I did not know was wrong.

My mother could have qualified for jail time for endangering the welfare of minors, but rich, beautiful women who live in fine houses and wear expensive clothes almost always evade the law.

Searching for my mother's approval was the major project of my childhood. It took me years to realize this project was hopeless. My mother could not love me the way I wanted. I would never, ever get her approval. My job was to learn how to love myself.

Granny Edey developed an ulcer in her fifties. Her doctors told her to drink heavy cream. Predictably, she had a stroke in her seventies, two months before we returned home from London. My mother took the next boat back, arriving the day Granny died. The rest of the family stayed in London. How practical. How devoid of feeling.

Nobody showed any sadness at Granny's death. Nobody mentioned her name again. Granny just... disappeared. I never got to say goodbye. My parents, wrapped up in their own affairs, never realized how much she meant to me. I lost two things when Granny died: Granny, and the person I was when I was with her.

I remember a few random facts about Granny. Her favorite artist was the symbolist painter Puvis de Chavannes, so she had a mystical, romantic side. She was famous for spitting out caraway seeds, which she detested, so she was a passionate woman with strong feelings. Her books are clever and amusing, so she must have been good fun. A man sitting next to her at a dinner party once said, "I hear you are a great wit. Please amuse me."

I eventually realized Granny never left me. She lives on inside me as the values that make up the very core of my being.

I cried for hours the night before we sailed back to the United States. London was my home now. I was not an American anymore. I was a proper British school girl. I had a photograph of the Queen pasted on my closet door. I was leaving behind freedom, art, adventure, an excellent education, my best friend, and the sturdy, old-fashioned British values. Granny's values.

CHAPTER FIVE

Foxhunting: A Granddaughter on Trial

Grandpa had four sons, and his first grandchild, Rick, was a boy. When his next grandchild turned out to be a girl, I suspect he had difficulty imagining a use for me. Remember what he said to my mother: "So the best you could do was a girl!" The only time he paid any attention to me was when I showed him my report card.

The Johnson boys had retired from fox hunting and polo by the time I was born. Their polo mallets ended up inside the medieval chests in the hall. Grandpa used one of those mallets to suspend Rick in the water when he was teaching him how to swim.

Grandpa continued to fox hunt until he fell off his horse and broke his collarbone in his late 60s. He missed fox hunting fiercely. He tried to take up golf, but this precise, slow-moving game was a poor fit for such an energetic, impatient man.

When Grandpa discovered I had learned to ride in England, I could almost see his mind taking me out of the category of "useless girl" and putting me into a new and improved category. I could fox hunt! A Johnson would ride to hounds again!

My parents were thrilled. As previously established, there were significant economic benefits to pleasing Grandpa. My mother plunged into the project of buying me a proper hunting outfit with enthusiasm.

Grandpa always went to Ireland to buy horses for fox hunting. He was too old now to take such a long boat trip. Instead, in the fall of 1957, Tom, his chauffeur, drove him and his horse van to Virginia. They came back with a retired racehorse, a thoroughbred chestnut mare called *Briar Time*. Knowing Grandpa, he haggled the owner down until he got a good price.

The Essex Fox Hounds held—and holds to this day—its biggest hunt meet of the year at Ellistan on Thanksgiving Day. The next Thanksgiving after Grandpa learned I could ride, there I was, the newest member of the field, perfectly turned out, sitting straight and proud on my new horse. The groom had braided red ribbons into Briar Time's mane and tail, polished her hooves with oil, and curried her chestnut coat until she shone bright as a copper kettle in the sun.

The trees had on their fall colors, and the leaves drifted lazily down like giant flakes of red and yellow snow. I had ridden Briar Time several times, but I had never jumped her. It was 1957. I had just turned fifteen.

The driveway rang with the sound of hooves as the riders trotted in. The men stood out in their "pink" coats, which are in fact bright red—the name comes from *Pinks*, the British store that makes them.

The four Galloping Grandmothers swept in, one by one, riding side-saddle, wearing long black skirts and black hats with black veils. These Far Hills matrons still rode to hounds, although they all had grandchildren.

The riders clustered around Tom, Grandpa's butler, while he passed out glasses of his famous "stirrup cup." He brought the ancient recipe with him from England. He made it from brandy, sherry, and rum infused with oranges and lemons, and he served it piping hot. It was strong enough to give courage to the most apprehensive rider—me. Grandpa strolled about, flashing his thousand-watt smile, greeting his friends, and enjoying their favorable comments about this new Johnson member of the hunt.

Then my mother showed up. Her camera was clicking away like a machine gun. I always wondered what I had to do to get that woman to notice me. Now I knew the answer—do something that impressed people she looked up to. That lit a fire in my belly. I would make something of my life. Then, my mother would have to pay attention to me.

Buster, the huntsman, the man who trains and works the hounds, was lifting his horn to his lips when I noticed a single female rider trotting up Grandpa's long driveway. About half the riders who hunted with the Essex Fox Hounds were women. That girlish smile—that orange make-up—it must be—it *was*—Jackie Kennedy. Her husband, Jack, was a US senator at that time.

Jackie's arrival was taken as a matter of course. Many eminent people hunted with the Essex in those days. Her smile never flagged. She never spoke to anybody—including me.

Buster blew the *"Moving On"* call. The hounds answered him with a chorus of high yelps. They were shivering with excitement. Forty riders tightened their lips, shortened their reins, and pushed their hats down on their heads. Forty horses pricked their ears and began to snort and jump around. One by one, their tails rose, and they deposited steaming piles of dung on the ground.

Buster led the hounds into a nearby wood. The whips spread out around the periphery. Suddenly, the hounds started to give tongue. A whip yelled, *"Tallyho!"* He had spotted the fox. Buster blew the *"Gone Away"* call. We were off.

I soon realized I was in deep trouble. There is an adage about horses—*"The purer the blood, the smaller the brain."* Briar Time was no well-schooled Irish fox hunter. She was only trained to race. All she knew how to do was to beat other horses to the finish line. She didn't even know how to jump. I was stuck on the back of a pig-headed idiot.

Horses have long, sharp teeth in front, which they use to nip up grass, and broad, flat teeth in back, to grind up grass. The bit is supposed to sit in the gap between these two sets of teeth. Briar Time had learned to push the bit between her back teeth and clamp down. Once she had the bit between her teeth, I could not control her.

When the field began to gallop, Briar Time decided this was the moment she should beat the other horses. I sawed away at the reins, tears streaming down my cheeks, as we streaked past the annoyed Field Master—the worst breach of fox hunting etiquette. I spent the next six hours clinging on, convinced I would die any moment.

I thought I was well prepared for fox hunting. I enjoyed riding. I had galloped many horses, and I knew how to get horses over a fence. I had no idea the sport was so dangerous or that my horse would be so unmanageable.

I never thought of leaving before the hunt was over. I knew Grandpa would be furious. I was more afraid of Grandpa's anger than I was of dying. Like Jackie Kennedy, I glued a fixed smile onto my face and spoke to nobody. I was so grateful to get off that horse alive that I almost cried.

I quickly gained the reputation of being a mad, keen fox hunter. Briar Time and I were invariably first in the field and first over every jump. Nobody suspected the truth—that I could not stop my horse.

Pictured: Me riding Briar Time at the Essex Fox Hounds meet at Ellistan, Thanksgiving Day 1959, next to a proud Grandpa Johnson. I am holding a glass of Tom's "Stirrup Cup", and the orange color of the E.F.H. is on my collar.

In record time, I was wearing the gold *colors* of the Essex on my collar and the black buttons inscribed *"E.F.H."* on my black coat. ("Colors" are an honor given to riders who have proven they are avid and bold.) When Grandpa saw me in colors for the first time, his smile almost split his face in two.

Fox hunting is dangerous even if you are riding a well-trained horse. Galloping that nitwit Briar Time up and down hills, stumbling over chicken coops, post- and- rail fences, and walls, plunging through rivers, and scrabbling over rocks, ice, and mud was lunacy.

Years later, when I mentioned Briar Time to Uncle Coddy, he said: "There was something wrong with that horse." If Coddy knew how crazy she was—and he had never ridden her—my whole family must have known, but there was a conspiracy of silence on the subject. Nobody was willing to tackle Grandpa, including my parents.

My father knew the dangers of fox hunting only too well. He had held a woman in his arms one day while she bled to death after she ruptured her spleen on the pommel of her side saddle. He did not try to stop me. Social success and pleasing Grandpa were so important to my parents that they willfully ignored the health and safety of their daughters.

My father had played polo and slept on an open porch all winter to please Grandpa. Now, it was my turn. Grandpa was proud of me. I did not dare complain. I did not think his love would survive if I stopped fox hunting.

Grandpa expected Lynn to fox hunt, also. The night before one hunt, she began to vomit. She vomited all night long. She wanted to stay in bed the next morning, but our father went into her room, told her to get up and get dressed in her hunting clothes, and get up to the stable.

Luckily, I only had one serious accident during the years I rode to hounds on Briar Time. One cold winter day, she stumbled while she was jumping over a ditch and fell. The icy ground came flying up to meet us. I was still sitting on top of her when she crashed over onto my left leg. As she struggled to get up, she ground my left hip into the frozen earth. The pain was so bad I blacked out. I was sixteen.

The next thing I remember is waking up on the library couch at home. Bolts of pain shot through my left leg when I tried to get up. I could not walk for several weeks, but eventually, my hip seemed to heal, and I assumed this was only a minor mishap. I had no idea this hip injury was a ticking time bomb that would blow up five decades later and plunge me into the worst pain of my life—as we will get to in Chapter Twenty-Two.

People who don't know anything about fox hunting probably assume that the point is to kill foxes, but that is wrong. If all the foxes get killed, there will be no more foxes to hunt. Foxhunters want the fox to give them an exciting gallop across country, and then escape so we can hunt it another day. Some fox hunts—I will not name names—buy foxes and seed the countryside with them each year.

I would have hated fox hunting even more if the foxes were killed, but they almost never were. The fox is the smartest creature out there. Foxes are wily. When the fox tires of the game, it simply goes to ground in one of its strategically placed burrows. The only foxes who get killed are either old, or sick. I rode to hounds for five years, and I never was in a hunt where the fox was killed.

The only part of fox hunting I enjoyed was going to Ellistan after the hunt to debrief Grandpa. I marched down the great hall in my mud-spattered boots to the wood-paneled library where Grandpa would be waiting for me by the fire, reading his latest book. The minute he saw me, he turned on his hearing aid. That was a compliment. He turned it off when he was with a person whom he thought was boring—which included me before I began to fox hunt.

He wanted to know every detail—who was there, where we met, where the hounds picked up the scent, and where we ran. The more mud I had on my riding outfit, the happier he was. His eyes shone as he re-lived his own days in the field.

I am probably alive today only because Briar Time was killed in 1961 by a bolt of lightning while she was standing in Grandpa's field during a thunderstorm. I tried to look sad when the groom told me the news, but I was cheering inside.

CHAPTER SIX

Boarding School, 1957-1960:
An Unhappy Spider, an Obedient Debutante

In September 1957, two weeks after we got home from London, my parents sent me and my horse Briar Time to St. Timothy's School in Stevenson, Maryland. I was fifteen. Boarding school was a rite of passage in my family. Escape was not possible. I was incarcerated at STT for the next three years, except for vacations, when I was expected to ride to hounds.

One of my friends told me he has a new definition of privilege since reading my memoir. It is going to boarding school with your horse.

This was the same all-girl boarding school my mother attended and hated. Why did she send first me, and then Lynn, to a school she loathed? My guess is STT had impeccable social credentials, and my parents were keen on high society. They did not know how unhappy I was at STT because I never told them. I knew they would not listen.

Two weeks earlier, I had been wandering, alone, around one of the biggest cities in the world. Now, I was only allowed to "walk the lane"— stroll down the driveway and back — if I signed out before I left, signed in after I got back, and took two friends with me.

What made me truly depressed was I had chosen this school myself. The day I visited; horses were grazing in sun-dappled fields on both sides of a long driveway lined with majestic old trees. *This is the school for me*, I thought.

I turned down blue-stocking Milton Academy in Boston, where I would have been much happier, because I visited on a windy day and a piece of dust blew under one of my contact lenses (My mother had me fitted with contact lenses—another miracle of sight.).

I was suspended between two cultures. I was not an American now. I was a British expatriate, with British manners, accent, customs, and clothes.

The stated purpose of STT was to produce *"Christian gentlewomen."* The school contained one hundred and twenty prospective Christian gentlewomen, all from genteel families, all white. I assumed we were all Protestant until I saw a handful of Catholic girls huddled in the courtyard one Sunday morning, waiting for the bus to take them to Mass.

Almost all the girls came from rich families. A few were on scholarship. I talked to one of these scholarship girls years later. She said the headmistress, Miss Watkins, made her wear second-hand uniforms so everybody would know she was a charity case. Miss Watkins reminded her of her inferior status on a regular basis. She hated the school even more than I did.

Every student at STT was arbitrarily assigned to one of two teams, called *"Brownies"* and *"Spiders."* She was thereafter expected to have a life-long, passionate loyalty to "her" team.
We wore uniforms at STT. During the spring and fall we wore green *(Spider)* or brown *(Brownie)* tunics with white short-sleeved shirts and black-and-white saddle shoes. In the winter, we switched to navy blue or grey wool skirts.

My mother was a Brownie at STT. Remember how sensitive she was to colors. She hated the color of her brown uniform. She called it *"tobacco spit"*. She thought it made her look ugly. She wanted me to wear green, so she signed me up to be a Spider. Good for her. She did not have any sappy, sentimental attachment to "her" Brownies.

The big treat of the fall term was the Brownie-Spider basketball game. I sat in a puddle of misery as eighteen girls I barely knew played, for what seemed like several days, an ancient form of basketball found nowhere else in the world.

Every Spider and Brownie was cheering with fanatic enthusiasm for "her" team. This was not a cause I could believe in. Cheering for a girl who was wearing a green tunic made about as much sense to me as cheering because she had blonde hair. I thought they were crazy. All those people transfixed, dazzled, screaming for some nebulous belief they did not understand? All that flagrant emotion for something so trivial?

Then I realized that I, too, was expected to cheer for 'my" Spiders, and feign allegiance to a cause whose values were not only unclear, but also trivial. My interest in this barbaric ritual was zero, but I cheered until I was hoarse. Things got worse after the game was over. All the Brownies and Spiders fell into each other's arms, tearfully congratulating each other. I am ashamed to admit that I even wrote a fight song for "my" Spiders a week later.

To be fair to STT, I was an overly sensitive, overly intense, overly intellectual teenager who was primed to dislike any other school I went to because I had been so happy at Queensgate.

I need to face the facts: I was a judgmental prig, too tense to let go and enjoy the commotion, too uptight to fit in, too certain my own values were right and theirs were wrong, too worried about proving myself to enjoy other girls' achievements.

Today, I forgive that fifteen-year-old for her hypocrisy. I had to conform to this grotesque school. I was too anxious about my parents' approval to complain. I knew my parents would not welcome me home if I did.

Lynn followed me to STT two years later. When she came home after her first semester, she fell on her knees and begged our mother not to send her back. Our mother asked Lynn where she planned to go to school and how she would get there. Lynn said she would go to public school in Bernardsville and take the bus. Our mother reminded Lynn that her parents went away to Florida for six weeks in the winter, and Lynn would have no place to live. Lynn said she would stay at Ellistan with Grandma and Grandpa.

I give my sister high marks for courage, but I knew her cause was hopeless. She went back to STT as scheduled, and so did I.

Most of the teachers at STT were widows or spinsters who had been at the school for years. They seemed more interested in the neatness of our clothes and room and the politeness of our manners than in the quality of our thinking.

Queensgate School was strict, but the rules were designed to help us learn. The rules at STT seemed designed to chop off all our individual quirks and remove everything that made us unique and interesting.

Our uniforms were under constant surveillance by the teachers. The slightest deviation from perfection brought down a punishment called a *"tidy cross."* The teachers inspected our rooms every morning. Poor bed-making or disheveled bureau drawers were another opportunity to get a tidy cross.

My first tidy cross came after I had been at STT for one month. One of the teachers gave it to me for "sloppy dressing." I was flabbergasted. All my clothes were new. My blouse was neatly pressed. The hem of my skirt was straight. My shoes gleamed with polish.

I tried to protest. The teacher told me the heel of one of my shoes was worn down. By using all my imagination, I could barely make out that one of my heels was indeed a quarter inch shorter than the other. "The paths at school wear down shoes quickly," she smirked.

There was an honor system at STT. Periodically, every student wrote a letter placing herself in one of three Groups depending on her conduct, which included the number of her tidy crosses. Our Group determined our privileges.

Group One was for perfect goody-goodies who did not have a single tidy cross and had not broken any rules—or for hypocrites who were clever liars. *Group Two*—where most of us resided—was for students who had broken only a few minor rules and had only a few tidy crosses. *Group Two Minus* was the final stage before a student was expelled.

I must have repressed this stage in my life—I cannot remember my Group. I suspect that begging and groveling to get into Group One seemed like a lost cause, so I automatically put myself in Group Two.

Students in Group Two Minus were sent to see the headmistress, Miss Watkins. This formidable woman had dyed purple hair pulled back in a severe bun, an enormous bust, three chins, and a permanent scowl of disapproval. Her cold, ice-blue eyes terrified us.

Rumor said Miss Watkins had never married because her one true love was killed in World War One. Many years later, I heard a more likely story. Miss Watkins was living, discretely, in a cottage near the swimming pool with her one true love—mannish, efficient Miss Bement, who managed the day-to-day operations of the school.

I did not think I would ever have any sympathy for Miss Watkins. Now I know about her burden of secrecy, I feel more charitable towards her.

Halfway through my first semester, I was in the study hall when one of the teachers ran in and whispered in my ear that Miss Watkins wanted to see me in her office, immediately. I ran up to the main building, my heart racing. I thought one of my parents had died.

"Your mother was a Brownie. We have made you a Spider. I apologize for this appalling mistake," she said. I sighed with relief, and explained my mother preferred green to brown. Those frosty blue eyes were not amused.

Sunday was the worst day at this bizarre holdover from Victorian times. One of the more peculiar rules was we were not permitted to do homework, listen to popular music, or wash our hair on Sundays. We were only allowed to read the Bible and listen to classical music.

Every Sunday morning, the whole school went to an interminable service at the local Episcopal Church. This was the only time the students were allowed to wear their own clothes, and they put on a fashion show—chic dresses, stylish hats, and high-heeled shoes with matching handbags. My dowdy British wardrobe was an embarrassment. Luckily, I sang in the choir, so I could wear a robe with a surplice and did not have to compete.

I studied the clothes of the other girls furtively, avidly, trying to figure out how they pulled off that casual, confident look. Fair Isle sweaters, circle pins, sweater sets, and penny loafers were new to me. I was even more intimidated by their sophistication about men. They talked casually about kissing their boyfriends—and more.

Sunday afternoons in spring, all the students in the school sat in a circle in the auditorium and sewed pieces of pink and blue flannel into baby nightgowns while Miss Watkins read aloud to us. Rumors flew these nightgowns were intended for the babies of the unwed mothers of Baltimore—a not-so-subtle reminder of the importance of always being a perfect Christian gentlewoman.

I am certain boys in their private boarding schools were not required to sew baby nightgowns. They were in training to be masters of the universe.

STT was training us to sew on their buttons. The only sewing I wanted to do was to fix injured people.

One day, one of the girls took me aside, saying she wanted to give me some advice. "At last, a friend." I thought.

"Drop that fake British accent and stop wearing long white socks with your tennis sneakers." she said. Then she added: "You are not smart. You are just a reader."

She sounded confident, but I did not think she was correct. I was a top student at Queensgate, which was a more demanding school than STT. I admired her rebellious spirit, and we began a wary friendship, but we did not stay in touch after graduation. I found out later she died young— a suicide.

Queensgate taught us science every year, but the only science at STT was a choice of either Biology or Physics, which we took during senior year. The school did not teach Chemistry. The math courses stopped dead after Trigonometry, and there were no courses in pre-calculus or calculus. I arranged to take Biology junior year and Physics senior year.

It was obvious STT did not expect their students to have to work– especially not in a job that involved science. Their husbands would have excellent jobs, and they would make the money to support the family. Presumably, Christian gentlewomen would not need to know chemistry or calculus while they were sewing on their husbands' buttons.

A few years later, this Christian gentlewoman was the only student in her college chemistry and calculus classes who had not already taken these courses in high school. This was a brutal experience. I barely passed both.

Back to my years at STT. At least I was able to study biology. The biology teacher was married, and she lived outside the school, so she had more insight into the minds of teenage girls than those elderly spinsters. She was a Radcliffe graduate, and she vibrated with energy.

Learning about the human body was bliss. I had learned the names of the organs of the human body at Queensgate. Here was my chance to find out how they worked. I read through the entire biology textbook before the rest of the class finished the first chapter. I took the lab mannequin apart and put it back together again until I knew every organ perfectly.

In the spring, the teacher gave each biology student a rat pickled in formaldehyde. The arteries were injected with red latex, and the veins with blue. I could not wait to get inside my rat.

The next day was warm and sunny. Miss Watkins announced a surprise holiday. Everybody cheered and headed for the lawn to get a tan. Everybody but me, that is. I headed straight for the school building. I spent my holiday in the biology lab under the glare of fluorescent lights— just me, my rat, the mannequin, and the medicinal reek of *formaldehyde.*

I was not popular at STT because I wasn't a real person, I was only a pathetic fake. I kept a perpetual grin on my face, like some masked actor in an ancient Greek play. I didn't tell anybody my thoughts or feelings. I put on the same act I put on back home…perky, pretending to be flawless. I made no lasting friends there, only acquaintances.

I kept my head down. I studied what the teachers told me to study and thought what they wanted me to think. I worked hard. I got good grades. I was Editor of the yearbook.

The most important skill I picked up at STT was to learn how to function when I was deeply depressed. I mastered the art of pretending to be happy when all I wanted to do was crawl into bed and put a pillow over my head. I graduated with a PhD in detachment. I was on track to do well in the operating room.

My sister was authentically herself at STT. Instead of a stiff, smirking robot, she was a genuine human being. She made many friends there, some lifelong.

When I went through some old papers recently, I discovered a few essays I wrote at STT for Current Events, Religion, and History. To my surprise, they showed that I was actively engaged in the subject matter at that school. The truth was I was happy there on an intellectual level.

The only college I applied to was Radcliffe, the female part of Harvard College. Radcliffe had the reputation of academic excellence, first-rate faculty, and excellent students. My Johnson family, especially Grandpa, valued being The Best. Getting into a good college was how I hoped to get the attention of my remote parents and grandfather.

I visited Harvard during my father's 25th reunion. I applied for Early Decision and was accepted. Only two other girls in my class got in.

In fact, Radcliffe existed in name only. Radcliffe women went to Harvard classes with Harvard men. They were taught by Harvard professors, they took Harvard exams, they were graded on the same scale as Harvard men, and they graduated with a Harvard degree. I went to Harvard.

I graduated from STT in 1960. Grandpa Johnson came to my graduation, beaming, in a blinding all-white outfit—white shirt, white tie, white linen suit, white Panama hat, and white shoes polished to a high shine. He charmed all my spinster teachers. I watched with amazement as he even got a smile out of Miss Watkins.

Years later, when I was an eye surgeon, STT invited me back to talk to the students about a medical career. Miss Watkins was long gone. As my taxi rolled past those two stone pillars and down that long driveway, I did not feel like an eye surgeon; I felt like a prisoner going back to jail. When I drove away, a wave of relief washed over me. I had escaped.

I saw Miss Watkins once more, many years after I graduated, when she came to my office for a second opinion about her retina problem. She said loudly as she walked into my room: "I know you will not be able to help me. I am only here because so many STT alumni have told me I must come." She did not ask me about my life or congratulate me on my career. Her eyes never met mine. I did not expect her to smile. She did not.

This was the woman who had terrified me when I was a STT student. Now, I saw her for what she really was: hostile, insecure, self-focused, and pathetic. She had no humanity. I felt sorry for her.

I almost did not go back to my 50th reunion, but I am glad I did. It was obvious that St. Timothy's was a far better school in 2010 than it had been fifty years earlier.

The school now teaches the International Baccalaureate Degree to students from forty different countries. The girls and teachers looked genuinely happy and excited. A shy fifteen-year-old with an intellectual bent and an international outlook—a girl like me in 1957—would feel right at home there.

I realized at my reunion those terrifying classmates of mine were figments of my imagination. Many of them confessed they were just as miserable at STT as I was. Underneath all those fashionable clothes were homesick girls like me. We were all putting on an act. We could not see each other through the walls we constructed around us.

After graduation, I became a *debutante*, i.e., an upper-class young woman who makes her first appearance in fashionable society. This involved purchasing an expensive strapless white dress I wore only once to my own party, and several other expensive dresses to wear to the debutante parties of my friends.

Pictured: Me as a debutante on the arm of my father, 1960.

I didn't take the debutante game seriously. It was one of the many rituals I had to endure on my way to become an adult —like going away to boarding school. I wasn't excited by the prospect. It was just another milestone I had to pass.

Buying ball gowns was a project my mother could believe in. We descended on *Saks, Lord and Taylor, Bonwit Teller*, and *Bergdorf Goodman*, and commandeered a saleslady and a dressing room. I danced the night away in high-heeled silver shoes. When the sun rose, trays of scrambled eggs and champagne were rolled in.

The best debutante parties had a *Lester Lanin* orchestra. Lester, a marketing genius, threw out colorful felt hats embroidered with his name at the end of the party. The men gathered around the band and fought to grab one of these trophies for their date.

I took out Lester Lanin's cataracts many years later. He handed his signature hats to every member of the operating room team. He gave me several CDs, and I played one of them during his surgery. When I asked him how he felt during the operation, he said he wished he had brought the trumpets in a bit louder.

For my own debutante party, my parents removed the furniture from the Ellistan living room, which provided room for several hundred people to dance. Dinner was in a tent outside the house. It started to rain hard, and the roof of the tent began to sag. My three uncles ran into the house, grabbed their polo mallets from the medieval chests in the hall, and pushed the water out to keep the tent from collapsing.

Nobody acknowledged it, but this expensive debutante ritual was a deadly serious mating game. I was presented to a group of socially acceptable tuxedo-clad bachelors as a choice piece of nubile female flesh, alluringly decked out in a strapless evening gown. These men knew my parents had money because they could afford my high-priced dresses and throw that expensive party. Uncles wielding polo mallets were a perfect finishing touch.

One of my friends asked her parents to give her the money for a trip to Europe instead of throwing her a debutante party. I was too anxious for my parents' approval to question their values. I had not yet learned to question authority—especially their authority. If they wanted me to be a debutante, I would be a debutante.

The debutant ritual worked in my case. One week before I went to Harvard, I met Malcolm MacKay, a rising sophomore at Princeton, at a debutante party on Long Island given by one of my STT classmates.

Malcolm was tall, dark, handsome, and brimming with ambition. I was impressed by his cocky air, his confident arrogance, and his no-nonsense energy as he piloted me briskly around the dance floor. He was charming, and, in my family, charm was held in high esteem. He was so alive he made *me* feel alive.

This man would go places. Here was an adult. All the other men seemed like the teenagers they were.

Malcolm had flawless credentials. He grew up on the socially acceptable North Shore of Long Island, and he graduated from St. Paul's School, the male equivalent of STT. He had the right accent and the right clothes—not too flashy, best quality, exclusively Brooks Brothers. His expensive shoes were polished to a high shine. His manners were impeccable. He leapt to pull out my chair, open the door, and help me on with my coat.

Best of all, he had the casual confidence of the St. Timothy's girls. He would be my ticket to social success. I would never feel inadequate again. In short, he had everything I believed—at that time—was important in a husband.

The next day, he invited me to crew for him in a sailing race. He got so far ahead of the boats in his own class he began to race the boats in the class ahead. I was impressed.

A storm blew up. I looked at the wind whipping his black hair and thought he would be the perfect skipper to take over my life. We came back soaked. Malcolm grabbed a towel and tousled my wet hair. He was so impudent and playful I almost laughed out loud.

CHAPTER SEVEN

Harvard, 1960-1964: Men, Eyes, Marriage

Until I arrived at Harvard, I always felt like an oddball when I was with girls my own age. They liked to shop for clothes and make-up; I was a bookworm who liked to stay home reading books. They knew everything about popular culture; I was clueless. They liked rock and roll and Elvis; I liked Bach, Beethoven, and Brahms.

I felt comfortable being myself the minute I got to Harvard Square. I didn't have to put on an act to fit in and pretend I was anything other than who I was. Harvard Yard was crawling with misfit bookworms just like me. A dinner topic my first night was whether Jesus, whose mother was a virgin, could have been born through parthenogenesis (– the answer is *no*).

The intellectual fizz in the air made me dizzy with excitement. I avidly studied the courses in the catalogue and the notices fluttering from bulletin boards—madrigal groups, debating clubs, opera societies, and Gilbert and Sullivan players. I felt like a kid in a candy store. I couldn't decide what to grab first.

My roommate, Lisa Stokes, and I connected immediately. Our childhoods had been uncannily alike—a great deal of privilege and very little attention from our parents. We roomed together for four years. We have remained close all our lives.

I was a pudgy, unpopular girl with frizzy hair and thick pink glasses for most of my life, but recently I had slimmed down in places and bulked up in other places. My man-repellant glasses were replaced by contact lenses. I didn't have to worry about wearing the right clothes because the other women had even less interest in fashion than I did.

My class had three hundred women and one thousand men. I was surrounded by smart, interesting potential boyfriends. The boys who made my life miserable in grade school were much nicer to me now. I was… popular with men! It went to my head like champagne.

There was an unstated purpose to my time at Harvard: I had four years to nail a socially acceptable husband. My mother was not subtle about drilling this into me. Many years before, one summer in Edgartown, I played with a boy named Natty Norton. She took a photograph of the two of us selling lemonade, pasted it in my scrapbook, and drew a heart around it. I got the message. A woman has value only if she can attract a valuable man.

I did not want to compete with my mother and get thirty-one proposals of marriage, but I did want to date as many men as possible to have a good selection. During my freshman year, I majored in Harvard men, with a minor in Princeton men.

All I had to do to find myself a boyfriend was wash my hair, shave my legs, and show up in the Great Hall at Widener Library wearing a skirt, sheer stockings, and heels. Another option was to wander the aisles of the campus store, the Harvard Coop, until I "accidentally" bumped into a promising suspect. If I really wanted to study, I headed for the Radcliffe Library in blue jeans.

There were many men I would happily meet for a coffee date, but I did not allow them to become my boyfriends. Only a narrow range of men were acceptable as romantic partners.

The freshman women enjoyed a free dating service called the *Radcliffe Freshman Register*, which listed our name, photograph, and dormitory, nine per page. The men studied it with enthusiasm. Some men set up betting pools where a pot of money went to the first man to date three across, three down, or three diagonally. This involved a difficult decision—go for the attractive women or for the ones who might be more available?

If a man telephoned our dorm when I was out, the student at Bells Desk put a blue slip with his name and telephone number into my mailbox. I saved all my blue slips, and, in the spring, I laid them out on the floor and gloated. I had over a hundred. I guess I was more like my mother than I like to admit.

The rules were clear for women in the early 1960s—no sex before marriage. The price for a woman's virginity was an engagement ring. Very few of my boyfriends got to First Base (kissing). Only a select few got to Second Base (touching my breasts). Nobody got to Third Base (the whole deal).

"Parietal Rules" established when men and women were allowed to visit each other's dormitories. Men were allowed into the formal rooms downstairs in my dormitory on rare occasions, but they were never, ever allowed upstairs into our bedrooms. If a man and woman were caught in a room together alone, both would be expelled instantly.

We had to be back in our dormitories by a certain time. I remember frantically kissing boyfriends on the dorm steps during the last five minutes before the witching hour.

One day, I heard the shocking news that a woman in my dorm had sex before she was married. I tried not to stare at her. She looked remarkably normal for a ruined woman. I was certain she would never find a husband. To my surprise, she found two.

Years later, my daughter Hope, a Princeton graduate, asked me how many men I dated at Harvard. I told her at least a hundred. "Mom!!" she said. She was shocked. She thought I had sex with all of them. In her time, if a woman and a man were dating, they were sleeping together.

I continued to date Malcolm during my four years at Harvard. I knew I would probably marry him, but I did not want to get tied down until I had tested other possibilities. He came up to Cambridge often, and I went down to Princeton. I telephoned him every Sunday night, sitting on top of the smelly shoes in our closet. We always talked about superficial things. We never discussed our feelings.

I did just enough work to avoid flunking out during freshman year. I memorized the words that danced up from the pages of my textbooks, spewed them forth on exams, and promptly forgot them. All those ideas just washed through me and out into the ether. None of them seemed important. It was just a game I had to play to stay around all those men.

Halfway through freshman year, I met an MIT engineering student at a *mixer* (a dance to introduce men and women). He was a free spirit, warm, and sensitive. He had a happy heart and a gift for enjoying life. He always knew what I was thinking and feeling. There was real depth to this man. I could really connect to him.

When he visited me in Far Hills, he was the only boyfriend who went out to the kitchen to talk to Tina. Tina told me afterward he was the man I really loved. She knew me better than I knew myself.

We began to kiss on the living room couch after my parents went to bed. As our kisses became slower and more languid, I began to feel strange. My breath became short. My brain clouded over.

"What is happening?" I whispered in an unsteady voice.

"You are aroused." he whispered in a voice filled with emotion. "There will be plenty of time for that in the future." Then he went up to the guest room.

I was falling for him, hard, but there was a problem—he was not acceptable marriage material. He grew up in a poor Southern family and he went to public school. He did not have the social credentials to fit into my upper-crust world. My parents would not approve of him.

I valued the pedigree, not the man. I was an immature snob who had not yet learned to think for myself. I called him and told him I did not want to see him anymore. He did not argue or get angry, but his voice sounded sad. He said something sensible and loving and hung up. I never saw him again. My face burns when I think about him. I know Larry has made some lucky woman very happy.

During my freshman year, I signed up for many—too many—extracurricular activities. I joined the tennis team, the fencing team, and the riding team. I sang in a madrigal group. I sang opera arias with a man who played the piano. Another man taught me how to play the guitar. I joined the Radcliffe Choral Society, and we gave concerts all over Cambridge and Boston, including the Isabella Stewart Gardener Museum and Sanders Theatre. We sang concerts with the Harvard Glee Club and the Boston Symphony Orchestra.

I joined the Gilbert and Sullivan Players. I played a lovesick maiden in "Patience," and picked up a boyfriend who was playing a soldier. My parents drove all the way up from Far Hills to attend opening night. This was a not-so-subtle signal about their priorities.

My mid-semester grades were alarming. Philosophy baffled me. Calculus was incomprehensible because I had not taken any of the preparatory courses. I was the only student in Inorganic Chemistry class who had not already taken the course in high school. I passed only because a boyfriend coached me through. Our relationship ended when Chemistry ended.

My heart sank when my "faculty advisor" asked me to come to her office. I assumed she wanted to discuss my grades. She looked up briefly from her desk and vaguely focused on me as I walked in.

"Are you having any difficulty coordinating your social life and academic schedule?" she said, stifling a yawn.

"No," I lied. I realized she had not even looked at my grades.

"Good," she said. She stood up. We shook hands. This was our first and last meeting. I had the strong impression she never wanted to see me again. I certainly did not want to see her.

I do not think my parents ever looked at my Harvard grades, either. They had no interest in my academic credentials. They wanted me to marry a man with good academic credentials. They never asked me if I was interested in a career after college. They would not have been happy if I flunked out, but it was almost impossible to flunk out of Harvard once you got in, back in those days.

I became a serious student sophomore year because I took a biochemistry course called Nat Sci (Natural Sciences) Five, taught by George Wald. My brain was on fire from my first moment in that course. I was studying about the human body again, so everything I learned seemed interesting and important. I spent a lot more time in the library and a lot less time on extracurricular activities. Now it was easy to get good grades. Much of what I learned in Nat Sci 5 has stayed with me the rest of my life.

Wald had a mellifluous, mesmerizing voice. His dark, soulful eyes glowed behind thick black glasses. Tendrils of curly hair sprouted from his head, which made him resemble Albert Einstein and announced his superior intelligence. I hung on to his every word.

The day finally came when Wald gave his famous lecture on the eye. When the first slide flashed on the screen, I sat bolt upright in my chair. I saw that diagram of the eye sixty years ago, but I still remember every detail. I remember where I was sitting in the auditorium. I remember the crisp fall day outside. I even remember the eye was looking to the right. I felt I had been struck by lightning. One lecture changed my life— although it took me a decade to realize it.

I could not believe how intricate the eye was. Charles Darwin had the same problem. The complexity of the eye made him temporarily question his theory of evolution. He found it hard to believe this extraordinary organ could have arisen through natural selection alone.

Wald's next slide was a diagram of the human retina. The retina has one hundred twenty million rods and six and a half million cones, he said. These tiny photoreceptors absorb light and convert it into an electrical signal, which is processed in the retina, picked up by nerve fibers, and carried to the brain.

He told us about the retinal molecule, *rhodopsin*, that changes light into electricity. All vertebrates, including humans, have rhodopsin in their eyes. The retina makes rhodopsin by connecting Vitamin A to a protein, called opsin. When light hits rhodopsin, it breaks apart again into Vitamin A and opsin, which creates an electric signal that races up to the occipital lobe in the back of the brain, which is where we see. Three years after I graduated, in 1967, Professor Wald won the Nobel Prize for discovering how rhodopsin generates that electrical signal when it breaks apart.

Humans cannot make Vitamin A, so they must get it from food. People who do not have Vitamin A in their diet cannot make rhodopsin, so they go blind. The first symptom of Vitamin A deficiency is *night blindness*, or loss of the ability to see in dim light.

An ancient Egyptian papyrus written three thousand, five hundred years ago describes night blindness and its cure— eat liver, which is chock full of Vitamin A. Many people in Europe during World War Two developed night blindness because their food supply was very limited.

I sat stunned, silent, in awe. After the lecture finished, I marched up to one of the handsome young course assistants standing by the wall. "I would like to work in your lab." I announced. John Dowling said kindly, "I would be happy to have you work in my lab." I did retina research in John's lab for the next three years.

John Dowling was, and is, a wickedly smart, easy, affable, modest, and unflappable scientist. His generosity to Harvard students is legendary. He is equally generous to men and women, which was not true of every Harvard professor at that time. He has inspired hundreds of first-rate scientists and doctors.

There is no advisory guidance structure for Harvard students. They are on their own. They must make their own luck. This system is not necessarily bad or good, but students who apply there need to know whether they would thrive under this system.

John was the best part of Harvard for me. Without John, I would never have become an eye surgeon. My years at Harvard were a success because I took the initiative to find him. Harvard did not work well for less entrepreneurial students, who felt lost and abandoned there. My roommate Lisa is a prime example.

George Wald discovered Vitamin A comes in two different forms. Animals that live on land, including humans, and fish that live in salt water, have *Vitamin A1* in their retinas. Freshwater fish have a different form of Vitamin A called *Vitamin A2*.

What about frogs, you ask, that start off as tadpoles in fresh water and then turn into land animals? Wald discovered tadpoles have Vitamin A2 in their retinas, but this changes to Vitamin A1 when they move to land.

How about salmon, which begin life in freshwater rivers, then migrate to the salt ocean, and then migrate back to freshwater to spawn? Wald found young salmon in freshwater have Vitamin A2 in their retinas. When they move to the ocean, they convert to Vitamin A1. Even more amazing, when they travel back to fresh water, they convert back to Vitamin A2.

John proposed a research project: create a rat with the eyes of a freshwater fish. We would put rats on a Vitamin A1-free diet until they went blind, then feed them fresh-water-fish Vitamin A2. He thought the rats would take up this foreign vitamin into their eyes and see like fish instead of rats.

A fascinating project had just fallen into my lap. I was no longer memorizing dry facts from a textbook. I was up to my armpits in a real project, asking a real question and trying to find a real answer.

John took me over to the Harvard Biology Laboratory. I thought this stark, ugly, C- shaped brick building was low-income housing until I noticed a life-size green statue of a rhinoceros on either side of the front door.

We went up to a room on the top floor. An overwhelming stench of urine greeted us when we opened the door. A scuffling sound stopped when we turned on the light. We were inside the famous Harvard Rat Colony, which had rows of shelves holding cages of genetically identical rats, from three weeks to two years old, waiting for any scientist who needed rats. The Colony still exists, but it now has many different strains of mutant rats.

We helped ourselves to twenty-five white, fluffy, sniffy, twinkly, three-week-old rats. I felt a bit sad about their doleful fates until three of their fat, malicious mothers bit me. Our project was on.

I fed the rats a Vitamin A1-free diet until they went blind. They could not tell me they were blind, but I found out by putting them to sleep, placing a small electrode on their eyes, flashing a light, and studying the electrical signal that came from their eyes. If their eyes gave off a signal, they could see. If there was no signal, they were blind. This clever technique is called *ElectroRetinoGraphy*, or *ERG*.

The ERG of my rats went down to zero after they had been on a Vitamin A1-deficient diet for several months. Then, I fed them Vitamin A2 and checked their ERG almost every day. Their ERG started to recover a few days later. They could see again!

I impatiently analyzed the Vitamin A in their bodies. As John and I had expected, there was no Vitamin A1 in their blood and livers, only Vitamin A2. However—to our astonishment—their retinas contained only Vitamin A1, not Vitamin A2. They did not have the eyes of a freshwater fish. Their eyes were the same as all other rats.

John and I had just discovered rats have an enzyme in their retinas that converts Vitamin A2 to Vitamin A1. It is, most likely, the same enzyme that salmon and frogs have. Why? John and I were baffled. Rats do not need to migrate from fresh to salt water and back again. This finding earned my thesis a *summa*.

John urged me to write a scientific paper reporting our results. Writing that paper would have taken very little time. The facts were laid out in my thesis, and all I had to do was cut and paste. He also invited me to join his lab and get a PhD. after I graduated. I did not write that paper or get a PhD. By then, I was officially engaged to Malcolm MacKay. Twenty years later, another group of scientists discovered the same enzyme and published their findings.

In the summer of 1963, between my junior and senior years, I got a National Science Foundation Grant to fund our rat project. I went out for lunch on the lawn on my first day at the lab. I noticed a tall, gangly, freckled man sitting next to one of the rhinoceros statues. He was eating a carton of *Dannon* orange yogurt with intense concentration.

Dannon introduced the world's first flavored yogurt that summer. It came in three flavors. The lemon was delicious. The lime was fair. The orange tasted like perfume mixed with axle grease.

I walked over, introduced myself, and told him he should switch his yoghurt flavor. He introduced himself—Jim Watson. I recognized that name immediately. Jim Watson co-discovered the structure of DNA, the molecule of heredity, in 1953. The year before we met, in 1962, every newspaper in the world had banner headlines announcing that Jim and two other scientists had won the Nobel Prize "for their discoveries concerning the molecular structure of nucleic acids and its significance for information transfer in living material."

Jim Watson and Francis Crick had made the most important biological discovery of the twentieth century. The Watson-Crick model of the structure of DNA gave us the key to life itself. A wealth of insights explaining how the body works followed Jim's discovery. It gave us information about evolution. It has led to the development of new drugs and diagnostic tests. It is routinely used to solve crimes: the DNA in a person's blood confirms guilt if it matches the DNA found on a crime victim. The DNA of a child tells who his father or mother is. And this barely scratches the surface.

When John Dowling came back from lunch, there was a Nobel laureate in his lab, helping me grind up rat livers. I was twenty. Jim was thirty-five.

What a summer. I worked in John's lab during the day, and I buzzed around Cambridge in Jim's black MG convertible during the evening. I was now dating two men: Malcolm, who planned to go places, and Jim, who had already gone places—the pinnacle of scientific success. Jim describes our summer together on pages 215–216 of his memoir, *Avoid Boring People.*

Jim told me he knew his DNA model had to be correct because it was so beautiful. Now I was involved in scientific research myself, I could understand why Jim used this word. This was not my mother's concept of beauty, but it was now *my* concept of beauty.

Scientific progress is not orderly. It is messy and wandering. A scientist thrashes around in a mess of seemingly random data until suddenly, clear as the ring of a crystal bell, a simple idea pops into his or her mind that explains everything. This scientist has opened a window and looked inside part of the universe, which was humming along in its own quietly miraculous way. Now, the scientist understands it in a new and—yes—beautiful way. This is what makes scientific research so addictive.

When Jim asked me to marry him, I was shocked, flattered—and tempted. Malcolm and I had talked about marriage, but nothing was official yet. I enjoyed Jim's off-beat humor, his integrity, and his constantly bubbling creativity. Here was a chance to live a life far from Far Hills.

I invited Jim to Edgartown to meet my parents. Neither of them was excited to meet this super-smart, world-famous Harvard professor. My father, as usual, barely spoke a word. My mother, who flirted aggressively with all my other boyfriends, flirted only half-heartedly with Jim. She didn't care a fig for his Nobel Prize, and she disliked his habit of sucking air through his teeth.

My parents could not appreciate Jim because he was too far outside their frame of reference. My mother was impressed by people who appeared in the society pages of the *New York Times.* Jim's name appeared all the time in the science section, but she never read that.

I began to see Jim through the eyes of Far Hills. He would not fit into my upper-crust world. I turned him down. Malcolm enjoyed telling people he won me away from a Nobel *Laureate.*

Five years later, Jim married a smart, gorgeous 19-year-old Harvard student, Liz Lewis. Liz has been a far better wife for Jim than I would have been. In addition to great warmth, she has superb cooking and decorating skills and a flair for stylish dressing—areas where I am deficient.

We have stayed in touch. I watched Jim and Liz transform the sleepy Cold Spring Harbor Laboratories into a world-renowned center of genetic and neuroscience research. In the late 1980s, Jim co-founded the *Human Genome Project,* which discovered the genetic blueprint of a human being. And that human being was Jim.

Pictured: Me (left) with Jim and Liz Watson, Cold Spring Harbor Labs, 1963.

A few months after I turned down Jim's proposal of marriage, on November 22nd, 1963, I was in a class in Harvard Yard when I heard the Memorial Church bell start to ring. It kept on tolling, tolling. That was a surprise. It never rang at that time or on that day of the week.

I ran outside and joined a knot of people gathered around a man holding a transistor radio. We heard President John Kennedy was shot and killed in Dallas. Nobody said a word. Everybody was crying. Harvard came to a standstill. All my classes were canceled. Day after day, I sat in my nightgown with my housemates, watching TV, barely able to speak.

Six years had gone by since I lived in London, and I had turned back into a patriotic American. Other countries might be pessimistic and cynical, but my country was young, vigorous, and optimistic, like our young President. I was naïve and complacent about politics until Kennedy was killed. Now, murder had struck at the very center of our country. I was so upset I could not think straight.

Two months after President Kennedy's death, Jackie organized a funeral mass at Boston's Holy Cross Cathedral. She invited the Boston Symphony Orchestra and its conductor, Erich Leinsdorf, to perform Mozart's *Requiem*. The Harvard Glee Club sent out an urgent message— did anybody know how to sing the Requiem? I did. I had sung it a few months earlier at Tanglewood, the summer home of the BSO.

The cavernous cathedral was lit by thousands of flickering candles. Every seat was filled with somebody famous. I had a direct view of the widow, dressed in black and wearing a thick black veil. I could not see the orange makeup she used in the hunting field, but I recognized her from her upright posture and dignity.

Leinsdorf conducted with even more passion than usual, boring his eyes into ours, fighting to hold back tears. During the quietest, most emotional part of the Requiem—the *Lacrimosa*, the eight measures Mozart wrote the day before he died—a priest started to swing a brazier of incense and chant loudly in Latin. Leinsdorf's face turned purple. I thought he might have a stroke.

During my four years at Harvard, the Swinging Sixties, with its drugs, free sex, civil rights movement, Beatles, and war protests, was exploding all around me, but everything went right over my head. Aside from buying one pair of bell-bottom pants, I concentrated single-mindedly on the all-important task of getting married within two months of graduation. I cringe when I remember I believed the government must know what it was doing when it invaded Vietnam.

I was a student at Harvard when Timothy Leary was giving my fellow students pills containing *psilocybin*, a substance made by mushrooms that alters a person's perception of reality and makes them hear or see things that do not exist. I ran into one of these students in front of Widener Library one day. I listened with disbelief as he told me how the drug made him see a lightbulb for the very first time.

In my sophomore year, I had tried to change my image from frivolous socialite to serious intellectual. I gave away my circle pin and my demure, pastel-colored blouses with round collars, and I bought a peasant blouse and a Greek book bag. Readily available around Harvard Square, these colorful wool bags were worn slung across the body as the badge of a non-conformist. They were really the badge of a conformist because everybody had them.

These items were mere window-dressing. They did not alter my deeply held beliefs about my future, or the type of man I wanted to marry. The only suitor who fit my vision of an ideal husband was Malcolm MacKay.

I was programmed to go into orbit around a man. Like my father, I subconsciously chose a spouse who would control me and give my life direction. Malcolm had a clear vision of what I should do with my life. He seemed so smart and capable I thought he would always make the right decisions. Instead of forming my own life, I accepted Malcolm's proposal of marriage, and put my life in his hands.

As the writer Toni Bentley said, "A man has always been a woman's best excuse to avoid her destiny."

When I first came to Harvard, I accepted the system hook, line, and sinker. I felt lucky to be there and grateful to be included among the elite. The thought never crossed my mind it was unfair to women and needed to change.

Over the years, I have come to believe there was a dark side for women at Harvard in the early 1960s. We sat in the same classes as the men. We had the same professors, read the same books, and took the same exams, but we did not get the same education. The school had different expectations for its male and female students. It celebrated its male students. It tolerated and ignored its female students.

The campus was not designed to welcome women. Many Harvard buildings were off limits to us, including Lamont Library. The male dormitories were much more luxurious than the female dormitories. The men had suites; we had rooms the size of their closets.

The women lived way up north in the Radcliffe Quad, a half hour away from the action in Harvard Square. When Harvard and Radcliffe formally merged in 1999, and men began to live in the far-off Radcliffe Quad, shuttle busses suddenly appeared to take students back and forth from the Yard.

I felt all the gravitas of male privilege at Harvard. The mahogany walls were what the news anchor Rachel Maddow has called "dude walls", plastered with portraits of white men with confident, self-satisfied expressions. There was not one portrait of a woman. I did not have one female teacher during my four years there. I got the message—men came first, and women were an afterthought.

Most of the intellectual life took place on the Harvard campus. Eminent professors lived in the male dormitories, and the male students socialized with them at meals. A harried, married music graduate student lived in my dormitory. I saw him only once when he fished one of my contact lenses out of a sink drain.

One woman in my class at Harvard said she did not know why we put up with it. I know the answer. We were programmed to take ourselves less seriously. A good mind was a liability in a woman back in those days. We played dumb so the men would not feel threatened by us.

If you want some evidence, listen to Leonard Bernstein's "One Hundred Easy Ways to Lose a Man" from the musical "Wonderful Town", which opened in 1953:

"Now the first way to lose a man-
You've met a charming fellow and you're out for a spin.
The motor fails and he just wears a helpless grin.
Don't bat your eyes and say,
"What a romantic spot we're in."
Just get out, crawl under the car, tell him
It's the gasket and fix it in two seconds flat with a bobby pin.
That's a good way to lose a man."

Funny—but not so funny when you think about it.

I didn't believe I could become somebody in the world, while the male Harvard students assumed they not only could, but would. Harvard gave me a priceless gift—a new vision of what I could do with my life—but I was too brainwashed by gender expectations to take advantage of it.

I graduated from Harvard with less self-confidence than I had when I arrived. I did not believe I could live alone, earn my own money, and support myself. I thought my most important job was to marry the right man, have babies, and follow my husband around. Like almost all my friends, I was engaged to be married before I graduated from college.

Like the heroine of a Jane Austen novel, I chose my life when I chose my husband. I was relieved I would not have to be the primary breadwinner. I expected to play a secondary role in our marriage.

My granddaughters, now at college, have a much healthier attitude towards marriage. Before they marry, they want to form their own lives and find their own way. Instead of getting their identity from their husband, they plan to first make their own identity.

I thought of the dating scene as a game of musical chairs. After graduation, I would no longer have access to all those smart, eligible men. If I did not find a husband before I graduated, other women would snap up all the good ones.

I married mostly to avoid confronting other choices. I had an intense need for security. I was in a rush. I was not confident enough to wait for Mr. Right to come along. Malcolm had a collection of attributes I admired. I made myself believe he was The One. My marriage was an arranged marriage where I was my own matchmaker.

I chose Malcolm with my brain instead of my heart. I did not see him as a human being with flaws and foibles, but as somebody who would take care of me, give my life direction, and make our money. I weighed his strengths and weaknesses against my other suitors. I selected him according to a checklist, as if I were buying a new car.

Scientists are supposed to make decisions based on careful observation. I did not follow the scientific method when I chose Malcolm. He was standing right in front of me, but I did not really see him, I imagined him. I saw the idea of him I had built up in my mind. I ignored the evidence right in front of my eyes that we were opposites in every way. I made myself believe we were a perfect match.

I did not think passion was necessary in a marriage. In fact, I distrusted it. I wasn't a silly goose who would be swept away by hot emotion. I was smart, cool, and dispassionate.

And yet…when I re-read the letters I wrote to Malcolm sixty years ago while we were courting, they catch at my heart. *"I'm half a person without my learned, laughing laddie (The scatterbrained half)."* *"Cambridge is sunny, efficient, and heartless* [without you]. *And my hair is very neat. And my shoulders are cold."* They are irrefutable evidence there was a strong connection between us. What went wrong?

I finally discovered a letter that answers my question. I am nineteen. Malcolm is twenty-one. I write: *"I wasn't communicating with you [on Saturday night]. You said, 'We're driving on.' and I didn't know why; I couldn't talk with you about it. I can practically always talk to you about everything. But sometimes the thread breaks, and then I'm miserable…. we suddenly go about 500 miles apart…I'm more scared of it than I am of any fault that you or I might have"*.

My heart was telling me there were serious problems with communication and compromise in our relationship, and we had completely different interests and emotional needs. Malcolm was not comfortable with emotions, and he could not express his feelings. My Armstrong ancestors gave me mercurial and intense moods. He disliked being physically touched. I express love by hugging and kissing.

I ignored my heart. I listened to my head. Malcolm checked all the right boxes. The point of marriage was not to be in love; the point was to marry a man with the right credentials. We got engaged in the fall of 1963.

1963 was the year Betty Friedan published her ground-breaking book, *The Feminine Mystique*, where she challenged the prevailing belief that marriage is necessary for women to be happy. Her studies showed many married women in the 1950s and 1960s were not happy staying at home and taking care of children, even though they were living in comfort. She claimed women would never be happy unless they lived independent lives as equal partners to men. She predicted that working mothers would produce happy children because they would be happy themselves.

I read "The Feminine Mystique" and discussed it at length with my female friends, but I did not believe it applied to me. I did not have the confidence to be an equal partner to Malcolm. I wanted him to be my skipper. I wanted to be part of his crew.

I graduated from Harvard in June 1964. A few days before I left, I went up to the attic to get my suitcase. I saw a pile of stuffed animals that had been left behind by previous women students. They had developed the confidence to be themselves and didn't need them anymore.

I didn't bring a stuffed comfort animal with me to Harvard, but I left with one—my strong, confident husband. I needed the support of a man to feel complete. It took many years and a medical degree before I developed the confidence to feel complete by myself.

Pictured: CJM (right) graduating from Harvard in 1964.

I knew nothing about sex before I got married except for what I gleaned from reading biology books and "Lady Chatterley's Lover."

"What happens during sex?" I asked my mother one day, when I was roughly fifteen years old. She immediately began to make her bed. "The husband puts a seed into his wife," she said, jerking up the sheets.

"How does he do that?" I asked.

"He just does." she said as she tucked in the sheets, *snap, snap*.

I had no interest in my wedding. I just wanted it to be over. I did not think there was much to celebrate. That should have raised a red flag. I would not let myself see it.
My mother took me shopping for a wedding dress. I fell in love with a supple, sophisticated silk dress that swished around my body. She talked me into a childish dress with a demure scoop neck, cap sleeves, and a bodice of white daisies. It felt stiff as a cage. She paid for it. I wore it.

My parents paid for my wedding. They invited the guests. I added Jim Watson at the last minute. I let my mother decide on the venue and the menu. It was her wedding, not mine. My parents kept the album of my wedding photographs in their house. I did not think I had the right to have my own wedding photos.

We were married on August 29th, 1964, in the small Episcopal Church in Edgartown, where my parents were married twenty-four years earlier. I was twenty-one. Malcolm was twenty-three. I was late for my wedding because I was buried in a book.

The local doctor announced loudly at our wedding reception, so everybody in the room could hear, Malcolm and I passed our *Wasserman* tests for syphilis. This test was mandatory for all couples at that time before they married. This was no surprise. We were both virgins. Like almost all my friends, the first time I had sex was on my wedding night.

We had no money to pay for a honeymoon, and our parents did not offer us any, so we kept it short, cheap and simple—we sailed a friend's boat from Edgartown to Oyster Bay, Long Island. The fourth day of our honeymoon dawned blistering hot. There was not one cloud in the sky, not one breath of wind. I could see my face reflected perfectly in the mirror-smooth water.

I suggested we wait until the wind came up, but Malcolm insisted we leave right away by motor. He wanted to get to Long Island in time to race the boat in a regatta. By the fourth day of our marriage, we were making decisions based on competing in a race and trying to win a prize instead of on comfort and romance.

We rocked down Long Island Sound for hours under a pitiless sun, breathing noxious gas fumes, until I saw a shiver on the smooth sheen of the Sound and felt a breeze caress my cheek. "I'll put up the jib." I sang out, as I jumped to my feet.

"You take the tiller," said Malcolm. "*I* will put up the jib."

"But I'm the crew, and the crew is supposed to raise the jib," I protested.

"I'm the captain, and you must do what I say," said Malcolm, through clenched teeth.

We argued until Malcolm was white with anger, and I was sobbing. We were not arguing about a sail. We were arguing about power. We were deciding who would be in control of this marriage.

I had to make this marriage work. Marriage was my only strategy for coping with adult life. I had nowhere else to go. The system I grew up in had not taught me how to be financially independent. I had no plans for how I might make money, and only a vague dream of becoming a doctor someday.

I had no idea where I would live if I did not have a husband. I knew my parents would not give me any money, and they would not welcome me if I asked to move back to Far Hills and live with them. My parents' marriage was a sealed unit that excluded their children. My problems were not their problems. My successes—if I had any—would not be their success.

I did not have a model of how to negotiate a compromise with a spouse because there was no give-and-take in my parent's marriage. My mother did exactly what she wanted, and my father never objected. It was quite clear my new husband would not tolerate challenges. I had to stop fighting with him.

I never let myself think I had married the wrong man. Instead, I thought there must be something wrong with me. I grew up placating difficult people—my mother, my father, Grandpa Johnson. If I remained upbeat, cheerful, and problem-free, we got along fine. It felt natural to do the same with Malcolm.

I knew our marriage would only survive if I played by Malcolm's rules. My need to have Malcolm take care of me was greater than my desire to have my own way.
Malcolm always knows best, I told myself. *"I will do whatever he wants and never question him. Then we will have a happy marriage.*

I put Malcolm on a pedestal. I signed on to be his lifelong worshipper. He signed on to give all the orders and make all the decisions. And for the next fifteen years, we had what I thought was a happy marriage.

Malcolm and I both came to feel squashed in our marriage. I felt childlike and ineffective because I had no power over our decisions. I believe that Malcolm, rigid and uber-adult, felt overwhelmed by his responsibilities.

If one spouse controls the other in a marriage, that is a form of abuse – unless that spouse wants to be controlled. For the first fifteen years of our marriage, I was fine with Malcolm making all our decisions. In fact, I liked the stability. I did not feel any need to control my life. Our marriage began to run into trouble only when I became a doctor and started to make my own decisions.

Superficially, it seemed as if Malcolm and I had close-to-identical backgrounds. However, there was one fundamental incompatibility we could never overcome—we had each learned different ways to express love.

Malcolm's mother molded him with a single-minded passion. She drove him fiercely to be a success. She picked out his clothes for him. She told him what schools to go to. She hopped onto his bed every night to help him with his homework. This mother-son relationship was not exactly intimate—it reminded me of the relationship of a drill sergeant to a private—but it certainly was intense.

Naturally, Malcolm thought love meant intervening constantly in the other person's life and solving their problems for them.

My parents were the exact opposite of Malcolm's mother. They had no idea what I was doing most of the time. They had no interest in which courses I was taking. They would have laughed at the thought they should help me with my homework.

Naturally, I thought love meant giving Malcolm the freedom to solve his own problems. Unfortunately, this made him think I did not love him. Malcolm was burning his brains out, trying to love me by telling me who to be and what to do, while all I wanted was the freedom to be myself.

Malcolm inherited his temper from his mother. I believe he did not know he was being harsh with me because anger was how his mother showed she cared. I grew up with my father's unpredictable eruptions. It was years before I realized we did not have a good marriage because anger felt so normal to me.

There was nothing wrong with the way Malcolm and I expressed love. The problem was we did not choose an appropriate recipient. This problem is depicted in Anton Chekhov's short story, *The Darling*. The heroine, Olenka, shows love by absorbing herself into her love object. This works well during Olenka's two marriages. Both of her husbands want and appreciate her single-minded, all-encompassing love. Both adore her and call her "Darling".

Her third partner, however, resents the way she clings to him and parrots his words, so he dumps her. Her fourth love object, a young boy who is the son of her third partner, finds her love overbearing and smothering and rebels against her.

In 1965, one year after Malcolm and I got married, Lynn married a charismatic, handsome Princeton architect, Harrison ("Pony") Fraker. She was twenty years old. They set up married life in Princeton, where he was a graduate student in architecture. A few years later, our brother Frank married a sensible, cheerful, warm woman, Jo Mason, who also came from Far Hills.

Lynn graduated from Wheaton College in 1966. Our parents came to my graduation, but they had a pressing social engagement and did not come to hers. Malcolm and I were the only family members there. Halfway through the ceremony, I noticed a commotion among the ranks of smiling young women standing proudly in their pastel-blue robes. Lynn, pregnant with Alison, her first child, had fainted. She was too polite to ask if she could sit down. If you were skeptical that Lynn and I were taught we must never ever complain, you probably believe me now.

After a decade and a half of marriage, Pony left Lynn for another woman. Lynn survived on the meager salary of a teacher of dyslexic children. She and her two daughters lived on powdered milk, peanut butter, and vegetables. She bought almost all their clothes at second-hand shops. She could afford one new pair of shoes for her daughters each year. No tennis lessons, clubs, music lessons, tutoring, fancy vacations. Our parents never gave her a dime, and she never asked them.

CHAPTER EIGHT

A Teacher, a Son, a Daughter

After our marriage, I put my life and my excellent Ivy League education aside and focused on Malcolm's career. We rented an apartment in Cambridge during our first two years of marriage while he finished Harvard Law School.

I got a job teaching Biology, Chemistry, and Physics at Dana Hall School in Wellesley, which paid for our rent and food. I did not think of teaching as a career but as something to fill time and keep me from getting bored. Malcolm's parents paid his tuition at law school.

Malcolm and I grew up with maids, so we had a steep learning curve during our first months of marriage. Before we married, Malcolm took off his clothes each night and dumped them on a chair, where his mother collected them and had them washed. When the pile on his chair reached a foot high, he realized he had to take them to the cleaners himself.

I did not know how to cook. For our first dinner, I bought what seemed like a great bargain—chicken necks. I served them with two heads of iceberg lettuce, one head apiece. I did not know sheets needed to be changed and houses needed to be cleaned. Our landlord stopped by after we had lived in the apartment for several months. He was so appalled by the dirt on the kitchen floor he mopped it himself.

After Malcolm graduated from law school in 1966, he got a job as an associate at the New York firm Milbank, Tweed, Hadley, and McCoy. We moved to Brooklyn Heights, a quiet, family-friendly landmark community with big old houses and big old trees south of the Brooklyn Bridge. By then, we had both learned the fundamentals of housekeeping, and I had learned how to cook.

Pictured: One perfect husband, two perfect children, in Brooklyn Heights.

I applied for a job teaching science at St. Ann's School. I was asked to come for an interview with Stanley Bosworth, the famously flamboyant founder and headmaster.

Stanley leaned his long body back in his chair, clasped his hands behind his neck, put his feet up on his desk, and sized me up with beady eyes that glittered behind his square black glasses. I felt like a fly trapped in the gaze of a lizard that was trying to decide whether to eat me for lunch.

Stanley began talking with machine-gun rapidity. He had a close-but-not-quite-right plummy British accent. He regaled me about his school's achievements at some length. He had created the perfect atmosphere for learning, he said, informal and stimulating. All his students were gifted. I could not get one word in.

Then he began to quote from the educator Jerome Bruner. I had taken a class from Professor Bruner at Harvard. I knew Bruner did not say what Stanley claimed. I managed to interrupt that torrent of words to describe Bruner's theories. Those lizard eyes blinked. "You are hired." he said. He offered me a salary of four thousand dollars a year. I accepted.

A few weeks later, I discovered Stanley had hired a male teacher my age with identical teaching credentials and offered him nine thousand dollars a year. I went to Stanley to complain. He was indignant. "Your husband is a lawyer who makes good money," he said. "This man has a wife and two children." I crept out of his office, feeling lucky to have a job—at less than half the pay of a man. I taught science at St. Ann's for the next five years.

I got pregnant after we were married for two and a half years. I didn't feel excited, I felt anxious. I didn't like babies. I could not understand why people cooed over those ugly, pug-nosed creatures who hollered and drooled and made messes. I thought dolls were grotesque. My favorite toys were my stuffed animals. Of course, I loved books most of all.

Then my body wasn't mine anymore. My abdomen inflated. Chunks of my hair started to fall out. A brown line grew from my navel to my pubis. My bloated belly trundled in front of me and threw me off balance. I felt more exhausted and lumbering every day.

In the fifth month, I felt a little blip in my belly. The blip grew into kicks and jabs. This naughty baby was getting its exercise—inside me. It proclaimed itself more and more each day. *This baby will grow up to be a great athlete,* I said to myself. And I was right. Rob became a US National Junior Squash Champion-twice.

At eight and a half months, my water broke, and I began to have contractions. Malcolm and I jumped into a taxi. The taxi driver took one look at me and drove to the hospital at high speed through every red light.

Everything was going too fast. "I need a break, right now," I said to my uterus, but this powerful chunk of muscle refused to listen. It kept on systematically ripping me apart, without permission, with increasing urgency, in a frenzy of purpose. It was so strong it could have easily ripped a telephone pole in half.

Then, I went into a primal state. The world went blank. They rushed me into the delivery room. Malcolm was beside me as I began to push. I pushed so hard I popped several blood vessels in my conjunctiva. I thought I might go into convulsions. I heard somebody screaming. It was me.

Then everything was quiet except for a sound like a cat mewing. I had never seen a newborn baby before. I thought mine would look like the chubby babies in *Gerber's* baby food ads—golden curls, plump pink cheeks, and a dazzling smile.

A nurse placed a small, bald, wizened stranger in my arms that reminded me of an elderly pixie. Its skin was coated with purplish wax. Its arms and legs were thin sticks. It had a grave, courteous expression. Its dark, almond-shaped eyes wandered around, then fixed on my face with a thoughtful expression.

It was a boy. What a shock. My female body had created a male body perfect in every detail, including ten fingers and ten toes, each complete with a tiny nail.

I need not have worried about loving this baby. When Rob started to cry, milk squirted from my rock-hard, enormous breasts. When this frantic, howling little man latched on, he melted into a trance. He gazed up at me with dreamy eyes as bluish milk collected at the corners of his mouth, and my uterus went into an agreeable spasm.

I had never felt this close to another human being. Love for this baby gushed effortlessly out of me. Making Rob comfortable made me happy in a way that was new to me. I even enjoyed changing his diapers. He opened my heart to all babies, to the entire human race. Now, when I hear a baby cry, I no longer feel irritated. I hear a helpless, desolate human being who has something simple that is bothering him, and I know how to help.

My breasts fed Rob for half a year. Then I fed him his first solid food, tiny white flakes of rice cereal that flew up into the air when I breathed on them. I felt a rush of sadness. For six months, his only food had come from me. This was his first step towards independence.

Pictured: Rob at one week old; I had never felt this close to another human being.

Every minute with this merry little fellow was an adventure. He was easy to please. He shrieked with delight when I hid my face in a towel, blew on his tummy, or tossed him in the air. We spoke a secret language. He babbled away, and I was the only person who understood him.

My parents almost never saw Lynn, Frank, and me when we were babies. They missed so much.

When Rob was six months old, I took him to Ellistan to introduce him to his great-grandfather. I was shocked when I saw Grandpa. His body was bloated, his skin was blue, and he was struggling for breath. My parents refused to discuss unpleasant things, so I had no idea he was dying from congestive heart failure.

When he saw Rob, he wheezed: "Hello, young fella!". My eyes filled with tears. He patted my hand and said: "Don't worry about me, Cynthia, you have your own life to live." It was sheer luck I got to hear those words.

He died that night. His last words were: "This has been the best day of my life."

Two years later, a delicate little pink girl arrived. As Hope and I drove home in a taxi, I thought, "I will rip apart anybody who threatens this baby with my teeth."

Grandma lived for another three years. Sunday lunches at Ellistan continued while this small, wrinkled woman with bright pink cheeks lay in her bed, watching soap operas on TV, tended by the butler, the cook, the upstairs maid, the downstairs maid, the laundress, the gardeners, the grooms, and the overseer.

At her burial, her coffin was piled so high with white peonies, her favorite flower, it looked like a mound of snow. A cold rain pelted down as her casket slowly slid into its slot in the slick clay. It left behind white peony petals like tears on the sodden grass.

Then Grandma died, and the Johnson center fell apart. Ellistan was sold. The twelve Johnson cousins left Far Hills and went their separate ways.

I taught science at St. Ann's School back in Brooklyn for five years. Then I began to feel restless. I did not want to teach science, I wanted to *do* science. I thought if I had to teach the Krebs Cycle one more time, I would go stark-raving mad. Then I turned thirty, which hit me like a brick. I was a grownup now, and I had to get serious. If I wanted to be a doctor, I had to apply to medical school right now.

Malcolm was supportive beyond my expectations. He encouraged me to take the Medical College Admission Test, or MCAT. My grades were so high they surprised us both. A young man with those scores would certainly be accepted to medical school, but I had three strikes against me: I was a woman, I was thirty, and I had two young children.

Malcolm and I talked over the pros and cons for weeks. I delayed. I agonized. I worried the time commitment would harm my children. He helped me fill out applications to all the medical schools in New York City and New Jersey. He trotted out to mail them while I lay in bed with a pillow over my head and tried not to think about what we were getting ourselves into. Neither of us had any idea of the challenges that lay ahead of us.

I would not have gone to medical school without Malcolm's full support. He was in control in our marriage, and he made all the decisions, and if he had not been on board, I would not have dared to apply. He wanted success for everybody in the family, and that included me. We went into this project together with high hopes and a strong sense of purpose.

I did not find a rich husband at Harvard, which my parents, if they thought about me at all, probably expected me to do. I found somebody even better: a man who helped me earn my own money. Few husbands would have been as supportive as he was.

My parents were not impressed by doctors. They put them in the same category as plumbers—boring drudges who did pedestrian, practical work. I had to reject their values to get where I wanted to go. It was easier to do this now I was married to Malcolm.

Malcolm respected hard work, and he admired doctors. He told the children that women can be doctors by declaring a marble bust of a woman, left to me by my great-uncle Ham Armstrong, was Elizabeth Blackwell, the first woman to graduate from a US medical school.

My medical school interviews did not go well.

The first interviewer said: "So, Mrs. MacKay, you want to be a doctor. Just who will take care of your two small children while you are in medical school?"

I dragged myself all the way up to Columbia Presbyterian Medical School, over an hour by subway, for an interview that lasted two minutes. The man told me they did not accept applicants older than twenty-eight.

Another interviewer said he would admit a male applicant with my credentials, but "women always leave."

Another interviewer told me when people reach the advanced age of thirty, they have "expectations of leisure time" so they don't work hard.

One by one, rejection letters arrived from the medical schools. Finally, a letter came from Brooklyn's SUNY-Downstate Medical School: "Happy to offer you a place..." I squeaked into medical school by the skin of my teeth.

The admissions director at Downstate, Dr. Parnell, prided himself in accepting what he called "unconventional" students, which luckily included me. Thanks to him, my class at Downstate was twenty percent women, which was more than most of the other medical schools at that time.

I learned later Dr. Parnell was less of a woman booster than I thought he was. He only admitted women with higher grades and MCAT scores than the average for men. He had another incentive to admit women. In 1972, the year I applied, *Title Nine* was passed, which said any institution that received federal funds could not discriminate based on gender.

Title Nine was more important than anything else, including the feminist movement, in opening medical schools to women. The feminist movement changed women's thinking. Title Nine changed their lives.

After I was accepted by Downstate Medical School, I got a letter from my college roommate, Lisa Stokes, that said: "You will only be yourself at medical school, which I suspect might be liberating since Malcolm's influence is so powerful". I had no idea how prophetic her words would be.

When I told Stanley Bosworth I was leaving, he asked me to recommend a new head for the Science Department. There were two candidates—a woman with three children who was an experienced teacher, and a young man who just graduated from Princeton.

Did I strike a blow for female equality and recommend the better-qualified woman? I cringe when I remember I did not. I was just as sexist as everybody else in my culture. I recommended the man. Stanley followed my recommendation, and both teachers quit. The woman was outraged by the slight. The man felt inadequate to the task.

When I told my parents I was going to medical school, my father, of course, said nothing. My mother said it was a shame I would not continue my sculpture career. I was speechless. My "sculpture career" consisted of producing one embarrassingly bad plaster nude woman during an evening class at New York's Arts Students League.

Did my mother really want me to be a sculptor? I doubt it. My family had room for only one artist, period. I suspect my mother was not pro-sculpture but anti-medicine. A demanding career like medicine would take my attention away from her, and she needed me.

When Malcolm went to law school, his parents, who had less money than my parents, paid his tuition while my salary paid for our rent and food. My parents did not offer to pay for my medical school, and I did not ask them to. I knew they would not give me the money.

They did not give Lynn any money when her divorce from Pony plunged her into abject poverty. Instead, they built a swimming pool at the Far Hills house. Lynn is a talented potter. Like all Johnsons, she is good with her hands. She made our parents a broad clay dish so swimmers could rinse the grass off their feet before they went in.

Our parents paid for our private schools and colleges, but after we graduated from college, it was as if they expelled us from the protection of the family. They had left us to our own devices all our lives, but now we were on our own in a way that would be considered extreme by most families.

I have asked myself many times why my parents were so averse to giving their children money. They could easily afford two thousand dollars a year for my medical school. Why didn't they give me something that would make such a big difference in my life? Perhaps they assumed I did not need money because adults make their own money, and they had thought of me as an adult since I was eleven.

My parents owned two houses, one in Far Hills and Granny's Eel Pond house in Edgartown. They had three cars, a cook, and a maid. They belonged to two country clubs in Far Hills and two in Edgartown. They spent six weeks in Vero Beach, Florida, during the winter. They traveled to Europe or South America for several weeks in the spring and fall, but they honestly thought they were poor because they had to keep up appearances with their rich friends, who had names like Dillon, Brady, Forbes, Engelhard, and Merck.

When my parents entertained (which they did rarely and reluctantly—they were better guests than hosts), they followed the Far Hills standards and hired a butler and two maids, in addition to their cook. At one dinner party, my mother's partner gave her a hot tip—the stock market was down, so this was a good time to buy racehorses.

My parents' focus was exclusively on each other. Their children were peripheral to their lives. They happily accepted the money Granny Edey gave them each month until she died, and the house and thirty acres of land Grandpa gave them, but they had no concept of investing money in future generations. We were on our own.

Malcolm and I paid for my medical school ourselves, using his salary and our savings. This turned out to be a blessing. When people ask me if I feel guilty about my privileged childhood, I say no, because I had to make my own way. I was raised in privilege, but I had to work hard for my money. This gave me a sense of purpose and gratification. I do not resent my parents. Their benign neglect set me free.

Lucky for us, the tuition at Downstate Medical School, one of New York's state universities, was one-tenth the tuition at the private schools, two thousand dollars a year. If I had been accepted at a private school, we would not have had the money to pay the tuition. We could have taken out a loan, but then we would have ended up in debt.

The main reason we were able to pay was we lived in a rent-controlled apartment. The ancient windows leaked so badly in the winter I had to change my babies' diapers in the only warm room—the laundry room. We could not afford to paint the apartment. Chunks of paint were peeling off the walls and ceiling until an elderly friend, Harold Hochschild, left us three thousand dollars in his will, just enough for a paint job. Harold was a generous supporter of many worthy causes, but I doubt any recipient of his charity was as grateful as we were. We were full of hope and purpose. We put up with the inconvenience, the cold, and the peeling paint.

PART TWO: LIFE AS A SURGEON

Part two relates how after four years of medical school, a year of internship, three years of eye surgery residency, and a fellowship in retina, I fulfilled all my dreams. I became a surgeon. I did retinal research. I set up my own private practice. I turned into a retina specialist, I was appointed a full professor, and I became an anti-LASIK advocate. I was happier than I ever dreamed I would be. Our two children, despite having a mother with a demanding career, married excellent spouses, and each had two children of their own. The only member of our family who was not happy was…Malcolm.

CHAPTER NINE

Medical School, 1973-1977: A New Sense of Purpose

I started medical school in September 1973. Malcolm was thirty-two. I was thirty- one. Rob was six. Hope was almost four. Both children were at private schools in Brooklyn Heights until 3 PM.

A live-in nurse was beyond our budget, so we hired a part-time cleaning lady. She came five afternoons a week, picked up the children on the days I got home late, and did some shopping and cooking.

I kept the house in order, bought the furniture, changed the light bulbs, arranged for repairs, etc., bought and cooked the food, and bought all the children's clothes. Malcolm paid the bills, kept the car in shape, and walked the children to school.

He obviously enjoyed spending time with the children without me. On weekends when I was away, he went to Rob's basketball games and watched Hope dance. He even bought Rob new socks one day. At the end of my first year of medical school, Hope said to him: "Pop, I used to be kind of scared of you, but now that I see so much of you, I'm not scared anymore."

Malcolm was supportive of my career to a degree that was rare for a husband at that time, but he did not shop, cook, or do laundry. Remember, his mother was a full-time homemaker. I was determined to have it all—

perfect family, perfect marriage, and perfect career—but I knew my career could not interfere with Malcolm's life. If our marriage was going to survive, I would have to keep the children dressed, the house clean, and dinner on the table.

When I got home from school, I rushed around the house like a demented whirlwind, driven to make everything perfect. I shopped on the way home, cooked dinner, gave both children a bath, picked up their rooms, tucked them into bed with a song and a story, and shoved several loads of laundry through the washing machine and dryer before I collapsed in bed.

Being a mother was exhausting enough. I had to get through the all-consuming experience of medical school at the same time without collapsing. Luckily, I have inherited a ferocious amount of energy and drive from my Armstrong ancestors. To be more specific, I have a mild case of mania. It shoved me through life until age seventy, when it almost destroyed me.

I was determined to be more connected to my children than my parents were to me. I rushed home from medical school as soon as possible, thereby missing the opportunity to get to know my fellow medical students. While they were chatting over lunch, I was studying in the library as I gobbled a sandwich. My notes had peanut butter and banana on almost every page.

Despite all my efforts, I always had a lingering doubt in the back of my mind – did my ambition to make it in the operating room make me a failure on the home front? Did my career have a negative impact on my children?

I got the answer many years later, when Hope went back to Princeton, her *alma mater*, to talk at a seminar about women who are juggling family and career. I fidgeted with nerves as Malcolm, and I sat in the audience. I had no idea what she would say. Relief flooded through me when she said she felt lucky she had a mother who gave her a positive attitude towards a job. I showed her a mother could work at something she loved and still raise happy, successful children.

When I was fifty-eight, I got even more feedback from Hope. She was thirty-three. Her daughter, Catherine, was two. My mother had just died.

Hope wrote me a condolence letter that said: "You have devoted your heart and soul to your family—always supportive, encouraging and giving more of yourself. Please know I have always felt your love and support. You do everything super- sized. I remember my birthday parties as a child when our house would be turned into a carnival. You would play the guitar and sing. There were lots of children, party favors, food, homemade piñatas…"

Hope was trying to cheer me up. She succeeded magnificently.

I assumed I would be the oldest person in my class. I was pleasantly surprised to find several students who were even older than I was. Two of the women—also Harvard graduates—were two and six years older than I. We became good friends.

The oldest student in the class, J, a six-foot-six Black man, was thirty-nine. I said to him one day it must be difficult to get back into the habit of studying after all those years out of school. "Hell, no, Cynthia, I just got out of college," he snorted. He started driving a cab when he was eighteen, built up his own cab company, taught his wife and four daughters how to run it, and went to college when he was thirty- five. J's four children and my two children were the total of the class children.

I was living in two worlds now: the stress of medical school from morning until afternoon, then the happy silliness of playing games and giggling with a four and six-year-old, and then back to the books after I tucked them into bed. Each world gave me perspective on the other.

I would not have appreciated medical school if I had gone directly from college. I didn't value college while I was a student. Now, learning seemed like a privilege. Sitting all day in a dark auditorium with two hundred students in their twenties put me in a time warp. I felt ten years younger.

We had to learn everything about the human body, no matter what field we planned to enter. One of my professors told me he thought this was a waste of time and money. He claimed it would be cheaper and quicker to ask us to steal an egg from an eagle's nest.

I did not have the experience or knowledge to answer him at that time, but I strongly disagree. I am an eye surgeon, but when patients come to see me, I cannot restrict my care to their eyes. There is no such thing as a routine eye exam. Most patients, especially the elderly, have other problems in addition to their eye problems. I have diagnosed, among other diseases, diabetes, high blood pressure, high blood lipids, and metastatic cancer by examining retinal blood vessels.

A few months after I started medical school, Hope said: "When I grow up, I want to be a nurse." I was so startled I forgot to remind her I was studying to become a doctor. "Would you like to be a doctor instead?" I asked.

"Women can't be doctors, Mom," she said.

"What about Dr. Weeks?" I asked. Dr. Virginia Weeks was her pediatrician. She pondered this for a moment. "Dr. Weeks is not a woman," she said firmly.

Medicine in the 1970s was so overwhelmingly male that the daughter of a female medical student thought all doctors had to be men. Hope eventually channeled her drive to help other people, not into being a nurse, but into becoming a social worker and therapist.

Girls today no longer think all doctors are men. Quite the contrary. When one of my patients gave her daughter a male doctor doll, the daughter said: "Mom, men can't be doctors," All the doctors she knew were women.

My Downstate classmates came from many worlds. There were nurses and pharmacists, chemists and philosophy majors, former teachers like me, actors, and businessmen. One was a professional tennis player whose knees gave out.

This motley group of people had one thing in common—we were determined to be doctors, whatever the cost. There was a quiet intensity of purpose in my medical school classmates that was unlike anything in my college classmates.

When I taught science, I was passing on scientific knowledge to other people. Now, I was using scientific knowledge to heal people. This seemed more important than anything I had ever done before, except for my two children.

Medicine seemed so certain, so black and white. All I had to do was master everything in my textbooks, or so I thought, and I could cure people. This was a cause I could believe in.

As I learned more and more about the human body, I began to feel a sense of purpose I had never felt before. Everything I learned seemed significant. If I randomly flipped open one of my textbooks, I read something that might save a life someday. I could not cut corners. I had to learn everything. If I did not, I might kill somebody.

There was so much to learn. I studied on the subway. I studied on the toilet. I studied in bed until I fell asleep sitting up. I started to grind my teeth at night. My dentist had to give me a bite plate.

I worried my thirty-one-year-old brain could not keep up with my twenty-something fellow students. My teaching experience saved me. I learned to present complicated ideas simply and clearly to my students, so I organized each medical school class as if I were preparing to teach a bunch of wriggly teenagers. This helped me focus on the big picture. Once I organized the facts, I could memorize them.

During our first year, we learned about the normal human body. In *Gross Anatomy*, we dissected a cadaver to study the parts of the body that are visible to the naked eye. In *Cell Biology*, we studied the tiny structures inside cells that are revealed by the electron microscope, and in *Physiology*, we learned how they work. In *Histology*, we examined thin slices of the human body, stained pink and purple, through a microscope. The artistic Armstrong side of my brain helped me recognize the different patterns.

Neuroanatomy was a new and more difficult problem. The brain is even more complicated than the eye, and we had to learn the different parts in three dimensions. I drew diagram after diagram. I went through dozens of sheets of paper before I figured it out.

Biochemistry was especially demanding because it was so abstract. My teaching experience saved me again. I managed to get the entire biochemistry course onto one sheet of paper that showed how every fat, sugar, and amino acid in the body is related. Then, I used my photographic memory to remember it. One of my medical school classmates noticed the diagram and asked if he could copy it. It soon began to circulate around the class.

We met our cadavers on our first day. Our Gross Anatomy professor was brief and to the point. "You are not allowed to take body parts home with you. You cannot use the cranium as an ashtray." he said. I felt a wave of nausea. Then he led us down the long green tile halls to the dissecting room. I could smell the *phenol* preservative from yards away.

My cadaver was waiting for me under a gleaming steel hood that resembled the ones that keep food hot at a buffet. When we rolled back the cover, I half expected to see a tray of chicken breasts with mushroom sauce and rice. Instead, there was a large man. He was extremely dead.

To become a doctor, I had to pass through a series of steps where the gruesome was transformed into the commonplace. Step number one was dissecting that cadaver. I picked up a scalpel, made a slice into the skin, and said to myself: *This will not bother a real doctor.*

My body did not listen. From that day on, I gagged when I looked at food. Meat was especially revolting. Chicken muscles are identical to human muscles, so when I saw a chicken leg, I made an immediate and repulsive connection to a human leg. My throat constricted, and my stomach shriveled. I lost several pounds.

Six weeks later, I had to go straight from the morning lectures to the dissecting room without time to eat lunch. As the afternoon wore on, I got hungrier and hungrier. My stomach began to rumble. I started to feel faint. Finally, I pulled out my peanut butter and banana sandwich and ate it while I sliced up the cadaver. From that moment on, I could eat normally again.

Five medical students worked on each cadaver. The phenol preservative seeped through my gloves and made my fingers numb. I cleverly assigned myself the job of reading the textbook out loud while I let my eager teammates do most of the chopping. When some crucial organ was revealed, I jumped in.

Our cadaver had seventy-eight organs, two hundred and six bones, and a daunting number of muscles attached to each bone. His nerves and blood vessels ran around in complicated mazes that looked like insane subway systems. I could not believe I had to memorize all their names and all their functions. I did.

To this day, I put myself to sleep by reciting, in order, the names and functions of the twelve pairs of cranial nerves that exit and enter the brain. Some are motor nerves (they make the muscles in the head and neck move), and some are sensory (they carry smell, taste, sight, and hearing into the brain). I rarely get beyond the sixth nerve (Abducens, motor, moves the eye out towards the ear) before I go to sleep.

During our second year, we learned all the gruesome ways this complicated mechanism can go awry. Medical students are famous for developing phobias during their second year. My family would not allow me to tell them anything about my day while we were eating dinner that year because, they claimed, it ruined their appetites.

In *Oncology*, we learned about more than one hundred different types of cancers in the body. Any cell in the body can become a cancer cell, including the skin, the lining of the digestive tract, and soft tissues such as muscle, fat, blood, and bone. This course made me especially paranoid. If Hope complained her leg hurt, my first thought was: *Osteogenic sarcoma of the femur.*

In *Neurology*, we learned how to diagnose diseases of the brain and peripheral nerves, such as strokes and multiple sclerosis, by performing a neurological exam. The neurological exam, when done carefully, reveals the exact location of the problem. Remember, this was in the days before MRIs and CT scans.

We began a neurological exam by asking the patients about the history of their illness. Then we tested their mental status, ability to move their muscles, sense of pressure, vibration and pinprick, and balance. We ended by checking their reflexes, twelve cranial nerves, and coordination.

Neurology fascinated me. What power. I flirted with becoming a neurologist. I even took a rotation in cancer neurology at Memorial Sloane Kettering Hospital during my fourth year. Eventually, however, I realized there wasn't much I could do to help neurology patients. I could diagnose the problem and, if they had seizures, give them anti-seizure medicines such as *Dilantin*. I wanted to heal people. Surgery would be more satisfying.

I was dazzled by *Psychiatry*. It dealt with profound subjects our other courses skipped. It had its own unique language and diagnostic system. The best and worst students in our class went into psychiatry.

Psychiatry introduced us to the *Diagnostic and Statistical Manual of Mental Disorders*, or *DSM*, which describes all the mental illnesses and their symptoms. Psychiatrists will diagnose a patient's mental illness by determining the symptoms and matching these symptoms with the descriptions in the DSM.

The first edition of the DSM, published in 1952, listed homosexuality as a mental illness. In 1973, the year I started medical school, the second edition of the DSM came out, and homosexuality was no longer listed. The DSM is in its 5th edition today.

As we learned about these different mental diseases, many of us, including me, began to think we had a mental illness ourselves. One of our classmates eventually figured out we were not mentally ill unless all our symptoms were on the same page.

Our psychiatry course included a lecture by Elisabeth Kubler-Ross. Her book, *On Death and Dying*, describes the five emotional stages dying people go through—denial, anger, bargaining, depression, and, finally, acceptance. Everyone in the class was in tears. I would soon be dealing with death. This was sobering.

Our psychiatry course also taught us about normal and abnormal sexual responses, as described by Masters and Johnson. We watched a movie of a man and woman making love, where the four stages of arousal were illustrated by sensors in the woman's vagina. Almost every teacher at Downstate was sitting in the back row, watching with interest.

In *Pharmacology*, we had to memorize the side effects, mode of action, recommended dosages, and interactions of every drug, from antibiotics to cancer drugs to psychiatric medications. This was hard slogging. My head began to swim. I could not get all these drugs onto a single sheet of paper. I felt lucky I had learned how to memorize in London.

Every teacher was a man during our first year. In second year, we had one female teacher who taught Pathology. She was clear, organized, concise, and the best teacher we had during our four years at Downstate. When she came in for her first lecture, several of the male students yawned conspicuously. Soon, they were scribbling furiously as she threw up slide after slide, running through the key points with lightning speed.

After the lecture was over, I heard one male student sneer to another: "How did you like that dyke?" He seemed to think a forceful and competent woman had to be lesbian. I got the distinct impression it would not be easy for me to make it in this man's world of medicine.

In *Pathology*, we learned how to diagnose diseases by examining organs with our naked eye and with a microscope. My Pathology lab instructor was a short, stocky, exuberant Russian called Dr Yermakoff. He placed specimens of diseased hearts, kidneys, lungs, and brains on his dissecting tray and sliced them up swiftly with a long, sharp knife, talking a blue streak as he did so. The black, shriveled lungs of smokers made an especially vivid impression.

When Dr. Yermakoff came to class on our last day, there was an unusual specimen waiting for him on his tray—a cake with a red heart on top. I had baked it to say: *Thank you.* He richly deserved it.

His face flushed crimson with pleasure. *"VE CELEBRATE!"* he roared. He cut up the cake with quick, deft strokes of his knife. He reached under his desk, hauled out a bottle of vodka and some glasses, poured out the vodka, and passed it around.

Parasitology was fascinating, sickening, and almost impossible to memorize. I discovered, to my dismay, I had to learn about three hundred different species of worms that live on and in the human body, including heartworm, whipworm, round worm, pinworm, threadworm, and tapeworm.

I found out some parasitic worms in the human intestine can grow to be thirty feet long. One example is the tapeworm *Diphyllobothrium*, which can be passed to humans when they eat raw fish. Cooks who taste *gefilte* fish as they prepare it, such as Jewish housewives, can pick up this tapeworm.

I can't begin to describe all the insects living on and in our bodies. They include head lice that live in our hair and drink blood from our scalp, face mites that live head down in the sebaceous glands of our hair follicles and wander around our skin at a rate of eight to sixteen millimeters per hour at night while we sleep, and scabies mites, transmitted during sexual intercourse, that live inside the top layer of our skin and cause violent itching.

Our bodies are host to seventy different species of single-cell parasites, invisible to the naked eye. We had to memorize how they are transmitted—some by water, some by insects, some by sex, and some by eating raw meat or fish. One of them, *Plasmodium*, the cause of malaria, dives into our red blood cells. *Giardia*, the cause of "Beaver Fever," goes for our intestines. *Acanthamoeba* enjoys our skin, brain, and eyes. Our skins teem with more than two thousand different species of bacteria, including an average of sixty-seven different kinds in our bellybutton alone.

Is your skin beginning to crawl yet?

Parasitology made me fanatic about bug repellent and hand washing. I also began to scrutinize my stools for tapeworm larvae.

I studied for months to prepare for my final exam in Parasitology. The night before the exam, I began to vomit. Done in by a parasite! I spent the night on the bathroom floor, periodically lifting my head to throw up into the toilet. I assumed I would have to take a make-up exam. The thought of re-learning the names of all those trypanosomes and nematodes and tapeworms and amoebae made me feel even more nauseated.

When Malcolm came home from work, he scraped me off the bathroom floor, threw me into the car, drove me to Downstate, waited until I finished the exam, and drove me home. I passed the exam. Have I mentioned that Malcolm was supportive beyond my wildest dreams while I was in medical school?

During our third year, we split up into small groups and went on rotations that included Surgery, Obstetrics and Gynecology, Psychiatry, Pediatrics, Neurology, and Internal Medicine.

We finally met real flesh-and-blood patients during third year. We were taught to interview them by asking open-ended questions so they would talk more freely. I listen to patients more than most doctors, but I ask pointed, relevant questions, or I would see very few patients.

Downstate Medical School and Kings County Hospital are at the center of what was at that time the poorest sections of Brooklyn—East New York, Bedford-Stuyvesant, and Brownsville. I saw medical disasters caused by poverty and ignorance that were galaxies away from anything in Far Hills, New Jersey.

My first third year rotation was Internal Medicine on ward E-62, the pulmonary unit at Kings County Hospital. The night before, I had a dream I was being slowly pulled down into a whirlpool. At the bottom of the vortex, I could hear patients calling to me and see the tiny figures of doctors in white coats rushing around. My husband and children were floating on the surface nearby. They looked at me reproachfully as I was sucked down. The feeling of descent was exhilarating and scary.

The pulmonary ward contained fifty women, mostly Black, all poor. These patients were under the care of two overworked interns, one overwhelmed fourth-year medical student, and one harried first-year resident who was also covering three other wards, all equally chaotic. Everybody was working flat out.

The previous day, an elderly lady began to bleed internally because her heparin dose was too high. She went into shock, from which only ten percent of patients recover. She was now in the ICU. Nobody visited her. Nobody had the time. Her fate was now in the hands of the ICU doctors.

As we went on morning rounds, I was struck by the machine-gun patter of the resident as he described the patients. They were problems, not people— "breast cancer with renal complications," "urinary tract infection not responding to ampicillin, switch to gentamycin".

We almost sprinted past the room that held the eight tuberculosis patients. They were admitted to the hospital to make sure they took their medicine. Some of them had been there for months. This room was dismissed in one sentence. Unless they became dizzy and nauseated from streptomycin or developed nerve damage from ethambutol, they did not need any attention—a blessing for the overworked doctors.

I was halfway into this new world of medicine. I spoke the language now, so I could understand what was going on scientifically, but my emotional reactions remained those of a layperson. I'm sure I was the only doctor who noticed how some patients managed to assert their humanity by bringing in bits and pieces of their former lives—cards, photographs, a bright African rug spread over a grey ward blanket.

One of my jobs during this rotation was to draw blood from the prisoners in the locked prison ward. Most of them were drug addicts. Their eyes were blank, like the eyes of goats. Almost every vein in their bodies was scarred down by years of injecting drugs. Luckily, they took pity on me and showed me their few remaining functioning veins. One man guided me to a tiny blue thread running between two of his toes.

My second rotation was obstetrics and gynecology. I watched the ob-gyn resident mismanage the second stage of a thirteen-year-old girl's labor because he never asked her if this was her first baby. It was her second. Fortunately, both mother and baby survived and did well. Another day, a young girl came to the emergency room complaining of "pains in her stomach." An hour later, she delivered a healthy baby boy.

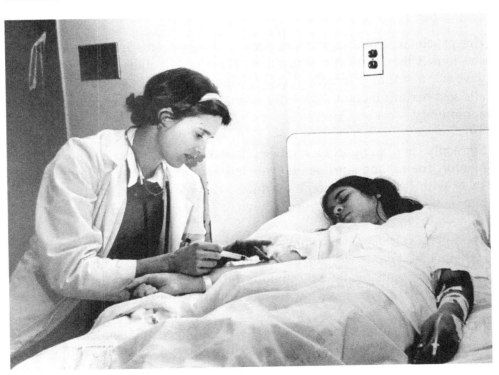

Watching a mother deliver a baby exhilarated me. I came home filled with energy, ripped down every curtain in the apartment, and washed it. I thought briefly of going into Ob-Gyn. A few moments of sober reflection on the unfortunate fact that babies are born at all hours of the day and night dampened my ardor.

Psychiatry was a whole new universe. Everything else in medicine could be photographed, observed, and proved right or wrong. Psychiatry dealt with forces that cannot be seen or measured—the disorders of the human mind. The job of psychiatrists was to replace the rigid, chaotic thinking of the mentally ill with rational, orderly thought.

The stark brick Kings County psychiatry building was crammed full of patients with serious mental illnesses. The first patient we saw was a woman in her late teens or early twenties. She was pacing swiftly up and down the hall, screaming that policemen parked outside the building were controlling her thoughts through radio waves.

Her psychiatrist told us she had been drifting towards mental illness until she joined the Jehovah's Witnesses. Their rigid beliefs and expectations gave her a strong external structure, which stabilized her inner world and allowed her to function—but only while she was safely inside the Witness community.

Suddenly, her stable community collapsed. An older man who was her mentor, friend, and spiritual advisor left his wife and the Church and ran away with the wife of another Witness. Her mind immediately collapsed into an acute schizophrenic breakdown.

I had great respect for psychiatrists after that rotation. I had no idea how to help that young woman whose mind betrayed her. I also had more respect for fundamentalist religions now I knew they could stabilize marginal people who have a tenuous grasp on reality.

During Psychiatry rotation, all third-year medical students took a *Rorschach* inkblot test. This test was devised by a Swiss psychologist. It reveals a person's personality traits. It cannot be faked—you look at the blots, and you have to say what they remind you of.

We worked in pairs. My partner, *M*, was an African American man who grew up in a rough neighborhood. He saw knives, guns, and coffins in the inkblots. I saw heraldic animals. I remember one especially well—I saw a rabbit running through a field with two buffaloes on its back. The psychologist was excited. Apparently, nobody had ever made that interpretation before.

I believe I saw heraldic animals in the inkblots because I survived my childhood by banishing the real world and living in a fantasy world. I transformed everything into something pretty, pleasant, and mythical. I filled the void left by my absent parents with flying-mane horses, clever dogs, elves, and magic carpets.

I flirted with becoming a psychiatrist—but I eventually rejected the field because it wasn't certain enough, the process took too long, and the outcome was neither measurable nor clear.

I got into a fierce argument with a senior surgery resident during Surgery rotation. He told me a woman who had children could never be a good surgeon. She would not have the necessary dedication because she would have other claims on her attention. His view was typical of doctors at that time. I argued passionately with him that my children gave me a connection to patients he could not begin to understand. I would not like to be a patient of that resident.

Doctors need to be empathetic because they are taking care of fragile, vulnerable people. Taking care of Rob and Hope taught me how to take care of my patients. Raising children has made me humble. It gave me a healthy skepticism about doctors. I know we are not all-knowing gods. When patients ask me a question I cannot answer, I do not pretend I am infallible. I look up the answer while they are in the room.

During the third year, we got up close and personal with patients. Step by step, we learned how to invade the body—into a vein; up a penis, a vagina, an anus; through a nostril and down into a stomach; through the mouth and down into the lungs; into the spine. We drew our first blood, started our first IV, did our first spinal tap, performed our first rectal exam, saw our first surgery, and delivered our first baby. No part of the body was sacred. We grew comfortable with feces, urine, vomit, blood, and snot.

I began to see people as organs surrounded by skin during the third year. When I talked to somebody, I surreptitiously measured his or her heart rate by timing the carotid artery pulse in the neck. I scanned the hands of subway riders, trying to locate a vein in which to start an IV.

We were introduced to a *potpourri* of different specialties during our third year. By the end of that year, we were expected to choose one as our specialty. I flirted with obstetrics, psychiatry, and neurology, but I could not forget my research project on rat eyes at Harvard. Healing eyes seemed more important and exciting than anything else. I decided to be an eye surgeon.

In our fourth year, we designed our own curriculum and signed up for rotations in fields that interested us. I took a month of ophthalmology with Dr. Austin Fink, an ophthalmologist in Brooklyn Heights who was the father of one of my St. Ann's students. Austin, a lovely and generous man, was especially helpful to me.

On my first day with Austin, I went into the OR to watch him take out a cataract. I had watched other operations during my surgery rotation, but this was the first time that I had seen an eye operation.

Austin began by sticking a needle around the patient's eye into the *orbit*—the bony box that contains the eye—and injecting Lidocaine, to prevent the eye from moving and feeling pain during the procedure. I never got to see that operation. When Austin plunged in the needle, the room started to swim. I barely got out of the operating room before I fainted. I spent the operation in the hall, with my head between my legs. I could not have imagined that two years later, I would be doing these retrobulbar blocks myself routinely, thinking nothing of it.

The very thought of operating on an eye makes people squeamish. Patients sometimes faint when I touch or even go near their eye. Many OR nurses will happily assist on surgical cases that involve the abdomen, the brain, the heart, or the limbs, but they will not assist on eye cases. The stakes are too high.

Right after my month with Austin, in the fall of 1977, when I was halfway through my fourth year, I found myself standing stiffly before the Admissions Committee of the Edward S. Harkness Eye Institute at Columbia-Presbyterian Medical Center. The (all-male) members of the Committee were staring impassively at a thirty-five-year-old woman with flecks of grey in her hair. I was interviewing for a residency in ophthalmology. Six months later, I would begin my internship.

My legs were trembling. My hands felt clammy. The next twenty minutes would be crucial to my career. I cursed my choice of clothes—preppy, conventional red blouse, leather- and-canvas belt, and gold *Ultrasuede* skirt. Why hadn't I worn something more professional?

I knew the row of male eye surgeons lined up in front of me in their crisp white coats must have serious reservations about me. Less than two percent of ophthalmologists were women in the 1970s. Surgery was, and still is, the most male-dominated field in medicine. Even today, only thirty-six percent of surgeons are women. Not only was I a woman, but I was ten years older than the other applicants. I had two young children. I was rejected by their own medical school four years earlier.

Ophthalmology was the most popular medical sub-specialty at that time because there were exciting new advances in the field, and it had more family-friendly hours than most other surgical specialties. Hundreds of top medical students applied for a vanishingly small number of eye residency slots. The Eye Institute was the best eye residency in New York and one of the best in the world. It admitted three residents a year.

A deep male voice came from the array of unsmiling white faces before me—why did I want to be an eye surgeon? I took a deep breath. I pulled out my only ace.

I heard my voice describing my research at Harvard with John Dowling, who was now world-renowned. Our Vitamin A deficient rats. Our use of the ERG. Our unexpected finding that rats have an enzyme in their eyes that converts Vitamin A2 to Vitamin A1.

I went home convinced they would not take me. When the Chairman called the next day to offer me a spot in the residency program, I was so shocked I could not speak. With an effort, I managed to pull myself together enough to stammer: "Take me; I'm yours!"

The Harkness Eye Institute was founded in 1866. I was their fourth female resident.

Why did I win this coveted residency against all odds? My bet is John Dowling's letter of recommendation. John wrote: "Cynthia Johnson MacKay is the best undergraduate who ever worked with me. I was very disappointed when she did not accept my offer to join my lab after she graduated." I had, of course, turned down John's offer because my number one priority at that time was to get married. I'm sure Jim Watson's succinct, complimentary letter helped, also.

I remember the expression on John's face when he saw the engagement ring on my left hand and how disappointed he was that I never wrote a paper reporting our research findings. John assumed I would not have a serious career once I became a wife and a mother. Now, I had almost finished medical school, and he believed I was serious. He was willing to give me a second chance. I vowed that nothing, but nothing was going to stop me from living up to John's recommendation.

I graduated from Downstate Medical School in 1977. My parents came to my graduation ceremony. They were happy to celebrate my successes, although they had no idea how to help me achieve them.

I stood proudly with my class as we recited the Hippocratic Oath, vowing we would uphold the highest ethical standards and never harm a patient. The President of Downstate, a friend of Malcolm, kissed me as he handed me my diploma. My mother instantly sensed romance. "You were the only one he kissed!" she whispered.

Our speaker was Dr. Lowell Bellin, New York City's chief health officer. I remember his exact words: "You must care for your patients. If you do not, somebody else will do it for you", he said.

That's a strange thing for him to say, I said to myself. *Of course, doctors care for their patients.* I learned later Dr. Bellin prided himself on being a "medical cop." He had unmasked scores of unethical physicians.

I eventually became a medical cop myself. I took on the entire ophthalmology establishment when I realized many LASIK surgeons fail to give accurate information about the possible complications of the procedure to their patients. But more about that later in Chapter 18.

There are four stages in a doctor's career.

The first step is medical school, which takes four years.

The second step is internship. Interns are paid to work as doctors in a hospital for one year. They work long hours, supposedly so they can see firsthand many kinds of medical conditions and learn how to treat them.

After internship comes residency, where doctors are trained in a specialty. Residency is three years for primary care physicians and many other specialties, including ophthalmology. It takes up to five years for some surgical specialties. Some surgical subspecialties require additional years of fellowship training after residency.

The fourth and final stage is to go into practice, either private practice, or as part of a group, or as a hospital employee.

Doctors need to pass three National Board Exams before they get their license to practice medicine. At the end of my second year of medical school, in 1975, I took and passed Part One. I took and passed Part Two at the end of my fourth year, in 1977. I would take Part Three during internship.

A nationwide computer system matched medical students with the hospitals where they did their internship. I matched with my first choice—a well-known teaching hospital on Manhattan's Upper East Side. My salary in 1977 was eighteen thousand dollars, roughly equivalent to $88,500 today. After four years of scrimping to pay medical school tuition, it was a relief to earn money again.

Medical school was challenging, but I was able to keep a more-or-less normal schedule. I knew internship is the most demanding year of a doctor's life. Rough waters lay ahead. *Just close your eyes, Cynthia, take a deep breath, and jump in,* I wrote in my diary.

CHAPTER TEN

Internship, 1977-1978: All Too Familiar with Death

I reported for internship at 8 AM on July 1, 1977, feeling excited, scared, and determined. The hospital gave me a beeper, two white coats with logos on the pocket, two white skirts, and a *DEA* number, which allowed me to write medication prescriptions. We wore our uniforms all the time while we were in the hospital.

My children were nine and seven when I started internship. They were both doing well in private schools in Brooklyn Heights, Rob at St. Ann's, Hope at Packer. I had no friends when I was their age, so I made a big effort while they were growing up to give them lots of contact with other children. As a result, they are both gregarious and socially adept, with many close friends.

I was determined to be the best mother I could during that year. I did not worry about Malcolm. I assumed he would cope well during my internship year, as he had done during four years of medical school.

I was naïve. Neither Malcolm nor I realized how overwhelming the internship year would be. This was a whole new level of time commitment and stress. I dropped off the edge of the world that year, barely surviving, one day at a time. I did not let myself recognize the strain this would put on our marriage.

Interns at that time worked a hundred hours a week, i.e., two-and-a half forty-hour-a-week jobs. We were at the hospital Monday through Friday from 8 AM to 7 PM. We "took call"—stayed overnight at the hospital—every third night and every third weekend. When I was on weekend call, I arrived at the hospital at 8 AM Saturday morning. I left at 8 PM Monday night, sixty hours later.

The hospital gave me a small room where I could sleep while I was on call. I almost never used it.

Internship devoured me. I lived under extreme time pressure that was intense and implacable. I lost track of the time, the day, the season. I never saw the sun or moon or felt the wind and rain on my face. When I was on weekend call, I gave up sleep, baths, and food. I could not take the ordinary activities of life at a normal pace. I had to plan when to do mundane things like wash my hair, take a bath, and cut my fingernails.

I was always in motion, darting from bed to bed, always under the glare of artificial blue light, always surrounded by noise—beepers going off, the PA system announcing codes, the steady tweet of patient monitors. The dream I had during the night before I began the third year at medical school came true. I was caught in a vortex, pulled under by powerful forces I could not control, fighting to catch my breath.

I spent that year in survival mode—teeth gritted, shoulders hunched, fists clenched. When I was at the hospital, I watched the clock and plotted when I could escape to go back home. When I staggered home, I tried furiously to make up for the time I missed with my children. Then I dove into bed and slept as if I was dead.

All that stress took a toll. For many years after my internship year, I was never able to fully relax. My mother said to me one day, "You are always rushing around, tense in the face. Why can't you just flop down and do nothing sometimes?" She was more perceptive than I thought.

The hardest part of that internship year was being away from my children. One day, I saw a girl in an elevator who was the same age as Hope. I ran to the nearest bathroom, cried, paced the floor, splashed cold water on my face, and carried on.

I lived with guilt. When I was at the hospital, I worried about my children. When I was home, I worried about my patients. One day, Hope put her hands on her hips and said: "Mom, are you loyal to the hospital or to your family? You spend more time at the hospital than you do with us." She was right. I was getting out of touch with my children's lives.

To keep myself sane, I began to keep a diary. Every night, no matter how late it was or how exhausted I felt, I wrote down everything that happened during the day. The diary helped me digest, absorb, and evaluate the torrent of experiences that were overwhelming me. After I described my day, I could detach from it. I had a voice. I existed. I had lived that day instead of merely surviving it. I relied heavily on my diary when I wrote this chapter.

Malcolm took over most of the day-to-day care of Rob and Hope during my internship year. Hope got sick at school one day when I could not get home. Malcolm, who was by then a senior vice president at New York Life Insurance Company, picked her up in the company Cadillac and drove her home. She told the chauffeur to drive slowly so all her friends could see her.

The first weekend I was on duty, Malcolm went into the kitchen to make lunch. He put three frozen hamburger patties in a pan and turned up the heat high. Smoke filled the apartment and set off the fire alarm. After that, he took the children out for all meals, usually to a restaurant called the New China Teacup. They somehow survived massive doses of monosodium glutamate without untoward effects.

The interns rotated through a different specialty each month. They included internal medicine, neurology, the cardiac care unit (CCU), the intensive care unit (ICU), and the emergency room (ER).

The interns, and the residents, who were two, three, or four years out of medical school, were collectively known as the *house staff*. The house staff took care of several floors of patients almost completely on our own, except for some supervision by senior doctors called *attendings*, who came in every weekday morning to review the patients with us. All the attendings were male and white. They strode through the hospital like gods, brimming with self-confidence.

Pictured: CJM as an intern during a talk by an attending, 1977.

Each floor had roughly forty patients. One resident and two interns were assigned to each floor. The resident was responsible for all the patients. We interns were responsible for half of them. All the patients were extremely sick, and new ones came in all the time.

I had dozens of patients under my care, and each one was a ticking time bomb. If I made a mistake, somebody would die. This was a whole new level of stress. Even when I was not at the hospital, I was working, worrying about my patients.

My beeper put me under the full control of the nurses. It took away my life as an autonomous human being. It went off every few minutes. I never knew what the nurse on the other end would say. It ranged from the ridiculous through to the mundane to the terrifying.

"Dr. MacKay, your patient just fell into a wastebasket. You must come to the floor and file an incident report."

"Dr. MacKay, your patient needs an order for a sleeping pill."

"Dr. MacKay, please order an enema for your patient."

"Dr. MacKay, your patient is having a seizure." In that case, I had to drop everything, rush to the room, wrestle the patient to the ground, get an IV started, and run in Valium until he or she stopped seizing.

Some of the male interns carried two beepers. When the second beeper went off, they hurried away. They returned half an hour later, looking a tad sheepish. They were supplementing their income by providing fresh sperm for the hospital's fertility clinic. Presumably, the sperm of a doctor had a high value. I worried some of their children would meet and marry as adults without realizing they were half- siblings.

Out of the several dozen interns, only three, including me, were female. We three women faced the loneliness and isolation of functioning as a woman in a man's world—always on display, always proving ourselves. Our ranks were reduced to two when one of the women made a suicide attempt that almost succeeded halfway through the year and dropped out.

The woman who left was young, brilliant, and strikingly beautiful. Her long, blond hair was always impeccably coiffed. Her lipstick and eye makeup were always perfect. She looked totally confident—far more confident than I felt. Why did she succumb to the grinding pressure while I did not... even though I was ten years older, with streaks of grey in my hair to prove it?

I believe my unusual childhood made me stronger than she was—strong enough to survive internship. I had to learn to be tough, to never give up, and to master fear when I was fox hunting and guiding my siblings around London. I was taught I should never show emotion. I was expected to solve every problem by myself. I was an expert on detachment. I also had an advantage she did not have—the diversion and entertainment of a husband and children.

Every nurse at the hospital was a woman. Many of the nurses flirted enthusiastically with the male interns and residents. Most of them were kind to me, but a few resented me. They pretended not to hear me when I asked for something. On a few occasions, I came across catty comments they wrote about me in the patient charts. Perhaps they believed that women should not be doctors?

The intern was the first doctor to interview each new admission. Our job was to take the patient's history, do a physical exam, order medications, order tests such as EKGs, blood tests, and X-rays, and write orders for the nurses telling them how often to check the patient's vital signs—blood pressure, temperature, and pulse. When a patient left the hospital, the intern wrote the discharge note and summary of the hospital stay.

I soon learned to write *prn* orders for medications for pain, sleeping pills, laxatives, and diarrhea medications, or I would get calls from the nurses all night long (*prn* is the acronym from the Latin *pro re nata*, or *as needed*).

Writing orders was a daunting responsibility. I had to be careful not to order a drug that was incompatible with other medications a patient was taking—for example, aspirin for a patient who had a bleeding ulcer. If I did a sloppy job, somebody would die.

All the doctors, including the house staff, went to *"M and M"* (morbidity and mortality) conferences once a week, where we reviewed every patient who did not do well or died while they were in the hospital. Soon, I was seeing patients who had been under my care. I have never forgotten these patients.

Doctors are human, and humans make mistakes. I had to make many split-second decisions during my internship. Most of them turned out well, but a few worked out less well. Doctors say we all have our own private graveyard.

By the third month of internship, I had treated patients with cancer, heart disease, venereal disease, anorexia, seizures, senile dementia, hysteria, psychosis, suicide attempts, morbid obesity, and alcoholism. One young man came in after he was bitten by his pet water moccasin. A young woman came in when she had a seizure caused by cocaine. She did not stick around long. The next day, she shot up with some heroin brought in by her boyfriend and walked out, hugging our floor radio in her arms.

I was exhausted by the time Christmas arrived. I did not have the time to do Christmas right—buy and wrap presents, put up and decorate a tree, decorate the house, and send Christmas cards. I dreaded trying to pretend I was feeling jolly. When the nurses put up Christmas decorations on the nursing stations, I wanted to take down each one and burn it to a crisp.

The dream of every intern and resident was to get a traction patient. The traction team strapped these patients into bed with weights hanging from their legs, to stretch out their spines and relieve pressure on their discs. The patients remained at strict bed rest for five, six, or seven days. There was nothing we interns had to do for these patients unless they developed a medical problem, which was rare.

Traction patients treated in hospitals for days at a time have gone the way of the dodo. We now know strict bed rest for many days causes muscles to atrophy and makes the problem worse. Traction for small amounts of time can be helpful, however. Chiropractors will sometimes put a patient's neck or back under traction for ten to fifteen minutes.

I was a woman on trial in a man's world. I tried to avoid looking feminine or stylish, as if I was inviting the attention of a man. My goal was to appear serious, competent, and professional. I adopted a brusque, no-nonsense manner. My outfit consisted of clunky flat shoes, a mannish Brooks Brothers shirt, iron-rimmed spectacles, and no makeup or jewelry.

Eventually, I managed to convince most of the patients, nurses, doctors—and myself—that I really was a doctor. To my surprise, it was the women, not the men, who had the most trouble accepting me.

One of my patients was an elderly Italian lady whose blood was drawn every day by the male medical student who worked under me. One morning, when he was on vacation, I went in to draw her blood. She glared at me. "I don't want the nurse to take my blood; I want the doctor," she said. I tried to convince her I was a doctor, but she would not buy it. She was only satisfied she had a "real" doctor when I asked one of the male phlebotomy technicians to help me out.

Being a woman turned out to be a plus instead of a minus one night when I got a late emergency admission, a middle-aged man with an infection that had spread to his bloodstream. This is called sepsis, and sepsis kills quickly. He needed immediate treatment with IV antibiotics. At this hour, there was no phlebotomy technician to bail me out. They all went home at five o'clock.

I grabbed an IV set-up and ran into his room. His high fever had addled his brain. He was pacing up and down, talking to himself and not making much sense.

"Please sit down, sir; I need to start your IV," I said.

"I'm damned if I'm going to let some #$@&%*! woman start my IV!" he bellowed.

"I'm not a woman, I'm a doctor," I said, in what I hoped was a seductive tone of voice, and I flashed him a flirtatious grin. He stared at me, and he began to laugh. I grabbed his arm, sat him down, and started his IV, fast, before he could change his mind.

Patients in the 1970s were like trusting children. They never researched their diseases. They did what their doctor told them to do, and they almost never asked questions. Malpractice suits and second opinions were almost unheard of.

Most patients were clueless about their medical problems. One day, I examined a new patient who had scars all over his abdomen. When I asked him what kind of surgery he had, he had no idea. "There was something wrong with my stomach," he said. Today, many of my eye patients go home, look up their eye problems on the internet, and pepper me with questions.

When I was a third-year medical student on my medicine rotation, I had been assigned to an elderly German lady who reminded me of Tina, our German cook. I stopped by her room often to talk to her. One day, she had a sudden massive heart attack. The emergency team rushed into her room, pounded on her chest, shocked her heart, and rushed out again when it was clear she could not be saved.

They left behind a mound of trash…and me. I stayed in her room and held her hand. I was upset for weeks, even though I knew there was nothing I, or any other doctor, could have done to save her.

Internship was a different story. A patient I knew died almost every day, and I felt…nothing. I was numb, all too familiar with death.

Doctors need to build defenses against the misery that surrounds us. We must learn how to live with suffering without being destroyed by it. When I re-read my diaries, I can see the distancing process build up as I start to describe the details of each case instead of the suffering and fear of the patients.

During my internship year, I learned how to suppress my empathy and put distance between myself and the patients. Like all other doctors, I described the patients not by their name but by their diagnosis and room number—for example, "The kidney failure in Room Four." Hospital gowns were helpful because they wipe out a patient's identity. Nobody looks rich, famous, or important in one of those ridiculous, flimsy, pastel-colored garments.

I did not allow myself to notice how vulnerable, pathetic, and scared my patients were. I ignored the worried faces that peeped out of the rooms. They seemed to be asking me: "Doctor, am I going to be all right?"

The interns did not have time to get to know our patients as people. Our job was to care for their bodies, not their feelings. Our focus was on the problem, not the person. If patients seemed upset or sad, we did not sit down and talk to them. We wrote *depression* on their list of problems and called in the psychiatry resident.

I felt like an expert mechanic who was tinkering with malfunctioning engines. I gave patients drugs to increase or lower their blood pressure and blood sugar, speed up or slow down their hearts, dry them out, or rehydrate them.

I have never completely lost this detachment. When somebody develops a medical problem – including me—I often catch myself focusing on the problem instead of showing the proper sympathy for what they are suffering.

Doctors are famous for misguided stoicism. We believe only patients are allowed to get sick. We ignore signs of illness in ourselves that would make us spring into action if we saw them in a patient. I ended up spending three weeks in the Pain Center of a major teaching hospital because I refused to recognize I had *Chronic Pain Syndrome* (more on that in *The Doctor Becomes a Patient*, Chapter Twenty-Two).

We interns had a lot of practice in diagnosing death. The most definitive way to find out if a person is really, truly dead is to look inside the eye at the retinal arteries. If the arteries are full of "box cars"—dark red rectangles of stalled clotted blood—the heart has stopped pumping. This line of what appears to be tiny red bricks is called "box cars" because it resembles the box cars of a freight train.

People say *the eye* is *the window to the soul*. The eye is, in fact, the window to the body. I marveled at how much I could learn about the body by looking into the eye. I felt excited when I remembered that, in only a few months, I would be looking at retinal blood vessels all day long.

On several occasions, I raised the dead, and each time, I felt like a god. One day, a diabetic man came in blue and comatose, in insulin shock. One IV of concentrated sugar, and he woke up pink and smiling. Another patient came in with a lethal heart rhythm, ventricular fibrillation. He was not breathing, and he had no pulse. A few shocks with the cardiac defibrillator, and he was alert and well again.

While I was on weekend duty, I did not have time to take a bath or change my clothes. I wore the same increasingly smelly shirt for three days straight. I was lucky if I snatched a few hours of sleep. My meals consisted mostly of custards left in the refrigerator as snacks for the patients. These custards were customarily gobbled down by starving interns, who customarily ate them standing up.

Nobody complained. Every doctor was expected to endure this trial by fire. This was our initiation rite. The purpose was to teach us to "think clinically," i.e., to develop a switch in our minds we could activate when we were faced with an emergency so we could perform what needed to be done without emotion.

This system worked. After I had been at the hospital for a month, I learned to walk briskly into the room of a new admission, ask a few key questions, slap my stethoscope on the chest, get a sample of stool, and escape to write a note. This kept me from developing any personal involvement with the patient.

There were no latex gloves on hospital floors in 1977. My hands were awash in blood all day, every day. Every night, I scraped blood out from under my fingernails. As I think back over that year, I am appalled by the danger I was in, and the danger to which I was exposing my family. Today, gloves are mandatory whenever a member of the hospital staff touches a patient.

At the end of the internship, the interns like me who were headed for a surgical residency had to take a blood test for *Hepatitis B*, a virus that is passed through blood and other body fluids. This virus attacks the liver. Ten percent of people who contract Hepatitis B end up with chronic liver failure and/or liver cancer.

My blood test showed I had antibodies to Hepatitis B but no live virus. Presumably, I caught the virus from the blood of a patient, but my body fought it off. I recovered without knowing I was infected. Fortunately, I did not have any live virus, or I would not have been allowed to become a surgeon. Today, Hepatitis B can be prevented with a vaccine.

After forty-eight hours on weekend duty, Monday morning dawned like a rainbow. The residents and attending doctors pranced in, rested and fresh, with the clear clinical judgment that comes from abundant sleep, to help us take care of all those sick patients. They would helpfully point out all the tests the exhausted interns had forgotten to order.

Thanks to a tip from my resident, I always drew a *"Didja"* tube on each of my new admissions. A Didja tube was an extra, red-topped tube of blood I kept in the refrigerator instead of sending it off to the lab. When the attending doctor asked me on Monday: "Didja get [such-and-such a test] on this patient?" I said: "Absolutely!" and I sent off the Didja tube, *STAT* ("to be processed immediately"). If the attending did not ask for extra tests, I discarded the Didja tube.

I learned to draw several Didja tubes when I was under the supervision of certain picky attendings. These fussy doctors always wanted to know what we called the "serum porcelain level"—i.e., some obscure test we had never heard of, did not have the time to research, which was of questionable importance.

I was never criticized for ordering too many blood tests and scans, only for ordering too few. I blithely ordered them without having the faintest idea of how much they cost.

I saw patient after patient with self-inflicted health problems. I saw alcoholics with liver and heart failure, peripheral neuropathy, dementia, and loss of balance caused by the death of cells in their cerebellum. We joked you could diagnose alcoholism by putting a stethoscope on the back of the skull and listening as the Purkinje cells—the cells responsible for balance— dropped dead and fell onto the floor of the fourth ventricle.

When I was in medical school, we watched a video of a white blood cell floating in normal plasma, followed by a video of the same cell in plasma that had a concentration of alcohol consistent with a patient taking two alcoholic drinks. The cell moved freely and purposefully in the first video. In the second video, it could barely move. White blood cells play a key role in the immune response against bacteria, viruses, and cancer. Anybody who saw that video would swear off alcohol for life.

I saw smokers who had strokes, heart attacks, leg gangrene, and many types of cancers, including lung. One patient lost both of her legs and one of her arms from smoking. She used her one remaining arm to hold a cigarette to her mouth.

I saw massively obese patients who had high blood pressure, diabetes, heart attack, stroke, breathing problems, and fatty liver disease. They were digging their graves with their teeth. Of course, like every other doctor, I told these patients not to drink/smoke/overeat. And of course, they ignored me.

There were several floors in the hospital where senior attending doctors took care of their own private patients. The house staff almost never interacted with these patients. Interns normally did not go to these floors unless they were called by a nurse.

One day, a nurse asked me to renew IV orders for a patient on one of the private floors. This was usually a routine matter of continuing the attending's orders. Luckily, I glanced at the patient's chart and noticed her doctor had put her on a blood pressure medication that raises potassium levels in the blood while he also ordered high doses of potassium in her IV.

High blood levels of potassium stop the heart. I ran a STAT (abbreviation of the Latin word *statim*, which means "immediately") check on her blood potassium. It was so high she would have been dead in a few hours if I had not immediately changed her IV and given her six Kayexalate enemas. This was a narrow escape. I was shaking.

All the other attendings at the hospital were competent. This doctor was sloppy and uninformed. I talked to the other interns and residents. They had seen other examples of this doctor's carelessness. They did not want to get the reputation of being a whistleblower because they planned to stay at the hospital. I was planning to leave. I was the ideal person to speak out.

This doctor had excellent bedside manners and a huge practice. He made a lot of money for the hospital because he brought in a lot of patients. I wrote a letter to the Medical Board of the hospital, describing what happened. My gutsy resident signed it. The Board told me the letter would be placed in the doctor's file. He remained on the staff.

I know he read the letter. His son, a senior resident I admired and liked, accosted me in the hall and berated me for writing it. He joined his father's practice the next year. Now, I knew the patients would get good care.

Not one, but two, of the residents who supervised me during the internship warned me separately I had too much control over my emotions. They were worried because I never showed any anger. They urged me to stop being so polite. "Express your feelings," one of them said, "or you will end up with migraines and ulcers."

They had never met a woman from my background before. My ability to express anger had been spanked out of me years ago by my nurses. I was a long way from Far Hills, New Jersey, but Far Hills was still right there, deep down inside of me.

I was able to control my emotions every day of internship except one, when I was on duty in the ICU, taking care of a post-operative patient of a surgeon who was notoriously eccentric. When he was bored, he went up to the roof of the hospital and hit golf balls into the street. He was a good surgeon, but we all knew he was tough on the house staff.

I was foolhardy enough to change this surgeon's IV orders. When he discovered that I had changed the orders, he started screaming at me. I surprised him and myself by bursting into tears. He muttered something like: "She's been working too hard." and let it go.

I spent the month of January in the most difficult rotation at the hospital, the Emergency Room. I was on duty from 8 AM to 11 PM the first day and 5 PM to 8 AM the following day. Then I had twenty-four hours off until 8 AM the following day.

The hospital scheduled twice as many doctors in the ER from 5 PM to 11 PM because this was the time when all the ugly secrets of the Big City floated up from the muck. Most of the mean, depressing cases came in then. The husband-and-wife fights, which meant wives who had been punched in the face or otherwise assaulted by their husbands. The muggers, who wanted us to sew up their cut hands. And—always—the *GOMERs*.

GOMER was our acronym for Grand Old Man of the Emergency Room. The GOMERs were alcoholic, mentally ill, drug-addicted, homeless men who slept in the streets. Sometimes, they wandered in looking for a bed and a square meal. Sometimes, they were brought in by the police. They always needed much more than a bed and food. Their thinking was so out of control they always had advanced medical problems they had not even noticed.

We began by ordering the poor nurses to give the GOMERs a bath. Then, we withdrew them from alcohol, managing their seizures with IV Valium. Often, they had serious illnesses, such as pancreatitis, and they ended up in the ICU for weeks. The GOMERs cost the hospital so much that we called them *Million Dollar Men*.

I was especially interested in one GOMER who went blind from a combination of poor diet and excessive use of alcohol and cigarettes. At that time, this disease was called *Tobacco-Alcohol Amblyopia*. It is now called *Nutritional Optic Neuropathy*. It is caused by cyanide in cigarette smoke, exacerbated by vitamin deficiency, especially Vitamin B12.

We treated this man by preventing him from smoking and drinking, injecting him with Vitamin B12 and giving him nutritious food and a multivitamin supplement. I lost touch with him, but these cases almost always resolve in a few months.

After many weeks in the hospital, the GOMERs were healthy again. They toddled out the door, waving a cheerful "Goodbye." They were—most likely—heading for the nearest bar and smacking their lips. In those days, there was almost no attempt at intervention.

I dealt with several patients who made suicide attempts. Most of them, fortunately, had taken a drug overdose. These we could help. We pumped out their stomachs and sent them to the ICU for observation. One was a strikingly beautiful, young, blond psychiatrist's wife with many gold chains around her waist and neck. Another was the daughter of a rich, prominent man. Occasionally, we got a person who had hung himself. There was not much we could do about a hanging suicide except talk to the family about organ donation.

The best nurses in the hospital worked in the *ER*, the *ICU* (Intensive Care Unit), and the *CCU* (Cardiac Care Unit). Only senior attending doctors argued with these nurses.

The ER nurses were the salvation of us interns. They never told us what to do directly. They simply wrote out the appropriate slips for the blood tests, EKGs, and X-rays they knew each patient would need and clipped them on the patients' charts, where they fluttered until we found the time to sign them.

My daughter Hope caught chickenpox during my month in the ER. Malcolm, Rob, and I had chicken pox when we were young, so we were immune. Hope did not get it until she was eight years old, so her case was more severe.

The week Hope was sick, I left the ER at 8 AM and rushed home to spend the day in bed with her. We had a cozy time together, dozing, chatting, and reading. It was especially difficult to go back to the hospital twenty-four hours later.

This was the only illness my children had during my medical training. I could not have become a doctor if my children had not been healthy.

One night, the hospital ambulance brought in a tall, unconscious, well-built man in a hockey uniform. We took a sample of his spinal fluid, the fluid that flows around the brain and spine, and it was full of blood. He had smashed his head and bled into his brain.

When he woke up, we told him he must stay in the hospital for several days so we could watch him closely in case the bleeding in his brain got worse. He got right out of bed and signed out *A.M.A.* ("Against Medical Advice"), which is the right of any patient in any hospital. We watched helplessly as he walked out, grabbed a cab, and went back to the hockey game. I do not know what happened to him in the immediate future, but I am certain he had chronic traumatic brain damage in his later years.

One of our best nurses came in one night, her face badly beaten by her handsome boyfriend. As we sewed her up, he paced up and down the hall in his Irish fisherman's sweater, tan chino pants, and Docksider shoes. I do not know if she went back to him, but I hope not.

Every night but one when I was on duty in the ER, I worked non-stop from 5 PM until dawn. One night, I was so tired I lay down on one of the gurneys, hoping to catch a few minutes of rest.

When I woke up, bright, clear sunlight was shining in through the ER windows. Two feet of snow had blanketed the city overnight. Outside, everything was blindingly white and silent. No buses were running. There were no cars on the streets. A few cross-country skiers were sailing down Park Avenue. Nobody came to the ER that night.

I became deeply cynical about human nature during my month in the ER. *Just what is your little secret?* I said to myself when I passed somebody in the street.

Living in New York City during the 1970s meant living with constant danger. The Big Apple was filthy, broke, riddled with crime, and stuffed with carcasses of burned-out buildings. The subway cars were plastered with so much graffiti I could not see out of the windows. I felt as if the cars were screaming obscenities at me when they rolled into the station.

The criminals were numerous and bold. People who set foot in Central Park after sunset had an excellent chance of being raped, robbed, and/or murdered—especially if they were female.

Everybody I knew who lived in New York during that time was the victim of many crimes, including everyone in my family. Thieves stole the radio from our car three times. My purse was stolen in the subway on four different occasions. A burglar broke into our apartment and stole my jewelry, my camera, and all our silver. I was especially upset about the silver. Some of those pieces had been in my family for two hundred years.

A man with a gun confronted Malcolm outside our apartment, but he ran off when Malcolm began to yell. Rob was attacked in the street by a boy with a knife, who forced him to hand over all his money. My suitcase was stolen from my parked car, twice. A homeless man ripped a gold necklace from my neck while I was standing on the 168th Street A train subway platform. I snatched it back and yelled. A crowd gathered and watched with interest. Nobody helped. The man strolled lazily off, leaving the necklace clutched in my hand.

When I was robbed at gunpoint in my office, I pretended I was having a seizure. I fell onto the floor, jerking, groaning, and gasping. I did not bother to wet my pants because I thought he would not know incontinence is inevitable after a seizure. The robber got flustered. He grabbed my bag—which contained all my best jewelry because I was going to a party that night—and ran off. He did not take the time to pull off my engagement ring.

We didn't even bother to report these crimes. That was the way things were in a city in the middle of a crack epidemic and a financial meltdown.

When I look back at that time, I wonder how Malcolm and I had the courage to live in that city. The answer must be a hefty dose of denial. My mother, who never worried about me while we were in London, remarked that whenever news of a rape, robbery, shooting, or fire came on the radio, it was always in Brooklyn. I suspect she worried about me more than I thought.

Only another doctor understands how stressful internship is. All that stress, poor diet, and lack of sleep and exercise takes a physical and a mental toll. Only my closest friendships survived my internship year. I barely had the time and energy to nurture my patients and my children during internship. I did not have time to pay my friends the small courtesies they expected. A handful of friends continued to care even though I ignored them. This was a good way to find out who really loved me.

Most of what I remember from internship year is what happened at the hospital. Everything else fades into the background. I put almost all my time and energy into my patients that year, while my family got leftovers. This was how I was raised, so it did not seem abnormal. My parents put most of their energy into their social life and work, and I got leftovers.

To my relief, Rob and Hope seemed to do just fine without me that year. They learned to be self-reliant. Hope made her own lunch on the mornings I was not home. She even made me lunch one day. She tucked in little notes saying things like, "Mom, these dried apricots are delicious. Eat them; you'll like them."

Malcolm sometimes brought the children to the hospital for lunch on weekends when I was on duty. My eyes devoured their bright eyes and red cheeks. I sniffed greedily the whiff of clean, cold, fresh air they brought in with them.

My children did not understand why I spent so much time away from them that year. On several occasions, they refused to talk to me when I got home from the hospital. I missed Rob and Hope even more than they missed me. I couldn't go to their sports events or plays. I couldn't tuck them into bed at night or read them stories.

I worried about my children all the time during internship. I didn't worry about Malcolm. I could stay on top of my work and somewhat on top of my children, but I could not give Malcolm the attention he wanted. He put a lock on the bedroom door to keep the children out at night, but I was so exhausted when I got home that all I could do was crash into bed and fall asleep. He complained he was always picking up the pieces and holding the family together—which was true.

Even before the internship, Malcolm and I did not have a relaxed, comfortable marriage. We were always rushing around and achieving. We cherished our careers. We did not cherish each other.

One night, we were invited to a dinner party that was important for his career. I could not get home in time to change, so Malcolm picked me up at the hospital, carrying my dress and shoes. I wriggled out of my uniform and into my evening clothes in the car. His enthusiasm for our joint project began to fade.

I was securely in orbit around Malcolm during the first fourteen years of our marriage. He was the one in control, the one who made the decisions. I was happy to let him do this. I was an easy-going, adoring wife whose first concern was Malcolm and his career. I thought about him many times every day. Now, I had other things to worry about. I was a hollow-eyed, smelly zombie who was dealing with life-and-death problems every day. I could no longer cater to his every need.

The price I paid to be a doctor was an increasingly shaky marriage, but I did not let myself see it. My parents taught me to put blinders on anything that was emotionally difficult. I was too exhausted to worry about my marriage.

Everybody who goes through an internship comes out a different person. I started to make my own decisions that year. I turned into a wife who took her career as seriously as her husband took his.

What I was required to do, on almost no sleep, was, frankly, insane, but I would have died rather than show weakness. All doctors must endure this ritual. Internship was a year of hazing. The attendings were hazed, so they passed the hazing on. They seemed to believe this year of extreme stress produced good doctors. I do not agree, and the dire consequences of leaving patients in the care of exhausted, overworked interns speak for themselves.

In 1986, eight years after I finished my internship, an eighteen-year-old college freshman, Libby Zion, was admitted to New York Hospital with a flu-like illness. Her intern and resident were covering forty—yes, forty—patients with almost no supervision from attending doctors. Libby did not tell the exhausted admitting intern that she was taking an antidepressant, and the intern was too overworked and harried to ask.

When Libby began to make strange, jerking motions, the intern ordered *Demerol* (an opioid) and *Haldol* (a drug designed for people with mental illness that has a sedative effect). These drugs interacted badly with her antidepressant. She had a cardiac arrest and died.

Libby's father, Sidney Zion, was a writer for *The New York Times*. He successfully pushed for a state law that limits the amount of time residents and interns can work. The *Libby Zion Law* mandates that house staff cannot be kept at the hospital for more than eighty hours per week, they can only be on duty for twenty-four consecutive hours, and a senior physician must always be physically present at the hospital. Many other states have passed similar laws. Thanks to Sidney Zion, patients now get their care from sane, rested interns.

Internship was a difficult year for me, but my lack of sleep and high stress level made it positively dangerous for my patients. I could have been that intern. Libby Zion could have been my patient.

One night, when I was on a weekend call, I was so frazzled, and sleep deprived, that I mistakenly wrote an extra zero in the dosage of a drug that can be dangerous at high dosages. The pharmacy immediately called to correct the order. The system at my hospital corrected my error, but other hospitals do not necessarily have a first-rate medication check system.

One day, I got an unexpected page from the front desk. I ran down, and there was my mother. "I'm in the city today getting some portraits framed, so we can have lunch." she said brightly.

It was clear she assumed I would be delighted to see her. I was not. How could she be so clueless as to casually drop by for lunch with a frantically busy intern in the middle of the day? I was a working woman, not some Far Hills debutante with time to kill. I had had no sleep the previous night. My hair looked like wet seaweed. A rank odor wafted from my armpits.

I never had time for lunch, but I handed my beeper to one of my friends for an hour and took my mother to the cafeteria. She launched into a detailed description of her new portrait commissions, interspersed with the latest Far Hills gossip. I did not expect her to ask about my job. She did not. Meanwhile, patients were dying on the floors above her head.

My mother's world was one of art and beauty and leisure and elegance and socially prominent friends. This had once been my world. I was no longer a part of this world of privilege and pleasure. I was in a new world that was harsh, rushed, ugly, and frantically busy, but far more meaningful to me.

Her world suited her well. My world suited me well. She could not understand my world, so she ignored it. My brain could barely navigate between these two worlds. I sighed with relief when she left.

Malcolm and I had built a "small business" marriage whose purpose was to produce success for everybody in the family. Our small business was flourishing. I was on my way to being a doctor. Rob and Hope were doing well in school and had many friends. Malcolm was a rising executive at the New York Life Insurance Company, where, luckily, he had regular hours.

Internship ended on June 30, 1978. I thought we interns would be bonded for life, like soldiers who went through battle together, but we scattered away to our new careers, where we were too busy to keep in touch. I admire my smart, dogged, dedicated fellow doctors, and I have professional relationships with some of them, but we did not have the time to develop deep friendships.

All through this brutal, demoralizing, lonely, stressful, unhealthy year, when I did nothing but medicine all day and night, I was sustained by a dream. Blind people would come to me, and I would make them see. Except for my two children, this seemed like the most important project of my life.

I left internal medicine without a backward glance. It was too slow and tedious for me. Every day, we made a small change in our patients' drug routine—push a diuretic, hold a cardiac med—and then sat back and waited to see how the patient responded. Surgery would be adventure and action. I would cure people. I could not wait.

CHAPTER ELEVEN

Residency, 1978-1981: Eyes Again

The first day of eye residency finally arrived on July 1st, 1978. Four excited, wide-eyed first-year residents, three men and me, spent the morning touring the operating rooms. The surgical instruments were surprisingly small and delicate. I could not believe how expensive they were. One forceps with a mouth the size of a grasshopper's jaw cost five hundred dollars, equivalent to two thousand dollars today.

In the afternoon, Dr. Gerald DeVoe, the former chairman of the Eye Institute, herded us into the auditorium. This eminent man stood over six feet tall. He was trim and white-haired. His pale blue eyes were almost invisible behind his glittering steel glasses.

He was the conscience of the Eye Institute. When he spoke at *Grand Rounds*, it was usually to remind us to focus on the best interest of the patient ("Grand Rounds" is a weekly meeting where doctors discuss challenging patients. "Rounds" is when doctors visit their patients in the hospital).

I learned later he was a meticulous and gifted surgeon. He wrote a detailed note, in minute, precise script, after every operation before he moved on to his next case. He was a man of few words. He almost never smiled. He had our complete attention.

Dr. DeVoe cleared his throat. "You are taking on a big responsibility when you operate on eyes." he said. "You must not do anything that could give your hands a tremor. Do not drink alcohol or do any strenuous exercise involving your arms the day before you are scheduled to be in the OR. On the day of surgery, you must not drink any coffee or tea. Most importantly, do not have any fights with your spouse the day before surgery." He turned and walked out.

No fights with my spouse. That will not be so easy, I said to myself. Malcolm was spoiling for a fight those days because he was so frustrated with my schedule.

Malcolm was my number one priority during our first fourteen years of marriage. He seemed so big and strong and capable and self-confident that I could not—or would not—let myself see he needed even more attention than our children.

He was supportive beyond my wildest dreams when I was in medical school, but neither of us had any idea how demanding internship and residency would be or how they would change me and my priorities.

Malcolm assumed he would get his wife back after I finished my internship. He thought I would pare down my work, avoid time-consuming projects, and focus single-mindedly on him the way I did when we were first married, and he would be in control of our life again.

I was on a different wavelength now. I had the job of my dreams. I was on fire, hungry to grow, to challenge myself. I had the chance to make a difference in the world. I was taking charge of my own life more and more.

Malcolm was getting more and more annoyed about the state of our apartment. He complained it was a chaotic, run-down mess. He never did any housework, shopping, cooking, or decorating, so he had no idea how much time and energy this took.

He grew up in a house decorated to perfection by his mother. It featured expensive antique chairs with white upholstery, gleaming brass and silver, and high-price oriental rugs. It looked like a museum. Every time I sat down in one of my mother-in-law's chairs, I worried I might break it.

Our rent-control apartment was clean because of our housekeeper, but in addition to peeling paint, it featured mismatched inherited furniture covered with stains, cheap frayed rugs, and faded curtains made from material I bought at a discount store. I thought it looked welcoming and comfortable. Malcolm said it looked "grubby".

I did not want to spend the time and money decorating our apartment to make it look like some grand colonial mansion. I wanted to spend all my time with our children when I was home. I wanted to do other things with our money.

I suspect Malcolm's anger at my lack of interest in decorating our apartment was displaced anger at what he thought was my neglect of him. I could not focus on Malcolm and our apartment with the laser-like intensity of his full-time homemaker mother. I no longer had the time, or the energy, or the interest to cater to Malcolm's every wish.

I had to become ruthless to be a surgeon, and not just in the OR. There were times when I had to put my patients on the front burner and put everybody else, including my husband, on the back burner.

Before I became an eye surgeon, I did everything Malcolm asked me to do. Now, like Grandma Johnson, I had to say no to my strong-minded husband. She did it by taking to her bed. I began with reason, and when that didn't work, I flatly refused. It was not until twenty-four years later, in 2002, when I was sixty years old, and Malcolm was sixty-two, that the cracks became so deep they busted our marriage into bits. For now, they stayed below the surface.

We had a running argument about swimming. Malcolm liked to swim on Tuesdays because it fit with his tennis and squash schedule. I operated on Wednesdays, and, as Dr. DeVoe predicted, if I swam in cold water the night before surgery, my hands had a tremor the next day. I drew a line— no swimming before surgery. Malcolm said I was being selfish and unreasonable. He seemed to think if I truly loved him, I would put his needs first.

I ignored the widening cracks in our marriage because life was so much fun on the home front. Our apartment was in a constant state of cheerful, barely controlled chaos, a never-ending party. I was blissfully happy.

Friends of Hope and Rob buzzed in and out like spinning tops, bouncing off walls, hooting and giggling, draping themselves over furniture, spending the night. The phone rang constantly. Music blared. Tweets and rustles came from the two cuddlesome guinea pigs in Hope's room. And for one day, until *Supermouse*, our perfidious cat, ate it, Hope had a loud, feisty quail chick she hatched in an incubator.

Food vanished from the kitchen hours after I bought it. Supermouse lurked around until Rob or Hope started to do homework on the dining room table, and then she settled herself comfortably on top.

Our careers had the positive effect of making our children self-reliant and organized. Hope forgot her key one day, so she had to climb up her balcony and through her window to get into the apartment. She never forgot her key again.

One weekend, when we were visiting Far Hills, we had lunch with a girl who was sitting for her portrait and her mother. After lunch was over, I said to Rob and Hope: "OK, guys, clear the table and put the dishes in the dishwasher." which they did. The mother was astonished. "How did you teach them to do that?" she said. I didn't teach them anything; their circumstances did. My children had to help because I was so busy.

Malcolm and my demanding schedules have made Rob and Hope close. Hope wrote one of her school essays about the day Rob vaulted over the school fence to walk her home as her friends watched with admiration and envy. She said it was the coolest way any girl had been picked up from school.

Rob told me having two overachieving parents made it difficult for him to achieve. He said whatever he did would never be good enough for his father. This, of course, describes Malcolm's relationship with his mother, who drove him passionately.

All the patients during my internship were seriously sick. The eye patients did not have any major medical problems, so they were easy to take care of. When I was on duty at the hospital at night during internship, the nurses beeped me every few minutes all night long. There were many nights at the Eye Institute when I did not get one call after midnight.

The attendings at the Eye Institute were eager to help the residents because that was the tradition there. They worked side by side with us in the Eye Clinic, so there was always a senior doctor present if we needed help. They also assisted us in the OR while we performed surgery. The senior residents were also happy to help the junior residents because they were not under any stress, and they had plenty of sleep.

Now I had time go to my children's school plays, squash matches, and parent-teacher conferences. Hope thought I was a cool mom because I came to her classroom one day with a surgical gown, cap, gloves, shoe covers, and sponge full of iodine soap and showed her classmates how surgeons prepare for operations.

Ophthalmology fascinated me. I was happy all day, every day. I read my eye journals with interest. Every patient was a fascinating puzzle to solve. I had the satisfaction of solving many small problems each day. I could make patients happy just by giving them the correct glasses. I had never forgotten the miracle of sight when I got my first pair.

One day, one of the other residents asked: "Are you taking anti-depressants?"

"No," I said. "Why do you ask?"

"You always seem so happy," he said.

I ran up to the library during every free moment to devour eye textbooks. I subscribed to, and read carefully, four different eye journals. I knew it would not be easy for a woman to make it in eye surgery. I knew I didn't have to be as good as a man to earn my place at this august bastion of white male privilege. I had to be twice as good.

My obsessive-compulsive-perfectionist traits were a big help. When I was not examining patients or in the operating room, I was reading textbooks and journals and filling box after box with notes written on index cards.

The accomplishments of the attending doctors and researchers intimidated me. They were the movers and shakers of ophthalmology: the journal editors, the presidents of eye societies, the ones who wrote the textbooks, the ones who invented new technologies and obtained new patents, and the ones who published the papers that drove ophthalmology forward.

Dr. Lazlo Bito invented *Xalatan*, a new class of medication for glaucoma.

Dr. Endre Balazs invented a technique for extracting hyaluronic acid (*Healon*), a natural viscous lubricant, from rooster combs. Healon has made eye surgery easier and safer. It has other uses as well. It is injected into arthritic knees to reduce inflammation and into aging skin to eliminate wrinkles.

Charles Campbell was the first doctor to use a ruby laser in a human eye, and Francis L'Esperance was the first to use an Argon laser in the eye. Fran also wrote the first eye laser textbook.

Ira Snow Jones wrote the definitive textbook on orbit tumor surgery.

Robert Ellsworth was the world's leading authority on retinoblastoma, a hereditary eye cancer in children. He brought down the death rate of this deadly disease from ninety percent to ten percent. When Bob got bored, he published a case report or invented a new instrument.

Jackson Coleman was the first ophthalmologist to use ultrasound to examine and treat the eye.

These were my colleagues and teachers. They would watch me while I performed surgery and listen as I presented a case at Grand Rounds. (A resident "presents a case" by describing the relevant facts about a patient—e.g., "Sixty-year-old male construction worker with a fifteen-year history of poorly controlled diabetes"—followed by the history of the eye problem—e.g., "sudden complete painless vision loss in the right eye"—followed by photos of the eye, and tests such as blood work, scans, etc.)

How would I live up to the standards set by these giants of ophthalmology? The answer turned out to be somewhat like picking wallpaper off a wall. I worked hard, I took it bit by bit and day by day, and I never gave up.

The other residents brought in videos and even musical instruments to amuse themselves during weekend call. I brought in stacks of journals—Ophthalmology, American Journal of Ophthalmology, Archives of Ophthalmology—and read steadily all weekend long. When the residents took the practice test for the ophthalmology board exam halfway through the year, my grades were the highest. One of the men failed.

Before we proceed, a short lesson on the structure of the eye might be helpful as we delve into my career and the many eye conditions I tackled over the years. The interested reader can refer to Appendix A to gain some basic knowledge about the eye and many of its parts.

Like all surgical residents, I learned on the poor. The patients who came to the Eye Clinic were all poor. They were treated by the residents, rather than the attendings, for a significantly discounted fee. This is a good deal for the poor. Studies have shown residents get just as good results as attending surgeons if they are carefully supervised.

My patients were the Hispanic people from the neighborhood around the Eye Institute who could not afford private doctors. Most were on Medicaid. A few were on Medicare. Others had no health insurance at all.

Most of them spoke only Spanish. My first patient was an elderly Hispanic lady who did not understand one word of English, although she had lived in the United States for the last thirty years. She brought her grandson with her to translate. She let loose a torrent of Spanish, and he piped up and told me what she said.

My Hispanic patients came in with dramatic complaints. I was not accustomed to dealing with people who complained easily and often; as I mentioned, my parents dealt with their own problems and expected us children to do the same. I quickly learned the Spanish for "excruciating headache," "horrible itching," "blurred vision," "terrible pain," and "I cannot see anything at all." Part of me wished I had permission to grumble as naturally as they did. I eventually realized my patients' problems were not as bad as they claimed.

The Hispanic women were ultra-feminine. They were always perfectly turned out in tight-fitting, low-cut blouses, short skirts, and high heels. Their gold hoop earrings were so large a canary could perch in them. Their long, black hair spilled down their backs in lustrous waves. One day, I saw myself in a mirror, sitting next to one of these ladies. Compared to her, I looked like a faded middle-aged man with frizzy hair and spectacles.

One day, one of my male patients said, "You must make a good salary." He was quiet for a moment. Then he said: "Will you marry me?" I realized he thought I was so ugly I did not have a husband, and I would leap at the chance to have him. I thanked him for the compliment and told him, unfortunately, I was already taken. He looked at me as if I had to be kidding.

Most of the Hispanic patients went south to the Caribbean during the winter. The slack was taken up by elderly Jewish patients, remnants from the time when the neighborhood was a Jewish enclave. They became depressed when the holidays approached, and they came in for reassurance they were not going blind. What they really wanted was somebody to talk to.

We first-year eye residents were on call every fourth night and every fourth weekend. During my first night on call, a nurse called me at 2 AM to tell me a male patient had urinary retention following general anesthesia, a common problem. "The doctor" had to come and insert a Foley catheter.

As I poked the long, slippery tube up the poor man's penis, which produced a whole bag full of urine, I wondered why the nurses were not allowed to do this simple maneuver. The next day, I learned the answer. This procedure was considered too "stimulating" for a nurse to perform. Now I was a doctor, I no longer qualified as an object of sexual desire.

I was nervous during my first months on call. I had not yet had any lectures on eye emergencies. I was responsible for the eyes of two-and-a-half to three thousand patients in Presbyterian Hospital, plus all the eye patients who arrived in the Emergency Room, located across the garden from the Eye Institute.

A few weeks into my residency, one of the medical residents in the Emergency Room called me at ten o'clock one night. "A forty-four-year-old woman has just walked in. She says she has suddenly gone blind in one of her eyes," he said. "Incidentally, she has a prosthetic mitral valve in her heart."

My heart started to pound. I was almost certain a clot had formed on her artificial heart valve, broken free, traveled to her eye, and blocked her central retinal artery. When an eye has a central retinal artery occlusion, the blockage must be reopened within one hour, or the retina will die, and the eye will be blind forever. It was crucial I make the right diagnosis because if she was forming clots, they might also go to her brain and cause a stroke.

I knew that nitroglycerin and carbon dioxide dilate retinal blood vessels, which could allow the clot to pass through more easily. The quickest way

162

to increase the concentration of carbon dioxide in the blood is to re-breathe in a paper bag. "Give her a nitroglycerin, STAT, and tell her to re-breathe into a brown paper bag," I barked at the ER resident. I slammed down the phone and ran to the Emergency Room. Rain was pelting down, but I did not bother to put on my coat. Minutes would make the difference between blindness and sight for that eye.

One of her eyes was, indeed, completely blind. It could not even see light. When I looked at the back of her eye with my ophthalmoscope, just as I suspected, her retina was chalk white and completely dead. She had a classic "cherry red spot" in her *macula*, the pin-head-sized area in the center of the retina where all detailed vision takes place (the macula gets its blood supply from the underlying *choroid* instead of the central retinal artery, so the choroidal blood vessels had kept it alive and pink).

I was only a month into my residency, but I knew more about the eye than anybody else in the hospital that night. I read about the best way to treat a central retinal artery occlusion in a textbook on eye emergencies. I knew what I had to do, but I had never done it before. I had seen surgeons perform a similar procedure in the operating room. It would be me or nobody.

"Get me a *TB syringe*, STAT," I said to the nurse. (A TB syringe holds one milliliter of fluid. The needle is 30 gauge, i.e., extremely fine.) I put a drop of anesthetic on her cornea, took a deep breath, plunged the needle through her cornea into the front of her eye parallel to her iris, and pulled out as much fluid as I could.

This procedure is called an anterior chamber tap. It abruptly lowers the pressure inside the eye. It is the fastest and most effective way to pull a clot out of a central retinal artery. Luckily, it causes almost no pain.

I heard a gasp. I looked around. The nurse was starting to faint, just as I did when I was a fourth-year medical student and saw Dr. Fink put a needle into a patient's eye socket. I had come a long way since that day. "Lie down on the floor, fast, and put your legs up against the wall," I told her.

Just then, the patient said: "I can see out of my eye!" My tap had knocked the clot out of her central retinal artery, and it had broken into small pieces and disappeared. She got back 20/20 vision in that eye.

This lady was lucky. Most central retinal artery occlusions do not get treated within an hour. Her eye went blind while she was awake, and she noticed it right away. She lived right next to the hospital, and she had the sense to come to the ER immediately. Because of the heavy rain, the ER was not crowded, so she was seen right away, and the ER doctor called me as soon as he heard her story.

A few weeks later, I was again called to the ER at night to examine a young woman who said she had "lost vision" in one of her eyes. This time, I was an afterthought. The ER resident called the psychiatry resident first. He thought the woman was crazy because when the nurse tested the vision in her "blind" eye, she saw 20/20.

Luckily, I got to the ER before the psych resident. The young woman seemed upset, but she did not seem crazy. I re-tested the vision in her "bad" eye. It did, indeed, see 20/20 when I tested it with a line of letters on the eye chart, but when I swung a flashlight from her good eye to her bad eye, the pupil did not constrict; it dilated.

Now I knew there was something seriously wrong with her bad eye. The pupil of the bad eye had dilated because that eye was sending less signal to the brain than the eye where the pupil constricted. This sign is called an *afferent pupillary defect*. It is not possible to fake an afferent pupillary defect.

I asked her if her "bad" eye hurt when she moved it. She said yes. *Aha*. Another clue. This told me she had inflammation around her eye.

I knew visual acuity and color vision are processed separately in the optic nerve, so one of these functions can be damaged while the other one remains normal. I tested her color vision in each eye separately. It was normal in her good eye, but completely absent in her bad eye. I tested her visual field. It was normal in her good eye but severely constricted in her bad eye.

"This woman has *optic neuritis*." I told the ER resident. "She almost certainly has *multiple sclerosis* ("MS"). I predict she has inflammation in other nerves, as well. She needs an MRI." He canceled the psych resident. An MRI the next day showed there were white areas in her brain typical for MS. I assume she was given high doses of steroids intravenously, to accelerate the recovery of her inflamed optic nerve.

The next time a medical resident called me to the ER at night, I was the one who made a mistake. A disheveled, smelly, elderly woman with dirty clothes was waiting for me. She was walking up and down, yelling, "Shards of broken glass are pouring out of my eyes!"

I glanced at her eyes across the room, and they looked normal to me—no redness, no discharge. I assumed she was mentally ill. I gave her a bottle of artificial tears and sent her home. I did not bother to examine her eyes with the slit lamp.

The next day, one of the attending doctors came to speak with me.

"A lady with EKC came to the clinic this morning," he said. "She claims you saw her last night. Why didn't you examine her eyes?"

I felt sick. I had failed to diagnose a case of *Epidemic Kerato-Conjunctivitis*, a painful, highly contagious viral infection that can scar the cornea and damage vision.

"I–I–I thought she was crazy." I stammered.

"Crazy people can get sick, too." he said.

The woman's eye infection resolved without any problems, but she taught me a lesson I will never forget. All doctors make mistakes. We need to forgive ourselves, learn from them, and live with them.

During my first year of residency, I assisted the senior attending surgeons in the operating room several times a week. I was not allowed to do any surgery in the operating room myself. I could only perform simple outpatient procedures, like lancing a stye or removing a lid growth.

Assisting the senior surgeons was invaluable. Nobody can learn how to operate by reading textbooks or watching videos. Surgeons learn by helping, or "assisting," other surgeons and by being helped, or "assisted." This process is intimate and sacred, like the laying on of hands.

The most important information I longed to learn was what to do if I had a complication during a case. I admit with every case, I prayed the surgeon would have a complication so that I would know how to handle it if I encountered a similar complication.

The second female eye resident at the Eye Institute arrived two years before I did. She was the one who had to deal with the Changing Room Problem. Changing rooms are rooms where surgeons change out of their street clothes and into their *scrubs*, which look like pajamas.

There were three changing rooms at the Eye Institute. Two were large, and one was small. The male attendings and residents each had a large changing room. All the nurses were jammed together in the small changing room.

The problem of where the first female resident would change was solved by shoving her in with the nurses. Now there were three female residents at the Eye Institute, and all three of us were crammed into the small changing room with the nurses.

On my first day in the operating room, when I went into the nurses' changing room to put on my scrubs, I was greeted by a short, stocky woman. She was as compact and sturdy as a fire hydrant. She put her hands on her hips and looked at me as if I was a fly she wanted to swat. She said loudly: "I never did like women surgeons."

This was my introduction to Robbie, the Head Nurse of the OR. She was formerly a nurse in the US Army, and nobody pushed her around. She was tough on all the residents, but she was toughest on the women. She worshipped Dr. DeVoe, and when he was operating, she curbed her sharp tongue and catered to his every need with silent devotion.

I think Robbie's comment had a purpose: she wanted to put me on notice that she would do everything in her power to test me and make me prove I was a competent surgeon. If I failed to live up to her standards, she would make my life miserable. I respected Robbie for that, and she could sense it. We both had one major concern—the welfare of the patients. It took several years to earn her respect. It took several more to earn her affection.

Most of the attending surgeons welcomed me as their colleague, but a few of the older ones treated me with barely veiled contempt verging on hostility. I assisted one of these men on my first day in the OR. When I walked into the room, he said loudly: "Lord save me, they've sent me one of those damn women."

When the operation was well underway, he suddenly told me a dirty joke. He timed it for the exact moment I was about to cut a suture. I saw his eyes swivel toward me over his mask. He was testing me.

I was not about to be intimidated by some male chauvinist surgeon. I cut the suture deftly. Then I retaliated by telling him several choice "dead baby" jokes that I had learned from my eleven-year-old son. In those days, all the eye surgery at the Eye Institute was performed with the patient under general anesthesia. Today, most eye procedures are done under local anesthesia, so the OR banter is considerably less X rated.

I mentioned this episode to the other residents. They told me he did the same thing to the two other women. The female resident one year ahead of me was shy, modest, and Catholic. He embarrassed her so much she blushed and got upset. One day, she started to cry.

Assisting most of the other attending surgeons was a pleasure, except for one man who was famously fussy. After a resident cut a suture, he would invariably complain it was either too long or too short. One day, one of my fellow residents asked him: "How would you like me to cut your sutures today—too long, or too short?"

A few weeks later, I was assigned to assist one of the eye cancer specialists as he removed a cancer-filled eye from a two-year-old girl. My job was to plunge my thumb into her orbit, the bony box that surrounds and protects the eye, the minute her eye was removed and press down hard on her central retinal artery to stop bleeding.

Maybe it was her blond curls peeping out from under the drapes. Maybe it was the rush of warm, red blood that swelled up around my thumb. Maybe it was the thought I was pressing on a thin sheet of bone that was directly in front of her brain. Maybe she reminded me of Hope. I started to feel faint. I pulled my thumb out of her orbit, excused myself, and sat down with my head between my legs.

The surgeon said: "Just my luck to be stuck with a wimpy girl." Not a woman. Not a female resident. A girl. I had confirmed all his worst stereotypes about women surgeons. Emotional. Unreliable. That did it. I never pulled out of an eye operation again.

Every attending had his own technique. Some surgeons took two hours to do an operation that others did in half an hour. While I watched each surgeon work, my mind was going a mile a minute, trying to decide what worked well and what did not, planning what I would do when I began to operate, taking the technique I thought was best from each surgeon.

As the year went by, and I watched the attendings operate repeatedly, I started to say to myself, *I can do that.* Then I started to say, *"I can do that even better."* while I was assisting certain ham-handed attendings. By the end of my first year, I was convinced I could operate as well as most of these surgeons and a lot better than some of them.

One attending, who had a huge practice, did not have the proper temperament for eye surgery. He was so clumsy, terrified, and inept the chief resident always arranged the schedule so one of the senior residents could "assist" him, which meant we did the case for him. Luckily, he had the sense to let us do this.

The warm-hearted Filipino nurses relieved the stress of the OR by throwing a party at the slightest excuse. They hauled in platters heaped with home-cooked Filipino delicacies. After the last case was over, we all jammed into the nursing office for a feast.

The nurses insisted I take a huge helping of everything. They had an unlimited capacity to laugh uproariously at my feeble attempts at humor. I had more fun eating Filipino food, with a plastic fork, off a paper plate than I had at any Far Hills cocktail party, making polite conversation as butlers passed silver trays of caviar, smoked salmon, and *pate de foie gras.*

Every normal eye has a lens. The purpose of this lens is to change the focus of the eye from far to near. When the lens becomes cloudy, we call it a cataract. Cataract surgery is the most common operation in medicine. I knew my first case in the operating room would be the removal of a cataract.

Early in my second year of residency, the day finally came when I was scheduled to do my first cataract operation. My patient was an elderly Hispanic man who had such a dense cataract he could barely make out the big "E" on the chart.

This was the moment I had worked for so hard during the last six years. This was my rite of passage. I was crossing the line. The night before the operation, I spent hours going over and over in my mind every step I planned to take and reading and re-reading *Cataract Surgery and its Complications* by Dr. Norman S. Jaffe. I had practiced the procedure on a real human eye that had been donated to the Eye Bank for surgical training purposes a few weeks earlier.

I began by scrubbing my hands with Betadine to kill all the bacteria. I would wear latex gloves, but gloves are not 100% reliable. There is always a risk they could be punctured. This happened to me many times.

The eye OR was the size and shape of a large living room. The air inside was filtered, and anybody who came in was expected to wear shoe coverings, hair covering, and a mask. The room was dark except for two lights the size of bicycle wheels hanging from the ceiling that were focused on a stark, simple altar in the middle of the room—the patient's bed.

The head of the bed was positioned directly underneath a jointed steel device hanging from the ceiling—the *operating microscope*. A gowned, masked, hooded figure stood ready next to a metal tray covered with steel instruments that were neatly organized into rows—the scrub nurse. The circulating nurse scurried about in the shadows, ready to bring me extra instruments if I asked for them.

The anesthesiologist crouched in semi-darkness next to a machine connected to several ribbed black rubber hoses that were attached to cylinders of gas. His job was to put the patient to sleep during the operation and revive him when it was over.

Dr. DeVoe, the former chairman of the Eye Institute, was sitting next to the head of the bed, gowned, masked, and gloved, ready to assist me. This great doctor would watch my every move – intimidating yet reassuring.

I walked into the eye OR with every nerve in my body humming.

The orderly brought my patient in on a gurney. The circulating nurse helped him slide the patient onto the operating table and strap him down. The anesthesiologist put an oxygen mask over the patient's mouth and nose, slipped *Pentothal* into his IV, injected *curare* to paralyze him, opened his mouth and throat with an L-shaped steel *laryngoscope*, and skillfully slid a plastic endotracheal tube down his windpipe.

The stage was set. Everything was ready for me to start the play. I was grateful my patient, like all cataract patients at that time, was under general anesthesia.

I began by cutting off the lashes. Then, I sterilized the lids, carefully wiping them three times with iodine and once with alcohol. The scrub nurse floated a sterile green cloth drape over the patient so the only thing visible was his eye. I gently slipped a lid speculum between the upper and lower lids to keep them open, and carefully adjusted it so it would not put any pressure on the eye.

The scrub nurse opened a sterile blue paper gown. I put my arms in, one by one, and the circulating nurse tied it behind me. Then, the scrub nurse held out a pair of sterile gloves, first right, then left. I plunged my hands in, one by one. We were partners in a familiar dance honed over centuries.

As I climbed into the draped surgeon's chair, the circulating nurse whispered in my ear: "Don't worry, Dr. MacKay. You will do fine. You have good hands." I would have hugged her if I were not in a sterile outfit.

She maneuvered the operating microscope until it was directly over the eye. I adjusted the focus. I closed my eyes for a moment. The scrub nurse handed me forceps and a pair of scissors. I began to operate.

And then...something happened I could not have predicted. The minute I grasped the *conjunctiva*, the moist, transparent layer filled with blood vessels that surrounds the eye, with the forceps, and made my first cut with the scissors, I felt a cog slip smoothly into place inside my mind. All my fear vanished. I felt relaxed, detached, and confident, as if I were floating.

I watched my hands move calmly and steadily. It felt as if I was looking at somebody else's hands. Two different parts of my brain seemed to be controlling these hands. My practical Johnson brain kept them steady and sure. My creative Armstrong brain kicked in whenever I needed to think up a new way to tackle a problem. I was a natural at eye surgery.

My ability to concentrate surprised even me. I became an obsessive-compulsive child in a futile attempt to earn the approval of my parents. I was so serious and driven I had no friends. I was so fastidious I cried when my parents first put me down on the sandy beach in Edgartown. Now these traits were paying off big time. Every move I made was flawless.

I used the cutting-edge technique of the time—*intracapsular cataract extraction.*

I cut off the lashes because we believed, at the time, this decreased the risk of infection. Usually, the lashes grew back normally, but sometimes they grew back crooked, which was an annoyance to the patient. A few years later, a prospective, randomized study showed that cutting the lashes increased, instead of decreasing, the rate of infection. Today, we use a thin plastic film that tucks the lashes out of the way.

 I sat down in the surgeon chair, and placed my left foot on the pedal that controlled the operating microscope hanging from the ceiling. With small motions of that foot, I moved the microscope forward and back, left, and right, and up and down to focus and decrease or increase the magnification.

After the scope was adjusted, I created a twelve-millimeter incision that cut the cornea halfway off. Then, I grabbed the cloudy lens, complete with its surrounding capsule, with a freezing probe, and slowly and steadily pulled it out of the eye in one piece.

Finally, I sewed up the wound with ten to twelve synthetic, braided *Vicryl* (Polyglactin) sutures. My first cataract operation had gone smoothly. My patient—like all cataract patients at that time—spent the night before and after surgery in the Eye Institute.

After the operation, Dr. DeVoe said: "Cynthia, you really have the touch. Not every resident does, but you do."

When I went to see my patient the next morning, my hands were shaking so hard I could barely pull his bandage off. A fervent prayer flooded through my brain—*Let this man see.*

The eye was perfect. The anterior chamber was deep. The cornea was clear. The pupil was round. Now, I knew I would be a good surgeon.

Intracapsular cataract surgery was the best we had in 1979, but it had significant problems. Surgeons had not yet invented a clear artificial lens to replace the natural eye lens, to restore the eye's focusing power. After the surgery, patients had to wear thick glasses to replace the focusing power of the lens, and these glasses distorted their vision. It was weeks before the eye healed and began to see well.

The incision was huge by today's standards. The *Vicryl* sutures I used to close it were stiff and scratchy. They were designed to be digested by enzymes in the tears, and were supposed to dissolve in four to six weeks, but sometimes, especially if the wound was not sewed up meticulously, and the sutures dissolved earlier than expected, the cornea sagged downwards, resulting in a sharper curve in one meridian of the cornea than the other. This is called *astigmatism*.

Given my obsessive tendencies, I sewed up every cataract incision with strict attention to detail. As a result, none of the cataract patients I operated on using the intracapsular technique developed astigmatism.

For my last ten years in the operating room, I used a totally different new technique to remove cataracts, called p*hacoemulsification*. It was invented by a series of daring and creative ophthalmologists during the previous twenty years. These surgeons dreamed up a method to remove the lens by emulsifying it. They could then remove this emulsified lens through a tiny incision that did not need any sutures, healed remarkably quickly and did not create any astigmatism. The procedure was close to painless, so eye surgeons were able to perform almost all cataract surgery under local anesthesia.

I began phacoemulsification by putting a numbing drop on the cornea and injecting *Lidocaine*, the anesthetic used to numb parts of the body and prevent pain, into the front chamber of the eye. After I adjusted the scope, the scrub nurse handed me a diamond-blade knife. I held it with a delicate touch—firm enough so it did not slip, gentle enough so there was no tension in my fingers.

I stabbed the diamond knife straight down through half the thickness of the far peripheral cornea. I then turned the knife horizontally and pushed it straight through the middle of the cornea for two millimeters. Finally, I turned the blade down again and pushed it into the eye.

This created a three-level incision with two overlapping flaps, which snapped shut and sealed itself when the probe was removed. A neat trick—no more sutures! I then made a smaller incision at right angles to the main incision to admit other instruments. Now, I was ready to tackle the cataract.

The human lens has a structure like a peach. There is a dense, hard nucleus in the center of the lens, like the pit of a peach. There is a layer of soft cortex, like the flesh of a peach, around this hard nucleus. A transparent skin, the capsule, covers the cortex like the skin of a peach. The main problem in taking out a cataract is dealing with the hard lens nucleus.

I began to remove the cloudy lens by tearing a circular hole in its front capsule with miniature forceps. Then, I slipped an ultrasound probe into the eye and put my right foot on the pedal. When I pressed down lightly on the pedal, the probe squirted saline. When I pressed down another notch, the probe squirted, and sucked. The third notch activated the ultrasound.

I pressed the petal down two notches, and sucked out the cortex until I had a good view of the nucleus. Now for the tricky part—removing that tough nucleus. I knew that if I executed this maneuver perfectly, the rest of the procedure would be smooth sailing.

I pushed the pedal down all the way. The probe squirted, and sucked, and waves of ultrasound radiated out from the tip. The tip of the probe started chewing away at the nucleus. It reminded me of a tiny mouth nibbling on a piece of steak. Slowly and steadily, I dug a trench in the nucleus.

Then, I raised my right foot, which stopped the ultrasound. The scrub nurse placed a succession of small instruments in my left hand. One was a tiny chopper that looked as if it was built for a grasshopper. One by one, I slipped these instruments in and out of the small side incision. I used them together with the ultrasound tip as if they were a pair of chopsticks. I pressed these "chopsticks" gently against the side of the trench, which cracked the nucleus in half. Then I chopped each half into half. Now the nucleus was in four fragments.

I pressed the petal down to the third setting again, which turned on the ultrasound. I fed the four lens fragments, one by one, into the mouth of the ultrasound tip, which steadily shattered them into a thick, creamy liquid.

I then raised my right foot slightly. The ultrasound stopped, and the probe only sucked and squirted. I sucked the slurry out as if I were sucking a milkshake out of a glass with a straw.

I was careful to keep the instruments well away from the back capsule of the lens. I needed to keep that capsule intact so it would form a living pouch to hold the new artificial lens.

Finally, the scrub nurse handed over the artificial lens, which was neatly rolled up like a taco. I gently shoved it into the eye through the two-and-a-half-millimeter incision and maneuvered it into the pouch formed by the remaining capsule. Finished.

I pulled the probe out and patched the eye lightly. Less than fifteen minutes.

You can watch a video of me performing modern-day cataract surgery on my website, *www.eyedocmackay.com*.

Patients who had their cataracts removed by the phacoemulsification method had excellent vision within a day or two after their surgery. Their eyes felt comfortable because they didn't have any scratchy sutures. The cornea never developed astigmatism because the wound was so small. The operated eye looked so normal when patients came to the office the next day, I had to look at the chart to remind myself which eye I operated on.

If you think the modern method of removing cataracts sounds far more difficult and higher tech than intracapsular cataract extraction, you are correct. Some of the older surgeons at the Eye Institute could not adapt to it. I will discuss this problem in Chapter Sixteen, *Medical Malpractice*.

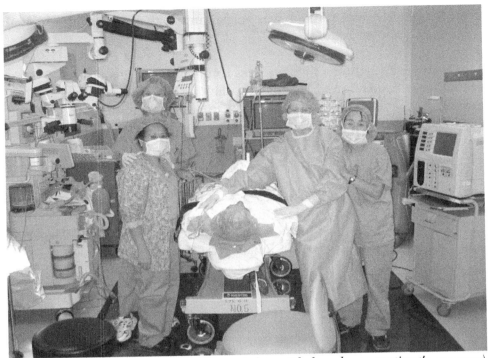

Pictured: CJM in the OR (center right, with hands on patient's gurney) after performing cataract surgery. Note this is an all-women OR team.

Surgeons need to make a transition inside our brains when we enter the operating room. We must activate a detaching cog that switches our mind from seeing the patient as a human being to seeing only the part of the body we plan to operate on.

I believe I developed my detaching cog when I was a child and was forced to cope with danger—guiding my sister and brother around London, fox hunting. I felt scared and inadequate, but I learned how to shut down my feelings and think and act quickly and decisively.

All good surgeons have that detaching cog. The cog will not function if a surgeon operates on somebody with whom they have an intimate relationship. Once they realize who they are operating on, they cannot dissociate because the stakes are so high. That is why surgeons almost never operate on members of their immediate family.

When I was having a colonoscopy, I greeted my gastroenterologist—an old friend—by telling him that he was the only man I would allow up my anus. He immediately told me not to kid around when he was about to do a procedure. He was right. I was interfering with his detaching cog. I should have known better.

I realized I was getting a reputation as a competent surgeon when I was a second-year resident, and I went in to help one of the attending doctors remove a cataract from one of his private patients. He turned to me and said "You can take out a cataract just as well as I can. You do it."

So, I did.

During my three years of residency, my mother mentioned I was training to be a surgeon exactly once. On Thanksgiving Day, when the turkey came out of the oven, she said: "You're a surgeon. You carve." That bird was a lot bigger than an eye, but I managed to slice it up somehow.

CHAPTER TWELVE

Retinal Research

I wanted to get involved in retinal research from the first day of residency. When I was a second-year resident, in 1979, and I had more time because I no longer took night call, I called John Dowling, my mentor at Harvard, and asked if he knew any retinal researchers at the Eye Institute. John suggested I talk to Dr. Peter Gouras. I did. We liked each other immediately.

Peter was one of the world experts in the *ElectroRetinoGram*, or *ERG*. The ERG captures the electrical signal the retina gives off when it is struck by light. This signal gives vital information about the health of the eye. Peter was the first scientist to show how the ERG can be used to diagnose retinal diseases.

I used the ERG at Harvard to find out if my blind rats could see again after I fed them Vitamin A. Peter and I spoke the same language. It would be easy to go from rat ERGs to human ERGs. I showed Peter my thesis on Vitamin A2 in rat eyes. He loved it. He asked me to join his lab. I jumped at the chance and joined his lab that day.

Going into retinal research was my passion, and I don't regret doing it for one second—but it was yet another activity that took me away from Malcolm.

Pictured left to right: Dr. Robert Lopez, CJM, and Dr. Peter Gouras: retinal researchers in front of the Harkness Eye Institute

Before Peter came along, the ERG was neither predictable nor reproducible. The light flashes came into the eye randomly, from many different directions. One lab could not compare its results with other labs. No researcher before Peter could figure out how to illuminate the eye evenly in all directions.

Peter's solution to this problem was simple. He took a Rand-McNally globe of the world, cut a circle out of one side, and placed the stimulus light inside this globe. Result: the flashes illuminated the retina evenly in all directions, and the responses were predictable. He called his invention the *Ganzfeld* technique, which is German for "whole field." Today, Peter's Ganzfeld technique is used by every ERG lab in the world.

Peter could have made a fortune if he had patented the Ganzfeld technique, but he didn't bother. He was interested in science, not money. He believed his invention belonged to humanity. He refused to make any money from it.

Peter and I did ERG research together for twenty-five years. All of this happened alongside my residency, and later during my clinical practice and surgical work. Peter became the father I never had—an older man who admired my mind and fostered my career. Years later, I paid him back by diagnosing his cataracts and restoring his sight.

Peter and I used the ERG to throw questions at the eye as if we were throwing nets into the ocean to discover new sea creatures. We explored how the different parts of the retina work in normal and diseased eyes by probing the retina with light flashes in four different colors: red, green, yellow, and blue, and in different intensities, dim to bright.

Our research took place inside a small, light-tight room painted black inside to absorb stray light. Patients put their chins on a chin rest inside a Ganzfeld globe fitted with a flash. We slipped a special contact lens into their eye, which picked up their electrical responses and fed them into an oscilloscope. Then, we printed the signals out and studied them.

Peter and I were doing *basic* research. We were trying to discover the fundamental properties of the retina. If we had been trying to make the retina work better, we would have been doing *clinical* research.

Basic research is not predictable. It doesn't work the way a car works, where you put in a certain amount of gas, and you know how far it will go. Some basic research pays off big time, like nuclear fission and fusion. Other basic research is interesting but has no practical consequences—at least, not yet.

The basic research I did with Peter allowed us to discover fascinating new information about the retina. However, we could not predict when or if one of our discoveries would be useful to patients.

People who are not familiar with scientific research probably think it is mechanical and boring. Nothing could be further from the truth. Good scientists are just as creative as artists, writers, and musicians. In fact, most of my ophthalmology research friends are musicians. Peter plays the recorder. Bob Lopez plays the guitar.

The essence of good science is to think outside the box. Peter was always willing to change his mind and admit his previous conclusions were wrong. He relished movement and discovery.

Scientific research is like putting together a puzzle, piece by piece, until a pattern is revealed. While we ponder a scientific problem, our brain works rather like a kaleidoscope. Different observations churn around and fall into different patterns. Most of this churning takes place when we are not even aware of it, when we are thinking about something else, or when we are sleeping. Finally, the pieces fall into a combination that suggests an answer.

Danger lurks when all the observations fit together—except one. It is tempting to ignore this outlier, but good researchers never do. That oddity could lead to an even more interesting discovery. Peter never looks for what he thinks should be true, only for what fits the facts.

Isaac Newton said he was able to see farther than other researchers because he stood on the shoulders of giants. Peter and I provided a small shoulder to the researchers who came after us, but every shoulder helps.

Peter and I spent every Monday for the next twenty-five years arguing happily about the retina. Three hundred hereditary eye diseases have been discovered. Peter and I discovered four of them.

One of our most significant discoveries was stolen by another retinal researcher.

Peter and I studied how the cone ERG responds to four different colored lights when these lights are flashed at different intensities. We needed an exceptionally stoic and quiet subject. I found this subject in my son Rob, who was a freshman at Princeton. He volunteered to spend a morning in our lab in return for some spending money.

Rob managed to sit still, his head in a lighted globe and contact lenses in his eyes, for over an hour while I flashed first white, then red, green, yellow, and blue lights into his eyes. In the end, I decided to re-check his response to the white flash. I could not believe my eyes. His response to the white flash had tripled in size.

Peter taught me to embrace the unexpected. I did not discard the data. Instead, I ran down and showed it to Peter. He could not believe it either.

We tested other people. The effect was real. We had just discovered the human cone ERG grows as the eye adapts to light. This had never been reported before. This finding is significant because ERG labs all over the world must account for this effect when they test patients.

Peter and I assumed this fundamental effect must have already been reported. We searched the literature. We found only one paper on the subject. John Dowling—my mentor at Harvard—had discovered the ERG of the skate (a type of fish) grows as it adapts to light. Nobody knew this happened to humans.

Immediately after we made this discovery, in 1985, we presented our findings at the world's number one eye research meeting, *ARVO* (Association for Research in Vision and Ophthalmology), which was at that time in Sarasota, Florida. We were so excited we did not bother to first write up the findings and submit them to an academic journal.

The other ERG researchers were just as fascinated as we were. A Japanese researcher listened especially closely. He went home and repeated our experiments. Then, he published them as his own work.

Our hands were tied. All the credit for a scientific discovery goes to the researcher who publishes first. I wanted to strangle that researcher. Peter was philosophical. "Everybody important in ERG research knows this discovery is our work," he said. "The only thing that matters is new discoveries are made, and science advances."

CHAPTER THIRTEEN

Good Hands, Good Head, Good Surgeon

Good surgeons never rush. They have no sense of urgency. They keep up a steady, leisurely pace. They appear to be doing very little. Their hands move deftly, efficiently, slowly, and deliberately, with a minimal amount of movement. They make surgery look easy. We say they have *good hands*.

A good surgeon is like a good carpenter. Both complete their first task and then move on smoothly to their next task. Good surgeons appear to have ice water in their veins. They act and think like impersonal technicians who are repairing a broken machine.

The hands of a good surgeon move the way my father's hands moved when he was shaving. He would have been an excellent surgeon.

Bad surgeons don't have a detaching cog. They cannot disconnect from the knowledge they are operating on somebody's eye. They are filled with anxiety. They feel uncomfortable operating, so they want to get out of that eye fast. They try to rush, but they end up taking longer than good surgeons. Their hands jerk. They do their first maneuver too quickly and begin to move on, and then they turn back and fuss over something they have already completed, which usually makes things worse.

Surgeons like to say: *God is in the details*. What this means is, we don't pray for a good result. We simply perform every step of every operation logically, calmly, and perfectly, beginning with how we sterilize the site and ending with meticulous closure of the wound. Perfect details, perfect surgery. There is no need for God to intervene.

An ophthalmologist friend told me he never got in trouble while he was performing surgery unless he broke one of his own rules. We try to stick to the same technique in every case.

Surgeons are like elite athletes. They must perform consistently at the highest level. Surgery, in general, is not easy. Eye surgery is the most challenging of all. Eye surgery must be PERFECT in every detail. One tiny wrong move— a fraction of a millimeter in the wrong direction – and an eye will be lost. A human being was using that eye to see.

Eye surgeons operate inside an object that is only the size of a large grape. The ceiling-hung microscope enlarges that eye to the size of a table. If there is the slightest tremor in our hands, they will vibrate like terrified jellyfish when they are viewed through the microscope.

We sew using nylon sutures that are one-third the thickness of a human hair. They are so thin they are almost invisible to the naked eye. The needles are the size and shape of a newborn baby's eyelash. The scrub nurse loads these needles onto a needle holder, which we grasp firmly but not too firmly.

We need *good heads* even more than we need good hands. Eye surgery is more of a mental challenge than it is a challenge of hand coordination. Each eye has its own peculiarities, and these differences become apparent only when we get inside. Eye surgery will never be performed by robots because a robot cannot adjust its technique to changing situations.

How did the circulating nurse who was in the room during my first cataract operation know I had "good hands"? It is surprisingly obvious. When I assist an eye resident for the first time, I can tell within a few minutes if he or she has good hands and a good head.

The tell-tale moment comes when the eye does not behave as expected. A resident with a good head will start to talk out loud. The resident will first say what needs to be done and then go ahead and do it in a logical sequence. That resident is thinking creatively. A resident whose head is not good will freeze and wait for me to explain what needs to be done.

If a resident has both good hands and a good head, I know this resident will quickly become an excellent surgeon. If a resident has neither good hands nor a good head, he or she will never become an adequate surgeon, no matter how hard he or she tries. I hope the resident will go into a sub-specialty like neuro-ophthalmology, where no surgery is involved.

If a resident has clumsy hands but a good head, he or she will eventually turn into a good surgeon. One of the best surgeons now operating at the Eye Institute had clumsy hands when he was a resident.

The residents I worry about are the ones with good hands but bad heads. They have a false sense of confidence. They have no idea what to do if a case goes anything less than perfectly.

I have trained hundreds of eye surgeons over twenty-five years. Excellent surgeons and less good surgeons were equally divided between men and women. I noticed only one minor difference—the women tended to be too timid and careful during their first case, while the men were often too brash and over-confident.

There is nothing more exhilarating than sailing smoothly through a case in the OR, healing an eye with your own hands. There is nothing more terrifying than an eye operation that starts to go wrong. Anybody can perform surgery if the eye behaves the way you expect. The challenge comes when you need to handle a complication.

Let me say this again: good surgeons must be creative. Every complication is unique, so a surgeon needs to invent new maneuvers with lightning speed. I will tell you the truth: the only way to never have surgical complications is to never perform surgery. If a surgical complication is handled well, the eye will heal just as well as it would have if it had not had the complication.

One day, as I was chugging along in the OR, the circulating nurse from the adjoining OR came into my room and whispered in my ear. Dr. Z, who was operating next door, was in trouble (I have given him an anonymous name because this story is embarrassing, and it might affect his reputation). Could I please help—as soon as possible? I finished my case, told the anesthesiologist to delay bringing in my next patient, ripped off my surgical gown and gloves, scrubbed up, and hurried into the adjoining OR.

Eight worried eyes swung over to greet me. Dr. Z looked as if he had been hit by a truck. I put on the gown and gloves the nurse held out for me and slid into the surgeon's chair to assess the situation.

I could see nothing because the pupil of the eye was constricted. I asked for dilating medication. After the pupil had dilated, I could see the cataract had broken up into many small pieces, and these pieces had fallen into the back of the eye. Some of them were sitting on the retina. The surgeon had no idea how to cope with this mess.

I asked the circulating nurse to bring me a *vitrector*, a miniature "roto-rooter." I made a tiny incision into the eye and slipped in the vitrector. Then I methodically cut up and sucked out every chunk of shattered cataract, beginning with the pieces that were closest to the front of the eye and ending with the ones closest to the retina. No drama.

After I removed all the lens fragments, I told the surgeon he could take over and insert the intraocular lens, and I went back to my next case. The eye healed beautifully and saw perfectly. I had never coped with this exact complication before, but I was able to adapt my surgical technique to solve the problem. That is creativity.

Every operating microscope in the Eye Institute has a video camera, which records every case. The video feeds into a large screen, so everybody in the OR can watch every operation. The nurse from the adjoining OR had watched me operate for years. She knew I could handle complications. By asking me to help, she saved the patient's eye.

When a case starts to go wrong, a surgeon needs to fire off commands quickly. Everybody in that OR must shape up, fast. The scrub nurse, the circulating nurse, the resident, and the anesthesiologist must all do their job with top efficiency. There is no time for *Please* or *Thank you.*

I was brought up to be polite, to never ask for help, to solve all my problems by myself, and to take care of others. Now, I had to learn how to order people to take care of me. Learning how to be assertive in the operating room was almost as difficult for me as learning to do eye surgery. Good manners had been drilled into me so thoroughly it was some time before I felt comfortable barking out orders.

People admire aggression in a male surgeon, but they often think an aggressive female surgeon is overbearing and difficult. I began my career in the OR as a polite Christian gentlewoman. I had to become, for the sake of my patients, just enough of a bitch to get respect.

I was working late in the OR one Friday evening, fixing an emergency retinal detachment. As the time dragged on, the anesthesiologist got more and more annoyed. He wanted to go home. Just as I was placing a needle into the wall of the patient's eye, he came up behind me and said in a loud voice: "How soon are you going to be finished?"

He startled me. My hand jumped, and I stuck the needle straight through the sclera right into the middle of the eye, thereby creating another retinal tear in a new location.

I knew what I had to do. I kept calm. I changed my technique. I sealed both the new tear my needle had created and the tear that had caused the detachment. The eye did well. It has 20/20 vision today. The patient came to my office every year, and every time I saw her, I remembered that moment.

As soon as I was finished, I let the anesthesiologist know directly and forcefully that I was furious. I told him he almost made somebody's eye go blind. He would not have dared to behave like that with one of the male surgeons. I could not request a different anesthesiologist for future cases, but I did not need to. He behaved perfectly with me from then on.

Each surgeon at the Eye Institute is assigned one day of the week to do their routine operations. My day was Wednesday. I usually did ten routine cases every week. If an emergency case came in—for example, a retinal detachment—on another day of the week, I did that case after the other surgeons assigned to that day finished their scheduled cases.

I began to prepare for surgery the day before I operated, getting my mind and body ready for an intense state of concentration. As Dr. DeVoe advised, I did not do vigorous arm exercises, I did not drink coffee or alcohol, and I avoided taxing social events.

On the day of surgery, every move I made, before and during surgery, was unhurried and smooth. I began by slowly and deliberately putting on my scrubs, cap, and mask. I slipped my feet in my clogs slowly and deliberately. I walked into the scrub room slowly and deliberately. I slowly and deliberately scrubbed my hands with a Betadine sponge—ten times down the side, back, and front of each finger and ten times on the back and palm of each hand. I held my hands above my elbows as I rinsed off the *Betadine* so water would run from a sterile area to a non-sterile area.

Then, I walked slowly and deliberately into the OR. I told the circulating nurse to turn on my CD player. Like many surgeons, I listened to music while I operated. Some surgeons like pop, some rock, some gospel. I liked confident, steady, controlled music because I wanted to feel confident, steady, and in control. This meant Baroque or Classical music.

The music I like best for operating has a steady beat. It is sure of itself. It is optimistic. It does not get too loud or too soft. It was composed during the Age of Enlightenment, when people believed in reason, scientific methods, and progress. My favorite was a medley of Baroque composers – Vivaldi, Bach, Handel, Purcell, Telemann, and Pachelbel. I never listened to Romantic music while I operate—too emotional, too exciting—or to a human voice—too distracting.

I asked the scrub nurse to hand me my first instrument. I paused for a moment. I was in no hurry. I planned to have fun. This will be an adventure.

Before I made my first move, I put my mind into another world. I consciously quieted it down. I banished any thoughts I was operating on a human eye and if my hands slipped somebody would go blind. I thought only about that first move. My concentration was so intense that I would not have noticed if somebody started to snip off one of my ears. I could go for hours without urinating—something I cannot do outside the OR.

I focused all my attention on making my first move perfect. Then, I focused on the second move. If something started to go wrong, I accepted it as a challenge. *This will be interesting*, I said to myself. *I can't wait to see how I am going to get out of this situation*.

I did not realize it at the time, but I was using a technique called *reframing*. You "reframe" an event by re-labeling it as something positive, a chance to learn, an opportunity for growth. Reframing allows you to convince yourself this is not a catastrophe, to transform it from something stressful into something that is not. It is no longer a problem; it is a situation.

Surgeons face stress all the time. If we did not know how to deal with it, we could not function. Reframing allows people under stress to think clearly, function well, and control negative emotions and panic.

Brain scans show that chronic stress changes structures inside the brain. It shrinks certain parts of the brain—the *hippocampus* and *pre-frontal cortex*—that are crucial to thinking well and creatively and keeping emotions under control. It ramps up the size and activity of the *amygdala*, the part of the brain that produces the *fight- r-flight* response - fear, panic, negative thinking, and reckless snap decisions.

You will learn more about the brain's ability to change, which is called *neuroplasticity*, in *The Doctor Becomes a Patient.*

This is good news. We have the power to heal our brains when they have been damaged by stress. We can reframe events that make us anxious. We can teach ourselves to be optimistic and calm instead of panicking and becoming pessimistic. Every good surgeon knows how to do this.

Once you start to control your mind, your mind becomes easier to control. Your hippocampus and pre-frontal cortex grow back up to their normal size and function. Your amygdala shrinks and starts to behave itself. These beneficial changes can take place in just a few weeks.

A surgeon friend of mine told me he felt "concerned" while he was operating. I think a better word is *vigilant.* I was calm and composed in the operating room, but I was never complacent. Cocksure, over-confident surgeons are the ones who get into trouble.

I was more alert while I was operating than at any other time in my life. My brain was constantly scanning back and forth like a laser printer, primed to catch the slightest deviation from normal. Is there more bleeding than expected? Is the cataract softer or harder than usual?

If you are scheduled for surgery, and your surgeon gives you the option of choosing the time, what time should you choose? I suggest you ask for the second slot. When I decided the order for my cases, if I had a patient who was of special concern—for example, somebody who had only one eye— I scheduled that patient as the second case.

I did not schedule that patient as number one because there was always a shake-down period during the first case of the day. The nurses needed to get accustomed to my likes and dislikes regarding the instruments and what settings I preferred on the machines. I needed to adjust the operating microscope, foot pedal, and chair the way I liked. The complication rate is not any higher for the first case, but the second case runs more smoothly.

A friend once asked me if I had ever performed an operation that failed. I immediately thought of a patient I operated on during my second year of residency.

The patient was an elderly man from India. He had longstanding diabetes, and advanced diabetic retinal disease. My attending told me to take out his cataract. I wasn't keen to operate on this man—I thought his main problem was his retina, not his cataract—but a resident does not argue with an attending.

He was too frail for general anesthesia, so I did the operation under local. The procedure went smoothly until I noticed the operating field was filling up with a watery liquid. It took me a while to realize he was crying. I suctioned up the tears and finished the case. The eye looked flawless the next day, but his vision did not improve. The operation was a success, but the patient remained blind. I felt like crying along with this poor man.

I am grateful I never totally blinded a patient. That is the horror of all eye surgeons. One eye I operated on, however, did go blind.

Early in my career as a surgeon, I began what I assumed would be a routine cataract operation. I had removed a cataract from this woman's other eye two weeks earlier. The surgery went flawlessly, and her vision returned to 20/20.

Not this time. The blood vessels in her body must have been especially fragile because she was old and overweight and had diabetes and high blood pressure. The minute I made the incision into the eye, a fountain of bright red blood spurted up from her choroid and surged underneath her retina, shoving her retina right out of her eye. This happened so quickly—a matter of seconds—there was nothing I could do to stop it.

This is called an expulsive hemorrhage. It was the most feared complication in cataract surgery at that time. There is no way to repair a retina once it has been vomited out of an eye. I sewed up the eye and went on to my next case. This was a severe test of my detaching cog. I was trembling with horror and mortification.

After I finished my other cases, I went with a heavy heart to talk to the patient and her family. I told them about the uncontrollable bleeding. I said the eye would likely never see again. I apologized profusely. I will never forget their nobility and kindness. They were sympathetic and understanding beyond my expectations. They were people who accepted life without complaining or blaming others.

I knew it was not my fault. The same thing would have happened to any surgeon who operated on that eye, but I did not sleep well for weeks. I was upset for years. Whenever I remember this operation, my stomach goes into a knot.

The risk of getting an expulsive hemorrhage during modern-day cataract surgery is—*zero*. The pressure inside the eye never drops suddenly, so fragile choroidal blood vessels never rupture and bleed. If I had operated on her eye with the modern technique, there would have been no sudden pressure change inside the eye, and she would not have had that expulsive hemorrhage.

CHAPTER FOURTEEN

I Decide to Be a Retinal Surgeon

I fell in love with the retina when I was a sophomore at Harvard. That passion lasted the rest of my life. Once I became an eye resident, I was hell-bent on performing retinal surgery, even though it is the most difficult of eye surgeries.

The retina is the most important part of the eye, the spot where a ray of light is transformed into a pulse of electricity. No retina, no sight—even if everything else in the eye is healthy. The rest of the eye exists only to serve the retina. The number one cause of blindness in the United States is retinal disease.

The retina is a child of the brain—quite literally. When a fetus is six weeks old, two bulges push out from the brain. The bulges turn themselves inside out and become two eyecups. The outside of the cup forms the wall of the eye. The inside forms the retina.

There was one problem with my love affair with the retina—it competed with my love affair with my husband. I wasn't thinking about Malcolm when I decided to be a retinal surgeon. I was thinking how important, interesting, and difficult this surgery was, and how I loved the challenge.

As I look through my diaries, I can pinpoint the exact moment when my marriage came to a crossroads. It was New Year's Eve, 1979. I was halfway through my residency. Malcolm and I had been married for fifteen years.

Malcolm said my New Year's resolution should be to spend more time with him and less time on my career. He told me after I finished my residency, I should get a part-time job at an eye clinic near home. I wrote down his exact words in my diary: "Your job is becoming more important and interesting than my job."

Malcolm put me on notice. He wanted a wife who would focus on his career, not hers. I had a choice—marriage or career. I could keep my husband only if I turned back into the deferential wife he had married. If I did not, our marriage would be in trouble. Not now—our children were ten and twelve, and neither of us would abandon them – but Malcolm would not be happy unless I scaled down my career.

After six and a half years of sacrifice and hard work, I was not about to settle for a part-time job in some clinic. I had a new vision of my life now—surgeon, teacher of surgeons, and retinal researcher. Like my Armstrong ancestors, I wanted to create something that would live on after I died.

This ambition would have been applauded in a man, but at that time, women were not supposed to have the fiery drive of men.

Was I a hard-hearted, selfish woman who put her own career ahead of her husband's career? I don't believe it. My career makes me feel alive, useful, and happy. If I gave it up for Malcolm's sake, he would have had a bored, resentful, depressed wife on his hands.

I thought I could keep Malcolm happy by letting him control everything else in my life except my career. I voted for the politicians he told me to vote for. I wore the clothes he wanted me to wear—grey or brown suits from Brooks Brothers. He liked to spend weekends playing tennis. I liked to explore new places, travel, camp in the wilderness, climb mountains, visit museums, and go to edgy Off-Broadway plays. We played tennis every weekend.

I did not apply for a part-time job at a clinic after I finished residency. Instead, I applied for and won a post-residency Heed Fellowship, which paid for a year of extra training in the retina and its disorders. This meant more time away from Malcolm because retina problems are emergencies. Once the retina detaches, hours will make the difference between blindness and sight.

Retinas detach because a small section of the *vitreous* , the clear jelly inside the back of the eye, is more firmly attached to the retina than the retina is attached to the back of the eye. When this section of vitreous breaks away from the retina, it drags that area of the retina along with it, creating a tear.

The ideal time to diagnose a retinal tear is before the retina detaches. At that point, I could treat it easily, quickly, and without knife surgery by surrounding it with a barrier of laser burns or freezing it with a cryoprobe.

Both heating (with laser light) and freezing (with cryo) stimulate the retina to form scar tissue, which welds the retina to the wall of the eye. Retinal tears are almost always in the periphery of the retina, so the laser and freezing treatments do not damage central vision.

I located retinal tears by using the *indirect ophthalmoscope*, which gave me a view of the peripheral retina all the way from top to bottom and left to right. Because the image is upside down and inverted, the indirect ophthalmoscope is notoriously difficult to use. I learned this the hard way when I treated my first retinal tear as a first-year resident.

I knew what I was supposed to do—use the indirect ophthalmoscope to locate the tear, place a freezing probe behind the eye directly under the tear, and depress the foot petal to shoot liquid nitrogen into the probe. The frozen probe tip would freeze the tear from the outside in, first freezing the *sclera* (the tough white outer wall of the eye), then the choroid, and, finally, the retina.

I had watched several attendings do this. It looked easy. It turned out to be close to impossible.

I located the tear easily enough, but it was not easy to stay on it. The indirect ophthalmoscope was attached to my head, so if I moved my head a fraction of an inch, the light zoomed right off the eye. In addition to keeping my head steady, I also had to keep my left hand, which was holding the condensing lens, still and upright at exactly the correct distance above the eye.

I shoved the probe behind the eye with my right hand, but it kept slipping. When I moved it to the right, it shot to the left. If I pushed it upwards, it zoomed downwards. I thought I would never be able to treat this tear.

A deep sigh came from the attending. I knew he had a bad back. I tried to move more quickly. I pushed the probe to a spot I thought was directly under the tear and depressed the foot petal. To my horror, I saw a ball of ice bloom in an area of perfectly normal retina. I was at least two clock hours away from the tear. I was mortified.

The attending didn't miss a beat. "That's your test spot," he said dryly, implying I had cleverly determined the proper freezing duration in this location before I went on to treat the tear itself. I almost laughed out loud. At least my "test spot" had not harmed the eye.

I went back to chasing that tear with renewed determination. My next freeze was in perfect position, surrounding and engulfing the tear, pasting it to the back of the eye, preventing the retina from detaching. Luckily, my patient was under general anesthesia.

If the tear was not treated in time, and the retina detached, how did I get it back on the choroid? The retina is a delicate, thin web of nerve tissue. After it detached, I could not grasp it directly and pull it back down onto the choroid, or I would shred it to bits. I needed to use something soft and gentle.

The softest, gentlest substance in the world is air. If my patient had a retinal detachment that had only one tear, and the tear was in the top third of the retina, I could treat it by injecting a bubble of air or long-acting gas into the eye. The bubble would float upwards and gently push the retina back on the choroid. I then sealed the tear with laser light or a freezing probe.

A neat trick. The retina was back in place, and the eye looked as if it had never been touched. I used this technique to treat a small retinal detachment in one of Joan Didion's eyes.

If the tear was large and it was in the bottom half of your retina, I took my patient to the operating room and performed one of two types of surgery.

One type of surgery is called a *vitrectomy*. I cut and sucked the vitreous out using a tiny roto-rooter. I then injected a gas bubble inside the eye. After the bubble pushed the retina back onto the choroid, I used a laser to place burns all around the tear. These burns turned into scar tissue that held retina in place. The bubble gradually absorbed over the next few weeks.

If the patient had giant or multiple tears in the bottom half of the retina, instead of pushing the tear back on the choroid using gas, I had to push the choroid up to the tear. I did this by creating a scleral buckle around the eye: I sewed a silicone band directly onto the sclera, and tightened it up, so the choroid touched the retina again.

Cataract surgery was a snap compared to putting on a scleral buckle. I began by cutting the conjunctiva off the eye to expose the six tiny muscles that move the eye. Then, I used the indirect ophthalmoscope to locate the tear.

Now came the tricky part. I sewed a silicone band the thickness of a rubber band directly onto the sclera. This band had to be precisely positioned so that when it was pulled tight, the crest of the indentation would lie directly under the tear.

This was high-risk sewing. Place a suture too shallow, and it would pull out; too deep, and the needle would puncture the sclera and create yet another retinal tear. Meanwhile, the eye was rolling around inside its socket like a greased ping-pong ball. The sutures had to be placed with obsessive-compulsive perfection.

After the silicon band was sewn into in place, I performed another high-risk maneuver—I deliberately punctured the sclera where the retinal detachment was highest. If I located this spot accurately, clear fluid from underneath the retina would flow smoothly out, and I breathed a sigh of relief. The exit of this fluid gave me room to cinch the band tight without raising the pressure inside the eye.

If I was off by less than a millimeter when I punctured the sclera, bright red blood would have gushed out, telling me I had punctured the retina itself and caused yet another tear. Luckily, I never did that.

And then…I looked inside the eye again, hoping the retina would be flat and the tear would be located exactly on the crest of the buckle. If not, I would have to cut the band off the scleral and start all over again. Fortunately, I never had to do it.

Retinal surgery is the most difficult, the least predictable, and the most stressful sub- specialty in ophthalmology, yet I was drawn irresistibly to it. Once I was adept at it, cataract surgery was too predictable and routine. It did not compare to the wild thrill of fixing a retina. I wanted the adrenaline and the challenge of using both sides of my brain to the utmost.

Once I became a retina specialist, I had to spend more time away from Malcolm instead of less.

He liked to leave New York every Friday after work and drive to our weekend house on Long Island, playing tennis at the Piping Rock Club on the way out. One month, I was in the OR three consecutive Friday nights, fixing emergency retinal detachments. We did not get to Long Island until Saturday morning.

Before I became a surgeon, I always did what Malcolm told me to do. Now, I was the one who controlled my schedule and decided how to spend my time. He was supportive beyond my expectations when I was doing something he valued and wanted, such as going to medical school. Retinal surgery and retinal research were outside his value system.

I had ambitions now, and Malcolm did not understand or approve of them. I was so excited and happy fixing retinas I didn't miss our social life. Malcolm did. He let me know he was not happy with my schedule. I can understand that. I was changing the ground rules of our relationship.

CHAPTER FIFTEEN

Setting Up My Private Practice Required Getting My Patients on Board

I wanted to set up my own private practice after I finished my residency and fellowship in 1982, but I had no idea how to begin. An average ophthalmology practice has between five thousand and eight thousand patients. Somehow, I had to convince thousands of people I was the perfect doctor to care for their eyes over decades and operate on them when they needed surgery, but how? Medical schools do not have courses on this subject.

The solution fell into my lap during my third year of residency, when I was preparing to assist one of the most famous ophthalmologists at the Eye Institute. I walked into the scrub room, hit the panel with my knee to start the water running, and grabbed a Betadine sponge. He walked in, hit the panel with his knee, and asked me if I planned to have any more children.

Another woman might have replied her childbearing plans were none of his (#$@&%*!) business. I was too polite to be that blunt. Besides, I was curious to find out why he asked me this question. I told him my husband and I had two children, and that was all we wanted.

His next remark surprised me so much the sponge flipped right out of my hands. He asked me to join his practice after I finished residency.

This doctor had a worldwide reputation. Even better, he was a retinal specialist—just what I wanted to be. He pioneered Argon laser treatment of diabetic eye disease. What an opportunity. I would be paid to learn about the retina from one of the great experts in the field. I knew he had not asked any of the other residents because they would have accepted him immediately.

He offered me $25,000 the first year, $75,000 the second, and $100,000 the third. These salaries were low, but I assumed after my third year, I would become his partner and make a percentage of the income I generated. This was so obviously the only fair arrangement I didn't even bother to discuss it with him at the time. I accepted with alacrity.

I began to work for him after I finished my residency. His office on the Upper East Side of Manhattan hummed with activity. Almost all the diabetic specialists in New York sent him patients.

I threw myself into his practice with energy and enthusiasm. I assisted him on every case he did in the operating room, and he assisted me. A year went by, then two, then three. By then, I had learned everything he knew about the retina. I thought we were close friends. I assumed we would work together forever. I had the perfect job.

During those three years, more and more patients came into the office who wanted to see me instead of this famous doctor. The diabetic patients liked me, and they told their diabetic doctors about me, and these doctors began to send their patients directly to me instead of going to him first. Malcolm and my friends, and our friends' friends, and their siblings, and their parents, and their parents' friends, and the family members of these friends became my patients.

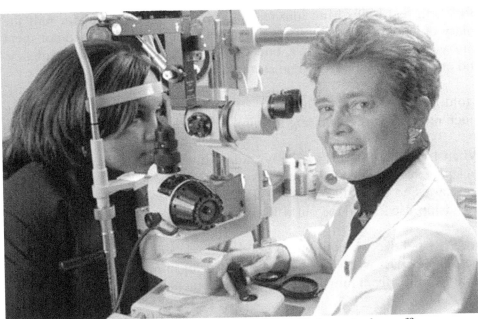

Pictured: CJM examining a patient with the slit lamp in her office.

I was making a name for myself. I was teaching first-year ophthalmology residents from all over the world at the Lancaster Course. I was lecturing at teaching hospitals throughout the New York City area. I was giving talks at ophthalmology meetings. Other ophthalmologists began to send me patients.

As my practice grew, I conveniently forgot Malcolm had complained my job was becoming more important than his job. I lulled myself into believing everything was perfect in our marriage. I refused to notice the deepening cracks between us.

Three years went by in a flash. I went to talk to the doctor about my future. He flatly refused to make me his partner. I would continue to get the same salary—$100,000 a year. I was shocked and angry.

In hindsight, I believe he picked me instead of a male resident because I was polite, a woman, and married to a man who made a good salary. He assumed I would be submissive and easy to control, and I would be happy to work for less than I deserved.

He had picked the wrong woman. Twenty years earlier, Stanley Bosworth had bullied me into teaching at St. Ann's School for half the salary of a man. This time, I was not about to be exploited. I had not spent four years in medical school, one year in internship, three in residency, and one in fellowship to end up as a salaried technician.

I told him this offer was not fair. I read the patient charts. I knew how much money I was generating for him.

When I came to the office the next day, my key would not work in the lock. He had changed the lock overnight. I felt sick. I had to ask the secretaries to buzz me in as if I were a patient. So much for our friendship. He kicked me out without saying thank you or goodbye.

Today, I believe we both had a good deal. He got what he wanted from me—three years when I made more money for him than he paid me. I got what I wanted from him—my own private practice.

I sublet an ophthalmology office at 69 East 71st Street and sent out notices to my patients about my new address. During my first year, I made twice what my former employer paid me. I rented that office for seventeen years. Then, I moved to my own office at 315 Central Park West.

I am retired now, but it was a privilege to take care of my patients. They believed in me. They gave me their most precious possession—their eyes—and assumed that I would give them the best care in the world. Their trust was an honor I never took lightly.

I want to explain to you what life was like when I took care of patients in my office. People are like onions. They have many layers of identity. The superficial layer is their age, skin color, clothes, job, gender, etc. As you dig deeper, the layers become more personal and intimate. Finally, you reach the layer that is their essential self. That nub of *self* is what interested me. This is what I tried to find in every patient.

Patients who are questioned with interest and sympathy by their doctors rate their relationship with those doctors highly. Conversely, doctors who know the most about their patients have the most job satisfaction and the least burnout.

Before I talked to a new patient, I took a look at the intake form. The medication list told me if they had AIDS, depression, obsessive-compulsive disorder, Parkinson's Disease, Alzheimer's, or cancer. My goal was to get inside the head of all my new patients and convince them I was on their side.

My antennae started to vibrate the minute a new patient walked into my office. Their body language—how they moved, whether they looked me in the eye, how confidently they sat down—told me whether they were angry, scared, hostile, in pain, insecure, lacking self-confidence, depressed, or happy. Now, I knew how to approach them. Now I could get to that nub.

It took only a few minutes to forge a connection with a patient. Once that connection was made, the relationship between us changed. Patients were not just coming in to get their eyes fixed. They were eager to help with their own healing. They were more compliant with taking the medications I ordered for them.

Before the advent of modern-day surgery and drugs in the twentieth century, doctors were able to cure very few of their patients. All they could offer them was sympathy and a correct diagnosis.

A study done in Canada in 2014 on patients suffering from chronic back pain showed that sympathy from doctors can have significant benefits. Half of the patients were given sham treatment, and the other half received sham treatment plus encouragement from their doctor. The patients who received sham treatment had a twenty-five percent reduction in their pain—i.e., there was a placebo effect. However, if this sham treatment was coupled with encouragement from their doctor, the reduction in pain shot up to fifty-five percent. In other words, an empathetic conversation with a doctor can relieve pain surprisingly well.

Today, doctors get more money for doing procedures than they get for talking to patients. I think this is a big mistake. It encourages doctors to do more procedures. It discourages them from taking the time to give their patients encouragement and counseling.

Studies show female doctors are better at listening to patients than male doctors. Male doctors wait an average of forty-seven seconds before they interrupt a patient. Women doctors wait an average of three minutes. A recent study showed that patients admitted to an emergency room were less likely to die if the first doctor who interviewed them was a woman—presumably because women listen more carefully.

I would love to show this study to the surgical resident I argued with when I was a third-year medical student. He claimed that women who have children cannot be good doctors. He was dead wrong.

Doctors who do not listen will not make the right diagnosis. I have often made a diagnosis other doctors have missed, not because I am smarter than they are, but because I listen.

I chose my words carefully. Every patient was different. Some wanted detailed explanations about what was wrong with their eyes. Others had no interest in the details. They wanted me to make the decisions for them. For the patients who wanted to make up their own minds, I told them what I would do in their situation and put the ball in their court.

If you were a fly on the wall, you would not believe what patients have told me. Once they realized I was really listening to them, they told me things they tell nobody else in the world. They knew if they held back information, I would not make a correct diagnosis.

Many of my patients were looking for a chance to unburden themselves. They opened wide when I asked a few questions and listened closely to their answers. Most people know doctors are forbidden by law to reveal anything patients tell them while they are in the office.

I had a peculiar one-sided relationship with patients. I knew a great deal about them, but they knew next to nothing about me. Whenever patients asked me a personal question, I felt awkward and embarrassed. "I'm here to focus on your problems, not mine," I told them.

The time sped by when I was in my office and the operating room. I was constantly busy, constantly amused, and constantly intrigued. As I solved their problems, I forgot my own. Helping patients filled my life with meaning.

My white coat was my magic cape. When I put it on, *Poof!* —I gained a gravitas that often surprised me. My parents' friends, who called me "Cynthia" all my life, did not call me "Cynthia" in the office, they called me "Doctor MacKay." I suspect they unconsciously wanted to see their doctor as infallible. They would not want a mere mortal operating on their eyes.

My white coat converted me into a rock that radiated positive energy. When patients complained, I did not take it personally. I knew they were frustrated or scared. One patient asked if he had offended me with his complaints. I told that him none of my patients offended me.

I could be magnanimous with my patients because I was not personally involved with them. My interaction was strictly limited to their medical and eye problems. I wish I could bring some of that steadfast goodwill into my personal life, but petty little emotions inevitably crept in when that white coat came off.

I had to learn how to set limits. One patient called me several times a week for months, asking the same question over and over. I knew he had plenty of money because he kept a yacht in the Mediterranean with a crew of twenty. I finally told him I had a new policy: twenty-five dollars per telephone call. He never called me again.

Our medical training teaches doctors to drive themselves beyond endurance and ignore fatigue and illness. As a result, doctors are often slow to recognize we might have a medical problem ourselves. See Chapter 22, *The Doctor Becomes a Patient*. Like many doctors, I am not a good patient. I think I know more than my doctors do, even when my problem is not eye related. If I am sick, I cannot wait to get back to my office, where I feel in control.

Often, new patients came in who had been terrified by something another doctor had told them. We call these patients: *word-wounded*. The most helpful thing I could do for a word-wounded patient was to explain, in simple, clear language, exactly what, if anything, was wrong and what, if anything, needed to be done.

Sometimes, all I needed to tell them was their problem was normal for their age. If they had a cataract, for example, they felt better when I told them everybody their age has, or will soon develop, a cataract.

I had the gratification of solving many interesting problems every day. One example: an 82-year-old man came to my office saying he was "going blind" in his right eye. He was no longer able to drive or read. His left eye was "lazy" because it had not been treated for far-sightedness and astigmatism with glasses and patching when he was a child.

He consulted an ophthalmologist, who told him there was "nothing of significance" in his right eye and sent him to a retina specialist. The retina specialist performed many tests, including an ultrasound and several different dye studies, and pronounced his retina healthy. His next stop was a neurologist, who did a CT scan, an MRI, a series of blood tests, and a carotid angiogram, all of which were normal. He resigned himself to blindness. Then a friend suggested he see me.

I did something very low-tech—I asked him a few questions. When had he begun to lose his sight? (*Many years ago*). How quickly did it progress? (*Very slowly*). Was his color vision affected? (*Yes—he had trouble seeing blue and purple*). Did he see better in bright or dim light? (*Bright*). Even before I looked at his eyes, I knew he had a cataract.

I was right. One quick look through the slit lamp, and the diagnosis was obvious—a dense nuclear cataract. Ophthalmologists sometimes fail to diagnose this type of cataract because it can only be seen if the slit beam is positioned to hit the lens at a forty-five-degree angle.

After cataract surgery, his vision was 'perfect' in his right eye. Color was back in his life, and he did not even realize it was gone. He could read the *New York Times* without glasses.

My patients and I were a team. It was my job to give them the proper diagnosis and encouragement. It was their job to take the medications I prescribed and have the surgery I recommended.

Patients are savvier than doctors realize. A woman who was the patient of a famous ophthalmologist came to me one day and asked me to take out her cataract. I asked why she chose me instead of this eminent man. She replied he had long, dirty fingernails. This woman assumed if her surgeon let this detail slip, he might let other details slip. One of my obsessive-compulsive habits is to keep my fingernails short.

Eye surgery was especially satisfying because I could look at an eye, see what was wrong, and—usually—fix it with my own hands. Another plus is that I followed my patients for many years, so I got to know them well. Surgeons in most other specialties usually see their patients immediately before and immediately after surgery. I cared for some patients for four decades.

Cataract extraction is the most gratifying operation in medicine. I performed cataract surgery on Wednesdays, so Thursday was my favorite day of the week. When I took the patch off and patients realized they were able to see again, they were as delighted as I was when I put on my first pair of glasses.

One day, my first patient burst into tears when the patch came off. The second fainted. The next, a man, kissed me. The last man told me a dreary subway station looked like a cathedral to him.

One lady told me her cataract surgery made her realize she needed to repaint her cracked, peeling walls, re-cover her tattered, stained furniture, and replace her torn dirty rugs. Another said she saw the world in *Technicolor* now instead of black-and-white. Another told me her sight was great, but she was not happy with all those new wrinkles I added to her face.

Because I followed my patients for years, I was able to see how surgery transformed their lives. An elderly woman crept into my office one day, practically feeling her way in. She stopped reading and driving years ago. She could barely see the images on her television set. Her favorite activity was needlepointing. Now that was gone, too. She felt depressed and lonely.

Before I looked into her eyes, I sent up a prayer —please let her have dense cataracts. I knew I could help her if her problem was cataracts. To my delight, she did have cataracts. After I took them out, she walked into my office confidently. One of my prize possessions is the door stop she needlepointed for me. It is fire-engine red, and it has an eye-catching blue-and-white eagle on top, wings spread triumphantly. She did not have to say a word. That eagle was screaming the news that her sight was back.

One of the things that made my job so exciting and fulfilling is that I did not just save my patients' sight, I also in many cases saved their lives. The eye is the only place in the body where a doctor can look directly at blood vessels. Most diseases eventually show up in the eye. The arteries and veins that run through the retina gave me important information about a patient's health. I have diagnosed high blood pressure, brain tumors, diabetes, metastatic cancer, and high lipid levels in the blood that the patients knew nothing about.

Ophthalmology gave me the opportunity to get to know people from many different backgrounds. My patients came from every walk of life—poets, policemen, professors, philosophers, truck drivers, movie stars, teachers, writers, actors, artists, doctors, billionaires, cleaning ladies, and CEOs of major corporations.

Many of my patients were celebrities. This was a good way to attract new patients. The downside was it raised the stakes of surgery. A bad surgical result on a person who appears often in the pages of the *New York Times* is visible to the entire world.

One day, a delightful elf with an impressive white beard, seriously bushy eyebrows, and a twinkle in his eyes came in, complaining he was having problems drawing. He was Al Hirschfeld, the man who drew caricatures for the *New York Times* and other publications. His drawings depicted actors, singers, dancers, musicians, politicians, and TV stars better than photographs. When Hope went to sleep-away camp, I sent her Al's caricatures every week so she could unearth the cleverly concealed names of his daughter, NINA.

Al and I made a deal—he would draw my caricature in return for cataract surgery. I thought this was a good deal for him. I changed my mind when I learned he charged fifty thousand dollars per caricature.

The surgery went well, his vision returned to 20/20, and a few weeks later, I went down to his gallery to pick up my caricature. I was pleased to see Al put five NINAs in my hair.

Then, the gallery attendant beckoned me upstairs to a room hung with Al's caricatures. He showed me how wavering and uncertain Al's lines were before cataract surgery and how crisp, confident, and flowing they were afterward. You could not ask for a better demonstration of the beneficial effects of cataract removal.

One day, Bob Hope came in with a retina problem. When I told him I needed to take photos of his eye, he immediately shot back: "I insist they be retouched." A few days later, a set of cocktail glasses arrived with his profile in gold and the inscription *Thanks for the Memory*. He sent me a Christmas card every year until he died. That man knew how to market.

Patients from my white, wealthy background almost always came in alone. When patients came in who were from other backgrounds, I was often surprised by how many people accompanied them. I needed more chairs in my waiting room than I thought to accommodate all those relatives and friends.

The difference between my patients' culture and my own was most obvious when I went to visit patients in their hospital rooms after surgery. The rooms of Black and Orthodox Jewish patients were crowded with visitors. The Italian patients had so many visitors they were practically falling out the windows.

One day, I operated on one of my aunts. There was nobody in her room when I went to visit her after her surgery. "You must have somebody take you home, or the hospital will not allow you to leave," I told her. "I will call my cleaning lady and have her pick me up," she answered. "I certainly do not want to bother anybody in my family." Did I mention the tradition in my family was: never make a fuss, never show your feelings, and solve all your problems by yourself?

One day, I noticed a patient had changed her address since her last visit. I asked her why. She told me her daughter had developed a mental illness, and she sold her house to pay for the daughter's care. I felt a twinge of sadness. I knew my parents would not do that. For starters, they never allowed themselves to recognize their children had problems.

People who do not get regular eye exams risk losing their sight. A smart, well-educated, successful man in his 60s came to my office complaining he had lost peripheral vision in his right eye. He founded and sold a successful company. This was his first eye exam ever.

The pressure in his right eye was a staggering *70*, normal being *8* to *22*. I was horrified when I looked through the slit lamp—the peripheral iris was plastered up against the back of the cornea. His eye was in the middle of an acute attack of *angle closure glaucoma*. The high pressure had destroyed ninety percent of his optic nerve.

Optic nerves, like all nerves, do not regenerate if they are damaged. If he had come to me for regular eye exams, I would have noticed his angle was dangerously narrow years ago and performed a laser iridotomy—which I did on an emergency basis that same day. Two days later, I did an iridotomy in his other eye, which saved it from the same ghastly fate. There was nothing I could do about the loss of vision in his right eye except prevent it from getting worse.

One day, an elderly lady came in for her annual check-up. She told me she was in the middle of a series of tests to find out why she was having eye pain. She went to her internist, who sent her to a neurologist, who sent her for an MRI, blood tests, and a CT scan. She was scheduled for a cerebral angiogram the following week.

One quick look through the slit lamp, and the diagnosis was obvious—severe dry eye. "Next time you have eye pain, see your eye doctor," I said as I handed her artificial tears and lubricating ointment. She canceled the cerebral angiogram. Bottom line: if you have pain in your eyes, see your eye doctor.

I have an advantage as a surgeon—I am a Johnson, so I can sing. This, after all, is what Johnsons do. If patients get restless during a laser procedure, all I need to do is belt out a few bars of: "Let's Do It, Let's Fall in Love," and they quiet down. They are too surprised to be frightened.

I performed laser surgery one day on an elderly lady with giant retinal tears in both eyes. The procedure was painful, and it lasted an hour. She had to hold still as I fired hundreds of shots of laser light into both eyes. To keep her quiet, I sang every gospel and calypso song I knew. She told me afterward she could never have endured this torture without music.

A professor who was slipping into dementia came to my office one day. He was in a bad mood. He refused to let me look at his eyes no matter how much I cajoled him. "How can I get you to cooperate?" I asked. "Can I sing you something?"

"Sing 'Chattanooga Choo Choo,'" he said with a triumphant smile. He thought he had stumped me. Little did he know that was one of my father's favorite songs. I sang out: "Pardon me, boy, is that the Chattanooga Choo Choo? Track twenty-nine, boy, you can gimme a shine." His cracked, quavering voice piped up: "I can afford to board a Chattanooga Choo Choo; I've got my fare and just a trifle to spare."

We traded verses until the song was over, his wife was in tears, he was meek as a kitten, and he allowed me to examine his eyes.

My patients give me books they have written, CDs they have recorded, photographs they have taken, and cookies they have baked. Their paintings hang on my walls. Two have written poems about me.

My most useful present came from a police sergeant, who gave me a piece of plastic the size of a credit card that states I am an Honorary Member of the New York Police Department. On it, he wrote: "Please extend courtesy." He told me to take it out if I was stopped by the police. I shoved it in my wallet and forgot about it.

Many years later, I was stopped for speeding. His card fell out while I was fumbling for my driver's license. The policeman looked at it and waved me on. He did not give me a ticket.

My job has allowed me to help people in ways that made a big difference in their lives. Every patient was a challenge and a learning experience. I had the job of my dreams. I felt happy and fulfilled all day, every day.

Our children were also happy. After they graduated from Princeton, they both married excellent spouses. They have lived useful and challenging lives. They dutifully produced four grandchildren who are also happy.

Malcolm was less happy. He tried several careers—law, insurance, university administration, executive search—but he didn't love any of them as much as he hoped. He did enjoy making significant contributions serving on many not-for-profit boards, including the Metropolitan Museum of Art.

CHAPTER SIXTEEN

Medical Malpractice

It didn't take long before I was involved in the medical malpractice system. One of the oldest attendings at the Eye Institute had been a renowned surgeon in his younger days. He wrote several textbooks and pioneered new surgical techniques.

By the time modern phacoemulsification cataract surgery came into general use, however, he was too old to learn how to do it. He didn't even know how to operate through a microscope. Even worse, he had macular degeneration. He was no longer doing good cataract surgery even with the old passé intracapsular technique. He was getting bad results with almost every patient, but he refused to retire.

I knew about this because he began sending me patients who had serious complications after he operated on them. At first, I could help most of them using a combination of laser surgery and medications. Then he sent me a patient who had one foot of the intraocular lens sticking out of his eye, which made me feel sick. The intraocular lens was tilted as well as displaced, which distorted the patient's vision, but not too badly.

I considered re-operating to push the intraocular lens back inside the eye, but there was a possibility the lens would dislocate and fall into the back chamber. There was also a risk of infection, which would have destroyed the sight in the eye. The exposed foot of the lens was covered by the conjunctiva, so the eye was not at risk of infection unless I opened it. I decided not to re-operate. I gave the patient new glasses instead, which helped somewhat.

The next week, he sent me a patient whose cornea had sagged downwards because he had not sewn the incision up properly. The eye had a whopping amount of astigmatism. The patient was a doctor who had only one good eye—the eye he operated on. I decided it would be too risky to open the warped eye to re-suture the wound. I gave him glasses instead. He was less miserable—he could read again—but he was not happy.

I called this surgeon. I praised the great contributions he had made to ophthalmology in the past. I begged him to allow me to come into the OR with him and "assist" him. He refused.

Anybody who wants to find out if a surgeon is competent should ask the residents. They assist every surgeon, so they know better than anybody else who is qualified and who is not. (Unfortunately, this is not possible for the average layperson.) The residents knew what was going on. They were just as upset as I was.

I went to the Chairman of the Department, explained the situation, and gave him a letter signed by every resident. The Chairman promptly revoked this surgeon's operating privileges at the Eye Institute. The surgeon promptly got privileges at another hospital and kept on operating.

The only way to get an incompetent surgeon out of the OR is through the medical malpractice system. Malpractice lawsuits are a ridiculous way to weed out incompetent doctors. They're expensive, inefficient, and unfair. Every surgeon will get sued—including me. Competent doctors who have done nothing wrong will get sued, especially if they appear aloof and arrogant. Incompetent ones may not get sued even if they have committed malpractice if their patients find them likable.

Lawsuits do NOT prevent malpractice. Troyen Brennan, a Harvard researcher, showed that only two percent of patients who received poor medical care will file lawsuits. Conversely, most patients who file a suit have not been victims of negligence.

I was sued once. An elderly dentist came to my office complaining his vision was blurred in his left eye. When I examined his eyes, I saw he had dry *Age-Related Macular Degeneration* (ARMD) in both eyes. ARMD is the number one cause of legal blindness in people over sixty-five in the US.

People with advanced ARMD only see big shapes and movement. They cannot read, drive, or recognize faces. If you want to get a feeling for how people with macular degeneration see the world, hold a tennis ball or a fist in front of your eye. Dry ARMD is relatively benign. It does get worse with time, but it rarely causes legal blindness.

His left eye had another problem that was far more serious—wet ARMD. There was a greyish mound of fluid under his retina at the edge of his macula. It had a fringe of bright red blood at one margin. Although only five percent of ARMD is wet, it is responsible for ninety-five percent of the blindness caused by ARMD.

I told the dentist the dry type of ARMD he had in both eyes was relatively benign and did not need any treatment. The wet macular degeneration in his left eye was another story. I warned him wet ARMD is famous for causing sudden blindness. These abnormal blood vessels would inevitably rupture suddenly and squirt a puddle of blood under the macula. He could sneeze, and—*boom*—his central vision could be destroyed. This could happen to him at any moment.

I told him I needed to treat his left eye with a laser right away. If I did not, there was a one hundred percent chance he would lose all his detailed vision in that eye. I also warned him the abnormal blood vessels were very close to the center of his macula, and even if my treatment was successful, he would have a permanent blank spot near his central vision. I explained even if I managed to destroy all the abnormal blood vessels, there was at least a fifty percent chance they would come back.

Our pre-operative discussion was as difficult as the laser treatment itself. I had to perform a laser procedure that was not only tricky but—even worse—had only a fifty-fifty chance of saving his sight. In other words, all the options for his eye were sub-optimal. He signed the consent form. I treated the patch of wet macular degeneration in his left eye with an Argon laser that day.

My laser treatment worked great for several weeks. The fluid under his retina went away, and his vision improved. I cautiously began to pat myself on the back. Then, the wet macular degeneration came roaring back in his left eye. This time, it was so close to the center of his macula laser treatment could not help. He brought a malpractice case against me, claiming I had destroyed his ability to make a living.

This was a *maloccurrence* – something bad had happened to his eye—but my laser treatment was not the cause, and what I did was not malpractice. Even though I knew I had provided the patient with the best care available in the world, I felt worried and upset. I have tried to be perfect all my life, and on some crazy level, I felt responsible. I wasn't sure I would be able to make a jury understand the laser treatment was appropriate and it was the only chance to keep the sight in his eye.

The day before I was scheduled for a deposition, my son Rob, an investigative journalist, sent me a magazine interview that quoted the dentist as saying business was booming and he was doing the best dentistry of his life. The article was introduced as evidence in the deposition. The case was thrown out of court with prejudice.

I was never sued again, but I have been involved in malpractice cases for over forty years as an expert witness. I have testified both for and against the plaintiff. I have concluded that the malpractice system is not fair, either to patients or to doctors. I have seen many examples of this. One of the most egregious involved a teenager sent to me by a malpractice defense lawyer.

A severely disabled young man, thin as a wraith, was wheeled into my office, slumped in a wheelchair. I touched him on the shoulder and said *hello*, but he did not raise his head. I realized he was deaf, dumb, paralyzed, and blind. I looked through his chart. He developed normally until he was three years old, and then he began to go downhill. He slowly lost his ability to speak, see, and move over the next twelve years. His parents sued the obstetrician who delivered him.

I knew even before I examined this unfortunate young man that his problem was not caused by the obstetrician. Babies who are damaged at birth show damage from the moment they are born. They never learn to talk and walk and then lose this ability later.
 It did not take long to determine the cause of this young man's problems. I did something no other doctor had done: I looked at his retinas. His maculas looked like targets—the center was darker than normal, and this dark center was surrounded by a ring that was lighter than normal, and around this light ring was another ring that was darker than normal.

Bingo. The diagnosis was as clear as if he had a neon sign inside his eye. I was one hundred percent certain he had *Niemann-Pick* disease, a rare and inevitably fatal hereditary degenerative storage disease. No other hereditary disease causes a bull's eye in the macula.

Niemann-Pick babies are born with a defective enzyme that normally breaks down fat. Without that enzyme, fat had accumulated throughout this poor boy's body, including his eyes, and caused his tragic decline. His problem was not caused by the obstetrician. It was genetic. Both of his parents carried a defective recessive Nieman-Pick gene without knowing it, and—by bad luck—they each passed their defective gene on to their son.

Storage diseases like Nieman-Pick are rare, but there are so many different kinds that one in one thousand people carries an abnormal gene for one of them. Treatment is available for some. Sadly, no treatment was developed for Niemann-Pick's disease, so a correct diagnosis and early intervention would not have helped him.

My report almost sizzled on the page. I told the defense lawyer he had a slam dunk case. I thought he would call to congratulate me after the trial ended. Weeks went by, and I did not hear from him, so I called him. He told me the case was settled – i.e., a cash payment was made to the parents.

Settled! I was so surprised I almost choked. Why?? In a weary voice, he told me that the plaintiff's lawyer put the obstetrician on the stand for four—*four!*—days. For three days, the doctor answered the lawyer's barrage of questions calmly. Halfway through the fourth day, he snapped and began to yell at the prosecutor.

The defense lawyer looked at the jury. Their faces were masks of disgust. They no longer had any sympathy for the poor, innocent doctor. Time to settle. Such a shame—one outburst negated the obvious innocence of the doctor and cost millions of dollars.

The only sensible solution is to scrap the present medical malpractice system and replace it with expert panels who really know how to determine negligence. These experts must be thoroughly vetted to avoid cronyism. Every time I took on a malpractice case as an expert witness, the lawyer first asked me if I knew any of the doctors personally.

I work with an honest, smart malpractice lawyer. He runs several potential eye malpractice cases by me every year. I review them without charge. I reject most of them, but if he sends me a case where I think there has been genuine malpractice, I help him in every way I can. This is the obligation of every surgeon. If we do not police our own, there will be no way to weed out incompetent surgeons.

This belief led me to campaign long and hard about the malpractice and misinformation surrounding the *LASIK* eye procedure. Telling the truth about LASIK became my passion. I am compelled to try to put an end to healthy eyes being made sick by an unnecessary and risky procedure. I cover my journey with LASIK in Chapter Eighteen.

CHAPTER SEVENTEEN

My Dream to Be a Professor Comes True—Eventually

My dream to be a retinal researcher came true. Over twenty-five years, Peter and I churned out two or three peer-reviewed scientific articles and abstracts every year. I traveled around the world, including Australia, Holland, Belgium, Portugal, Switzerland, and Italy, giving lectures about our discoveries. On almost every trip, I managed to sneak in a visit with Elizabeth Craig-Cooper, my British school friend in England. My dream to become a retinal surgeon also came true.

Another dream of mine was to pass on knowledge to other ophthalmologists. That, too, came true, mostly because I learned how to give a clear, interesting talk during my nine years teaching high school science, and because of my reputation as an academic researcher.

I began by teaching the first-year Eye Institute residents at the Basic Science Course in 1982, after I finished residency. The residents wrote evaluations of their teachers at the end of the course, and they gave me good marks. I often presented cases at Grand Rounds at the Harkness Eye Institute. Other teaching hospitals in the New York area needed guest lecturers. Soon, I was presenting at Grand Rounds at hospitals around Manhattan and on Long Island.

My teaching talents eventually came to the notice of the Lancaster Course. This course, run by the Massachusetts Eye and Ear Infirmary, teaches fundamental eye information to roughly one hundred first-year ophthalmology residents every summer over seven weeks during July and August. It meets at Colby College in Waterville, Maine. Ophthalmologists from all over the world come to the Lancaster Course to teach, and ophthalmology residents from all over the world come to learn.

I taught color vision, ERG, and retina at the Lancaster Course for seventeen years. During that time, I helped train half the ophthalmology residents in the United States every year—thousands of ophthalmologists.

ROW 1 L to R: J. Brown, H. Hammond, R. Bannon, F. Bannon, R. Osborn, D. Guyton, J. Hammond, H. Albin, C. MacKay, M. Walluck. ROW 2: H. Hacker, G. Vukmar, C. Mattox, T. Hunter, S. Ann-Lee, D. Corallo, D. Lennaun, C. Harris, P. Sarfarazi, L. Yakubus, J. Spitzer, G. Smith, M. Tremblay, D. Sherman, M. Mercantetti, L. Nouyen, G. Pretsko, W. Walton, M. Bertini. ROW 3: C. Hulburd, M. Natatta, S. Parke, E. Heon, E. Hassman, P. Duguay, R. Condon, A. Terabush, L. Maioli, D. Messina, D. Morrison, C. Joseph, T. Chiu, R. Des Roches, R. Carignan, W. Brawner, O. Hakim, I. Hardy, D. Bergeron, L. Keys, S. Mayers, R. Foster, S. Shah. ROW 4: S. McClatchey, P. Branch, S. Kerrick, J. Berland, M. Tanenbaum, J. Ferris, L. Gyugyek, P. Matthews, B. Britton, D. Bregman, C. Burgoyne, D. Vittoria, D. O'Conner, M. Sevitt, J. Shovlin, G. Heslen, A. Assallah, J. Stock, R. Tourigny, D. Falvey, C. Sirois. ROW 5: D. Belyea, R. Baldovi, F. Falck, J. Perlecon, G. Lane, A. Brown, P. Maguire, H. Cummings, C. Slade, R. Vallar, M. Kahn, J. Chessman, D. Gibbon, M. Erasmus, C. Sherrod, H. Saras, M. Vocol, J. Wisey, R. DeBarge, F. LoRusso, M. Weiner.

Pictured: The Lancaster Course year photo for the class of 1989, Colby College, Waterville, Maine, 1989. CJM is in the front row, wearing a lobster shirt, second from the far right.

My favorite lecture was color vision, probably because my mother was so interested in color. Color vision defects are hereditary, and common. One out of every twelve men has a color vision defect.

One day, a young man in his twenties stormed into my office, angry and upset. His dream was to be an airplane pilot. Before he went to flight school, he went to an ophthalmologist who checked his refraction, cornea, and retina and told him his eyes were perfect. The ophthalmologist did not check his color vision. After two years in flight school, when he was one month away from graduation, he took a color vision test and failed it. The school told him he could not graduate.

I did a test that showed he was color-*weak* instead of color color-*defective*. I wrote a letter certifying that he could accurately identify the color of landing lights. He graduated on schedule.

Every young boy should have a color vision test. Men who are color weak, instead of color blind, often have no idea they have a color vision problem. Most of the residents at the Lancaster Course were men during the seventeen years I taught there, so every year I picked up one, two, or three who were color-defective and did not know it. That got everybody's attention.

When I was giving my color vision lecture one summer, I noticed a large man standing in the back of the room. He was listening intently, and he

216

never took his eyes off me. He made me nervous, especially when he walked up to me after the lecture. I didn't know what he was planning to do. Perhaps he was planning to attack me? I realized with relief he was an elderly janitor.

He told me he was color blind. I tested him and discovered he was a *deuteranope*, i.e., his green cones were defective. About one percent of men are deuteranopes. I knew deuteranopes use brightness, instead of color, to distinguish objects, so they can pick up the differences between camouflage and background. I told him he could see through camouflage. He took a deep breath and told me an amazing story. His deuteranopia helped the Allies win World War II.

He was a private in the Army during the war. He was standing in the US with his squadron as they watched a camouflage demonstration. He remarked to a friend the system was no good—he could see everything. An officer standing nearby overheard him and told him to point out what he saw. He accurately picked out every plane, machine gun, and tank.

The officer realized this private had a talent that could be useful. He shoved him on the next plane to Belgium, where the Battle of the Bulge was raging. A spotter plane flew him over the battlefield. A squadron of bombers followed close behind. He pointed out every target the Germans had carefully camouflaged, and the bombers blew them all up. The Germans had no idea their nemesis was a color-blind man.

He told his story to the class the next day. I did not have to remind the residents that color vision is important.

My final dream was to become a professor. Every doctor at the Columbia University College of Physicians and Surgeons has a title. As doctors rise through the ranks, their first title is *Instructor,* then *Associate,* then *Assistant Professor,* then *Associate Professor,* and finally—a title given rarely—*Professor.*

When I finished my residency in 1981, I was given the lowest title— Instructor in Clinical Ophthalmology. Then, I began the long climb up. Eventually, I got to the second-to-last step, Associate Professor. To become a professor, a doctor must be a first-rate researcher, surgeon, and teacher, and to contribute to the Eye Institute in significant ways. By the late 1990s, I thought my credentials were good enough to be appointed Professor.

I published many scientific papers with Peter Gouras. I taught at the Lancaster Course, which brought prestige to the Eye Institute. (I was the only Eye Institute attending who was invited to lecture there.) I was a member of prestigious ophthalmology societies. I received the Honor Award for Excellence in Research and Teaching from the American Academy of Ophthalmology and the Master Teacher Award in Ophthalmology from my alma mater, Downstate Medical School. Castle Connolly named me one of the "Best Doctors in America."

Even better, I brought a lot of money into the Eye Institute. When Peter and I started to do retinal research, I wanted to raise money to help fund our projects, but I did not know how to begin. I had wealthy patients because of my background, but the thought of asking them for money made me cringe with embarrassment.

Then, some friends of mine from St. Timothy's School—yes, I did make a few friends at that school—started an organization called *Women and Money.* One of the lectures was about how to ask for money. I listened intently as the speaker—an accomplished fund-raiser—said he saw himself as an advisor for rich people. They did not know which recipients were worthy of their donations. He did.

This talk gave me the confidence to ask my wealthy patients to steer their money into retinal research. They didn't know the difference between good research and research that was silly or just plain wrong. They would believe me if I explained it to them clearly and simply.

I decided to raise a *chair* for Peter. "Chairs" are sums of money that pay the salaries of researchers, who then get grants to fund their work. A chair at that time cost roughly a million dollars. I managed to raise not just one, but two chairs—one for retinal research, the other to study the genetics of glaucoma. No other doctor at the Eye Institute had raised two chairs. Most of them hadn't raised any money at all.

I was recognized by the world but not by my ophthalmology department. I remained stuck as Associate Professor of Ophthalmology because Dr. *X* was chairman of the Eye Institute. (Dr. *X* has since died.)

I found out when I was a second-year resident that Dr. *X* was one of the attendings who did not think women should be eye surgeons. When he assisted me with a cataract operation one day, he said after the operation was over: "You are one of the most gifted surgeons I have ever seen. Isn't it a shame nobody will want you to operate on their eyes because you are a woman?"

Dr. *X* forgot about *transference*, which means that people tend to "transfer" feelings from people they knew during their childhood to people in their adult life. Children who have had a good relationship with a female authority figure—usually their mother—will "transfer" these positive feelings to female authority figures when they become adults. Patients with positive feelings about female authority figures preferred a female doctor. One of them was an eminent doctor who was President of Downstate Medical School when I was a student there. He chose me to take out his cataracts instead of one of the famous male surgeons. All his doctors were women. I found out later he adored his mother and had no use for his father.

One day, Dr. *X* called me into his office. I thought he wanted to congratulate me on the recent publication of a scientific paper Peter and I had written. Instead, he said: "Perky [Miss Perkovitch, our beloved clinic nurse] is retiring. Buy her a retirement present. The Department will reimburse you".

I could not believe my ears. I was an Associate Professor of Ophthalmology, and Dr. *X* was ordering me around as if I was a Woman-Good-For-Running-Errands. He had just ordered me to do a personal chore that would have been insulting to his secretary. He never would have asked one of the male attendings to do this. A male doctor should spend his time on loftier pursuits.

My childhood training in good manners kicked in. I did not tell him to buy his own (#$@&%*!) present. I said, "I know just where to go. The Metropolitan Museum of Art shop sells wonderful presents." I spent half a day picking out a present for Perky—who I dearly loved.

Dr. *X* was a good surgeon, but as Chairman, he was promoted beyond his abilities. He did not have a driving dream for the Eye Institute because he did not do research, and he did not keep up with scientific discoveries. He was not a good fundraiser, probably because he had no idea of what to do with the money. The skills of a good surgeon are different from the skills of a good administrator. Hospitals should recognize this when they choose administrators.

Dr. X badly mismanaged one of the chairs I raised. I convinced one of my patients, who had glaucoma, to donate a chair to fund the salary of a researcher who would study the genetics of this disease. I told her if we could find the gene that causes glaucoma, we could diagnose and treat it better and possibly even find a cure. She gave the Eye Institute a million dollars in my honor. Dr. X could not get this research project off the ground. Years went by, and the money was not spent. Eventually, the Eye Institute had to give back her money.

Dr. X was promoting men whose academic credentials were much weaker than mine. These men hadn't published any scientific papers, they did not attend international research meetings, they did not teach courses, and they hadn't raised any money for the Eye Institute. I was running rings around them, but it was clear he was not going to promote me.

Friends told me this was unfair. They urged me to talk to Dr. X. I did. He sat and looked at me. He said nothing, and he did nothing. When Dr. X retired, one of the first things the new chairman did was to tell me to apply for a Professorship. Six months later, in 2003, I was Clinical Professor of Ophthalmology at the Columbia University College of Physicians and Surgeons.

CHAPTER EIGHTEEN

I Could Not Live with Myself Unless I Spoke Out About LASIK
(as you read this chapter, please look at the book I co-authored, 'The Unsightly Truth of Laser Vision Correction: LASIK Surgery Makes Healthy Eyes Sick' and the movie 'Broken Eyes' for which I am the Executive Producer)

Granny Edey taught me to speak up against wrong. I am one of a handful of ophthalmologists willing to speak out about LASIK. I have been telling the truth about this dangerous eye procedure for thirty years. I get no money or fame for doing this. It takes up a lot of time. I get nothing but criticism from my colleagues. However, I could not live with myself unless I did.

LASIK is a cosmetic surgical procedure that re-shapes the corneas of healthy eyes with an excimer laser to get rid of distance glasses and contact lenses. It does not prevent or treat eye disease.

Eyes are vitally important, so the rate of serious complications from LASIK surgery should be zero. In fact, the complications are multiple, disastrous, untreatable, and permanent. They include blindness, life-long pain, disability, and, in some cases, these have led to suicide. Out of a 8,000-member LASIK   support group, at least thirty-five patients committed suicide after LASIK. This number is certainly an undercount.

The risk of developing serious LASIK complications is at least thirty percent. Since 40 million people in the world have had LASIK, at least twelve million people are suffering today from these life-destroying complications. Seven years after LASIK, fifty-five percent of patients say they wished that they never had the procedure. You can learn more about these complications by going to my website, *eyedocmackay.com*.

Unfortunately, many LASIK surgeons do not adequately inform their patients before their surgery about the possible complications of LASIK.

LASIK affects me like a gut punch because I have spent my life as an eye surgeon saving and restoring vision. The thought that an eye procedure is causing blindness and pain makes me sick to my stomach. I have talked to many LASIK-damaged patients, and the stories they tell me are appalling. The lives of these poor people have been ruined by my own colleagues.

Let's take a moment to clear up the misconceptions about eye lasers; I do not condemn the lasers that are used in the treatment of actual eye disease. Most people do not know that there are five different lasers used by ophthalmologists to treat the human eye. Allow me to briefly discuss my experiences with each of them before we move on to LASIK.

The first laser invented to treat the human eye is the *Argon laser*, which is used to treat retinal diseases, including diabetic retinopathy, retinal tears, and macular degeneration. I started using the Argon laser during my first year of residency. It did not look very impressive at first glance, just a black box connected to a slit lamp with a chin rest and attached to a foot petal. Once I started to use it, however, I was blown away.

I sat down opposite the patient and slipped a contact lens into the eye. This allowed me to gaze down into the inside of the eye, admire the glistening perfection of the retina, feast my eyes on its gleaming marvels, and watch the dark purple veins pulse.
When I triggered the Argon laser by pressing down the foot petal, a tiny spot of green Argon laser light shot into the retina with stunning accuracy. Unbelievable. I felt like a machine gunner mowing down enemy troops.

In 1976, two years before I started my residency at the Eye Institute, the results of the first prospective randomized trial to treat diabetic retinopathy with the Argon laser were published. The researchers stopped the trial early because it was blazingly obvious the patients who were treated with the laser were doing better than untreated ones.

We forget today how revolutionary this study was. Before the invention of the Argon laser, all diabetics with retinopathy went blind. Thanks to the Argon laser, they almost all keep their sight – if their retinopathy is diagnosed and treated early.

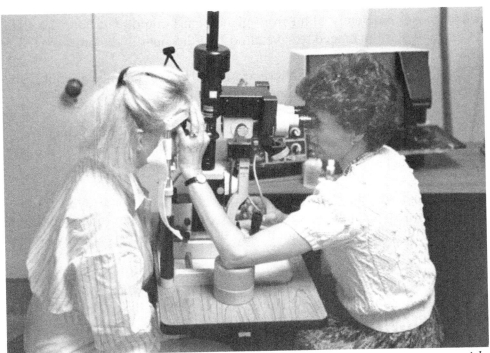

Pictured: CJM performing an Argon laser treatment on an eye with proliferative diabetic retinopathy.

Another laser used to treat the eye is the *Selective Laser*, which I used to treat open-angle glaucoma. I shot spots of laser light directly onto the *trabecular meshwork*, which is the place where fluid drains out of the eye. The laser spots tickle the trabecular meshwork cells and stimulate them to change shape and produce new chemicals, which improves their ability to drain fluid out of the eye. This lowers the pressure inside the eye, which stops damage to the optic nerve.

Glaucoma is hereditary. My Johnson family is a good example of the inheritance of glaucoma. Grandpa Johnson had open-angle glaucoma. His glaucoma was not diagnosed and treated early, so he had almost no peripheral vision when he was older. He smashed up his car whenever he tried to park it, which is one reason he hired a chauffeur.

Uncle Bobby Johnson didn't know glaucoma was hereditary, so he did not get regular eye exams. When he was middle-aged, he came to my office for his first eye exam ever. I realized to my horror one of his eyes was almost completely blind from glaucoma. I couldn't restore the sight in that eye, but I managed to save almost all the sight in the other eye.

One of Bobby's daughters inherited her father's glaucoma. Luckily, she was diagnosed and treated promptly, so her sight was saved.

The third laser I used in ophthalmology is the *Nd:YAG laser*, which treats narrow angle glaucoma and secondary cataracts that form after modern cataract extraction.

The fourth laser, the *femtosecond laser*, is used by some eye surgeons during modern cataract surgery. It provides no better outcomes than surgery with phacoemulsification, and it is very expensive. I have never used it.

I used Argon, YAG, and Selective lasers for forty years to treat retinal diseases, glaucoma, and secondary cataracts. I never have, and never will, use the fifth laser on our list: the *excimer laser*.

Eye surgeons are supposed to make sick eyes healthy. The excimer laser, in the hands of LASIK surgeons, can make healthy eyes sick. There is nothing wrong with eyes that need glasses. They see well with their glasses before the procedure. Given that patients already have a treatment for their poor vision (glasses or contacts), LASIK is purely cosmetic. It removes the need for glasses or contact lenses. The patients ought to see equally well after the procedure, but they often do not.

The worst thing about LASIK is that patients are not warned about just how much risk the procedure involves—and what a gamble they are making on something as precious as their sight—all for the sake of merely not having to use glasses or contacts anymore.

I was one of the first people in the world to hear about LASIK. In the late 1980s, I was working in the Edward S. Harkness Eye Institute clinic when one of my colleagues, Steve Trokel, rushed into my room and shoved a piece of paper into my hands. His paper showed a cornea with an exact rectangle sliced into it by an excimer laser. It was hot off the press—quite literally—still warm from the printer.

Steve told me this laser could re-shape human corneas and thereby eliminate the need for distance glasses. He told me he was planning to call his procedure 'LASIK" (the acronym for *Laser-Assisted In Situ Keratomileusis*).

I thought Steve was crazy. I knew the excimer laser would not only re-shape, but also thin and weaken, the cornea. The cornea has more nerve endings than any other place in the human body. The laser would cut these corneal nerves, causing pain in all patients and excruciating pain in some patients. It would produce scar tissue, which would destroy vision. Anybody who knows anything about corneal healing knows these complications would be inevitable, disastrous, and untreatable. I thought LASIK would never catch on.

I was wrong. I underestimated how much people want to get rid of their glasses. I also did not predict that the complications would not be adequately explained on the consent forms, with surgeons obfuscating the reality of the procedure, and the fact that almost no ophthalmologists would speak out against it.

As a surgeon myself, I know we are obligated to explain the risks, benefits, complications, and alternate treatments to every prospective surgery patient. Unless these complications are explained in words the patient can understand, and the percentage risk is stated for each complication, a consent form is useless.

LASIK patients started showing up in my office soon after the FDA approved LASIK in 1995. Many were happy—at least, in the short-term immediately following their procedure. Others had poor vision, glare and halos in dim light, chronic pain, and ruined lives. They all told me when they asked their surgeon about LASIK complications, the surgeon *never warned them* this could happen to them.

I soon developed a reputation as one of a small number of ophthalmologists who was willing to warn the public about LASIK. In 1994, Dan Dorfman, the infamous CNBC "stock picker," called me out of the blue and asked my opinion about LASIK. I told him the procedure was "experimental and unpredictable" with "worrisome complications," including "over and under correction, fluctuating vision, poor vision at night, and pain." *Bloomberg* reported my comments, and the stock price of the excimer laser companies plunged tens of millions of dollars.

I continued to speak out against LASIK at Grand Rounds, in my office, and to anybody who was contemplating the procedure.

In May 2008, I went on *CBS* news and explained LASIK complications to the chief medical correspondent. The LASIK surgeons retaliated by claiming that I was "naïve" and did not know what I was talking about.

In 2010, the campaign to tell the truth about LASIK gained a recruit who is far more effective than I am—Dr. Morris Waxler. Morris was the chief scientist in charge of FDA clinical research trials. He was head of the FDA committee that approved LASIK.

Dr. Waxler realized he had made a ghastly mistake in approving LASIK when he met Paula Cofer. Paula was a successful banker until she had LASIK in both eyes in 2000. Today, she lives with severe, constant eye pain. Her vision is so blurred and distorted she can no longer work. She survives on disability.

Paula did not commit suicide, although she considered it. Instead, she dedicated her life to telling the truth about LASIK. She set up a Facebook page called *LASIK Complications Support Group*, where other LASIK-damaged patients can share their problems and get advice on how to live with their ruined eyes and lives. This support group has close to 8,000 members. She also created a website, *www.lasikcomplications.com*, and a not-for-profit called *VisionAdvocacy.org*.

Paula introduced Dr. Waxler to other LASIK-damaged patients and their families. Morris realized, to his horror, that the clinical trials submitted to the FDA by the LASIK surgeons only looked at how well the patients could read an eye chart. They failed to pick up serious long-term side effects, including night vision problems and chronic dry eye, because the number of patients was small, and the follow-up was short.

The LASIK surgeons assured Morris that these problems were "temporary side effects." Morris realized they were permanent and devastating.

He took a second look at the original data from the trials. Then, he reviewed all the papers on LASIK complications in the scientific literature (he was able to look at medical research papers not readily available to the public).

Morris realized the original data submitted to the FDA by the LASIK surgeons showed that twelve months after the procedure, sixty percent of patients had fluctuating vision in dim light, fifty percent had gritty eyes, forty percent had sensitivity to light, twenty percent had fluctuating vision in both dim and bright light, and fifteen to twenty percent had problems driving at night because of glare and halos.

Morris heard that I was a (rare) ophthalmologist who was willing to speak out about LASIK. He called me, and invited me to come to Washington, D.C., with him on September 22, 2010, to testify before the FDA about the dangers of LASIK.

As Morris and I rode up the gleaming escalator of the shining brand-new main building of the FDA complex in Silver Springs, Maryland, I thought it would be a slam dunk to convince the FDA to ban LASIK. Dazzling minds must work in this dazzling palace. LASIK was a serious public health problem. Once the regulators knew the facts, they would surely ban LASIK.

Morris told the FDA how the focus on short-term rather than long-term data had tricked him into recommending LASIK, and why he now believed it should be banned. I explained how the cornea behaves when it is wounded and why the side effects are unavoidable and devastating. We both described patients whose lives had been permanently destroyed by this procedure. *ABC* ran a special about Morris's testimony that evening.

Three months after our testimony, on January 6, 2011, Morris filed a citizen's petition with the FDA. It is thirty-two pages long. It includes ten figures, six tables, and one hundred and one references from peer-reviewed scientific literature. Every one of Morris's statements is based on scientific evidence. Now, that is good science. It is readily available online—simply Google *Morris Waxler FDA LASIK*.

Morris concluded his petition by stating: "LASIK risks and long-term consequences outweigh the benefit of reduced dependence on corrective lenses." He urged the FDA to withdraw its approval of LASIK, issue a Public Health Advisory, and recall all LASIK devices.

The FDA response was a drop in the bucket. The FDA website recommends that LASIK patients obtain a copy of their medical records, including the consent form. It cautions prospective patients their vision at night will be permanently reduced after LASIK, even if they have 20/20 or better vision in bright light. It also warns that visual outcomes of LASIK decline over time. The FDA did not ban LASIK.

Morris and I did not give up. Eight years later, on September 13, 2018, we went back to the FDA. We brought three other people with us—Paula Cofer; a medical doctor, Nancy Burleson, whose son, an only child, committed suicide after LASIK; and another LASIK-damaged patient.

Morris, Paula, Nancy, and I went out for dinner the night before our testimony. Paula could not see once we walked into the dark street, so she grabbed my arm. I will never forget the feeling of her hand reaching out to mine. I had to warn her about steps. She could not read the menu when we were in the restaurant. I had to cut up her food. This was a woman whose sight and life had been destroyed by one of my fellow ophthalmologists. It made me sick and angry.

The next day, Morris, Paula, Nancy, and the other LASIK-damaged patient gave vivid, searing, and well-documented testimony about how LASIK destroys eyes and lives.

I asked the committee members if they wanted their legacy to be blindness, pain, and death, and I gave everybody a copy of a consent form that explains, in language a layman can understand, the risks of LASIK, with the percent chance for each risk. I told them their duty was either to ban LASIK or require all LASIK surgeons to give this consent form to their patients at least two weeks before surgery. The FDA did neither.

Pictured left to right: CJM., Paula Cofer, Morris Waxler, and Nancy Burleson M.D. in front of FDA building immediately before their testimony in 2018.

I co-authored a book, *The Unsightly Truth of Laser Vision Correction: LASIK Makes Healthy Eyes Sick*, with Morris Waxler, Paula Cofer, and an optometrist called Ed Boshnick who has treated thousands of LASIK-damaged patients with scleral contact lenses. We dedicated the book to the millions of people who have suffered appalling eye disorders caused by LASIK. Every penny of profit will go to helping LASIK-damaged patients.

I personally interviewed and wrote the stories of most of the LASIK victims who appear in our book, because they could no longer read, write, or use the computer since they had LASIK. They all told me the same thing: we trusted our doctor would not do this surgery unless it was one hundred percent safe. The surgeon claimed there was a back-up plan for every complication. There is not.

Many TV and newspaper articles have told the stories of LASIK-damaged patients. Many scientific articles have appeared in the literature that provide ample evidence of the inevitable and catastrophic complications of LASIK. Our book puts the two together.

New data continues to come out about the dangers of LASIK. In 2023, two high-quality studies—i.e., prospective, randomized, and done at academic institutions—reported the frequency and risk of complications after LASIK.

One, *Ocular Pain After Refractive Surgery* from Bascom Palmer Eye Institute and Oregon Health and Science University, showed that ocular pain increased from seven percent to twenty-four percent after LASIK, and sixty-five percent of patients reported an increased use of artificial tears.

The other, *Patient Reported Outcomes with Wave-Front Guided LASIK From a Single Institution* from Stanford University School of Medicine, found that twenty-five percent of patients reported a decrease in quality of life and visual well-being three months after surgery, and thirty-two percent had new symptoms such as halos, double images, and dry eye.

Put the results of these new studies together with the risk of complications from the original trials the LASIK surgeons submitted to the FDA and explain each risk in a language patients can understand, and you get the following consent form, which I wrote and which I urged the FDA to adopt.

What follows is an excerpt:

LASIK IS AN ELECTIVE COSMETIC PROCEDURE

If you have LASIK, you have up to a 50% chance of developing dry eye, *which means your eyes will feel as if sand is pasted under your lids, and they will burn as if they have hot pepper sauce in them. There is a 100% chance this pain will be with you for the rest of your life. The 'dryness' is nerve pain caused by damaged corneal nerves.*

You have up to a 60% chance of developing fluctuating vision in dim light, a 50% chance of glare, a 40% chance of sensitivity to light, a 20% chance of fluctuating vision in both bright and dim light, and a 10-20% chance of difficulty driving at night due to halos around lights and ghost images. These problems will never go away. You may have to stop driving at night and going to the theatre and movies. If your job requires you to function in dim light, you could be permanently disabled.

The LASIK flap never heals completely. You have a lifetime risk the flap could dislocate after minor trauma, and infection could creep underneath the flap.

The cornea is not inert, like a sheet of plastic. It is a living structure that grows and remodels throughout life. 20% of LASIK eyes do not remain stable. They either go back to being nearsighted or go in the other direction and become farsighted, or else they fluctuate from one to the other. Some eyes continue to fluctuate for as long as twenty-five years.

If LASIK surgeons were required to give this consent form to every prospective patient, I question whether many people would consent.

Because LASIK surgery is cosmetic, it is not covered by insurance, which means it is not subject to price limits set by insurance companies. *Medicare.com* says: "LASIK is not considered medically necessary; therefore, it is not covered." *LASIK.com* states: "Most insurance companies don't cover LASIK … it is nearly always considered an elective or cosmetic surgery." This means LASIK surgery is highly profitable.

When I talk to ophthalmologists in private, they readily admit the dangers of LASIK, but they refuse to criticize this multibillion-dollar industry. They know there will be serious pushbacks. This happened to me.

On June 12, 2018, the *New York Times* published an article exposing the dangers of LASIK. I convinced a friend, a former *NY Times* editor, it was the duty of his paper to write it. I worked with the writer, Roni Caryn Rabin, to back up each statement with peer-reviewed science. The article received over one million page views (one hundred thousand is considered impressive). Roni quoted me in the article. Two days later, I appeared on *Good Morning America*. Today, most people have forgotten about it.

The assault from my colleagues was immediate, personal, and lacking in scientific evidence. One accused me of "fake news" and said I am "no scientist". Several colleagues pointedly ignored me at a professional meeting. One told me I wasn't qualified to criticize LASIK because I am a retina specialist. Three filed letters of complaint with the president of the society. Fortunately, the society did not expel me.

Notably, however, no one disputed the facts: LASIK inevitably causes complications, some mild, some so severe they have led to suicide.

The LASIK flap is attached to the eye only as strongly as a contact lens. The bond between the LASIK flap and the rest of the cornea is so weak bacteria can easily creep under it and invade the cornea, even years after surgery. Even mild trauma—rubbing the eye, being hit by a wave, contact sports—can dislodge it. As soon as the flap dislocates, the eye instantly loses clear vision. The flap must be replaced surgically as soon as possible. It is now much more likely to dislocate again.

I tell all my LASIK patients they must not rub their eyes, and they must wear eye protection when they play contact sports and goggles when they go swimming. This is not my job. It should be the job of the LASIK surgeon. It should be mentioned in the consent form.

LASIK surgeons often urge their patients to have both eyes done on the same day. Some offer discounts for the second eye. This violates a universally accepted rule of eye surgery—to always let an operated eye heal for at least two weeks before you operate on the second eye.

Could it be that LASIK surgeons know that one-eyed LASIK patients will compare the vision in their operated eye to their unoperated eye, and they will realize the operated eye has blurred vision, distortions, glare, etc., so they may not schedule the second eye?

Ophthalmologists—including LASIK surgeons—measure visual acuity with high-contrast black letters on a white background. This isn't the way we see objects in the real world. Objects are not all pitch black with straight, crisp sides against a white background. Our eyes need to distinguish between subtle gradations of color, brightness, and form.

LASIK surgeons usually define "success" as being able to see 20/40 using high-contrast black letters on a white background without glasses. Using this criterion, they claim the "success" rate of LASIK is ninety-nine percent. If they asked the LASIK patients themselves, they might discover more than half of these "successful" patients do not agree with this definition of "success."

As of this writing, roughly eleven million people in the US have had LASIK. I am not aware of any report by the LASIK surgeons on the number of complications from this procedure.

The LASIK surgeons like to say with new, improved techniques, the complication rate has gone way down. However, the new techniques— like the old technique—invariably cut corneal nerves, thin the cornea, and cause scarring. The simple fact is this: If cutting and removal of tissue is the root source of these medical complications, the most advanced technique in the world will not stop the complications. The nerves and tissue are still being cut; the root source is still the same. And another point of consideration: If the LASIK surgeons do not collect any data, how do they know the complication rate has gone down?

I knew LASIK would cause eye pain given that nerves would be cut, but I had no idea how bad that pain would be. Many LASIK surgeons call this pain *dry eye*, but I question this because eyes with post-LASIK pain do not have any signs of dryness, such as corneal staining and tear debris. Instead, they look completely normal and well-healed. What these eyes really have is much worse—corneal neuropathic pain.

Neuropathic pain typically develops sometime after LASIK surgery—at least three months, and sometimes years, afterward. It is caused by damage to the small corneal nerves that run through the cornea.

The job of corneal nerves is to keep the cornea healthy. Once these nerves are cut, they never grow back normally. They develop persistent low-grade inflammation that is readily visible on scans. In some unlucky patients, these nerves start to fire constantly, causing unrelenting, unbearable pain. The same phenomenon can occur after a patient loses a limb. In this case, it is called *phantom pain.*

Neuropathic corneal pain causes severe foreign body sensation, burning, and dryness. Walk into any drug store, and you will see bottles of artificial tears labeled, *For LASIK Dryness.* LASIK patients have been falsely told by their LASIK surgeons that their eyes are dry, so some patients put wetting drops in their eyes several times an hour, trying to alleviate the pain. Yes, I mean every hour. The irony is that these artificial tear drops do not help the patients because their eyes are not dry.

I know all about chronic neuropathic pain because I had it myself in 2012. It almost caused me to commit suicide. I will tell you all about it in Chapter 22, *The Doctor Becomes a Patient*.

Would you agree to have surgery that has a thirty-plus percent chance of leaving you with moderate to severe pain for the rest of your life, for the sake of getting rid of your eyeglasses?

Many ophthalmologists feel the way I do about LASIK. They are aware LASIK destroys eyes and lives. Dr. Ray Jui-Fan Tsai, the ophthalmologist who introduced LASIK to Taiwan, now refuses to do it. A surgeon friend of mine who once did LASIK told me he no longer performs it because, "–if something goes wrong, you can't do anything about it." Another friend, a corneal specialist who was a pioneer of LASIK surgery, now won't go near it. Yet they refuse to speak out and tell the world the truth.

In Japan, public skepticism about LASIK has caused a significant reduction in the number of laser vision correction procedures. There has been a shift from approximately four hundred thousand refractive procedures annually, before anti-LASIK campaigns, to about one hundred thousand in 2023, and another procedure where intraocular lenses are placed into an eye that still has its own natural lens now accounts for nearly half of these.

The LASIK situation is like smoking causing lung cancer, or *Oxycontin* causing addiction and death due to overdose, or concussions causing chronic traumatic encephalopathy. The emperor has no clothes. Nobody has the guts to say the obvious.

If we can get the truth out about LASIK, I will feel my life was worth living.

Paula said it best: "How the FDA has let this continue for over twenty years—a harmful medical device that is used for a completely unnecessary eye surgery on previously healthy eyes without adequate warnings, a scheme to make some eye surgeons very rich—is simply impossible to fathom."

PART THREE:

LOOKING INWARD: PHYSICIAN, HEAL THYSELF

Surgeons have great power. We hire them to cut into us, but we don't know much about their private lives. In this third Part, I cut myself open to reveal the woman underneath the surgeon's gown.

CHAPTER NINETEEN

My Parents: A Reckoning

In the 1990s, while I was busy with my husband, children, growing practice, research, and increasingly negative opinions about LASIK, my parents started to develop debilitating health problems. I realized that I had to get more involved in their lives.

I was lulled into a false complacency about my mother because she refused to act her age. She cultivated friends who were my age and—even harder for me to accept—the age of my children. She would not let her young friends meet me because, she claimed, if they saw me, they would realize she was older than they thought.

This annoyed me at the time. Today, I admire her spunk. She never lost her zest for life or her belief she was special. As I get older, I realize how difficult that is.
I resented my mother's single-minded focus on her art when I was a child. I always took second place after those stupid portraits. I am proud of her when I look at them today. I can understand and forgive the demons that gnawed at her and drove her into her studio because I have the same demons. She felt most alive when she was creating art. I feel most alive when I am working.

Plato, the Greek philosopher, said artists have what he called a "divine madness." Artists are interesting and fun, but I know only too well they can be difficult parents.

In her best portraits, my mother went beyond getting a likeness and revealed the true personality of her subject. As a poet friend of mine said, "She creates a matter-mirror of their spirit-mirror."

Her self-portrait has a cool, haughty gaze. Here is a woman who does not tolerate people she considers beneath her notice. My father's portrait shows his sweetness. I look alert and anxious to please in my portrait, as if I am trying to win the approval of the painter. Hope flashes an optimistic, outgoing grin. Rob is quieter and more introspective.

My mother's ability to create art came from the right side of her brain. This side works in images, not words. It goes to the big picture, so it sometimes forgets to deal with details. It is the side that recognizes faces and picks up social cues. It allows us to recognize three-dimensional forms in space. It is also where musical talent is located.

The left brain is the logical side. It is all business, all nuts and bolts. It chugs along like an efficient machine, analyzing, organizing, plotting, and planning. It is the side that handles language, reading, writing, and mathematics. It can be a bit of a nag, but it gets things done.

My mother had a strong right brain, and my father had a strong left brain, so they each supplied something the other lacked. I think this is one reason why their marriage, despite all the bumps, stayed so strong for so long.

Artists cannot explain their creativity because the right side of the brain has no language. Edward Hopper refused to explain his paintings, saying, "The whole answer is there on the canvas." Cezanne said, "If I think while I am painting, everything goes to pieces." An artist friend once told me she knew a painting was finished only when she saw her hand starting to paint black lines around it.

My mother's early paintings are my favorites. I can sense her excitement as she captures a landscape in strong, simple brush strokes.

Her brush strokes became more tentative when she switched from landscapes to portraits. She wanted to please, so she ignored what was before her. She flattered. She removed scars, moles, and wrinkles. She made her customers look years younger and pounds lighter.

She began to work from photographs when she switched to portraits. She even painted a few posthumous portraits from photographs. Photographs helped her get a good likeness, but they took the spontaneity and freshness out of her work. I don't like her late portraits as much as her muscular early paintings.

My mother was a good artist, but she never became great because she did not develop her own style and make her own statement. She simply imitated the style of the great painters. Her early landscapes look like Thomas Hart Benton. Her middle paintings look like Cezanne. Her late portraits are in the style of Monet. She would have made a great forger.

I learned a lot about marketing by watching my mother in action. She was a brilliant self-promoter. She never left a cocktail party without bagging a commission for a portrait. She paid for my delivery by painting a portrait of her obstetrician's wife. She met the Duke and Duchess of Windsor at a charity event, and, somehow, the next day, they ended up in her studio sitting for their portraits.

She boasted about her portraits so much I thought they were keeping the whole family afloat financially. Today, I know that she never made much money from them. She had to charge what the market would pay, and that was not nearly enough to support us. In her best years, she might make enough money to buy a few pieces of furniture for our house.

She often disparaged businessmen—as boring, narrow, and only interested in money. My father, the businessman who was paying our bills, listened without a word of protest.

My parents were at their best as grandparents. They were not responsible for raising their grandchildren, so they could relax and enjoy them. They were able to give them what they could not give their children. They missed all of Lynn, Frank, and my milestones—first words, first steps—but they made up for this with their grandchildren.

Pictured:CJM's mother, Helena Edey Johnson, painting a pastel portrait of CJM's daughter, Hope MacKay Crosier, in the late 1970s.

My famously impatient father had a patience that never flagged when he was with Rob and Hope. He crawled around for hours on his hands and knees while they fought to ride on his back, shrieking with delight.

He never took me, Lynn, or Frank fishing, but he took my children out in the Whaler for hours in Edgartown harbor, where they caught small fish called scup. He methodically scaled and gutted the scup on the lawn, and we cooked them for lunch. "Delicious!" we exclaimed as we picked through the dense thicket of needle-sharp bones for a few scraps of sweet pink flesh.

Pictured:CJM's father as a grandfather, with Rob on his back.

Was this the same man who never said a word while I watched him shave or went with him on runs in London?

My mother set up tea parties on the lawn for Hope's stuffed animals. She took Rob and Hope to art exhibits. She spent hours creating a coloring book for Hope by making black-and-white drawings of paintings by her favorite artists—Matisse, Picasso, Renoir, Van Gogh, Gaugin, and Monet.

Was this the same woman whose daughter had a heavy German accent when she was a child because her mother never spoke to her?

I was delighted to see how much my parents loved my children, but I was sorry they could not show the same love and attention to us when we were small.

I struggled all my life to become a success to impress my mother. This backfired when I became an eye surgeon and became her rival for the world's attention. She did not tolerate rivals.

One day, she was introduced to a famous writer and political figure. She expected him to say: "So you are Helena Edey, the famous portrait

239

painter!" (She used her maiden name, Edey, to paint.) Instead, he said: "So you are Dr. MacKay's mother!" I could tell by her miffed tone of voice that she felt humiliated.

She had that same tone in her voice when she told me one of her Far Hills dinner partners raved about Dr. MacKay, telling her I saved his sight. I was getting more attention than she was. Being the center of attention was proof she mattered. This was not a happy situation for a woman who wanted to be the only star in the sky.

Then I did something she could never forgive nor forget. I let Bill Draper paint my portrait in exchange for some eye surgery. She was apoplectic with anger and jealousy.

Bill was one of the top three portrait painters of his time. He was my mother's nemesis. He grabbed all the big portrait commissions— presidents, movie stars, CEOs of major corporations—she thought should rightfully be hers. Everybody in my family was expected to say when the name of Bill Draper came up: "He is not nearly as good at painting portraits as Helena Edey."

Bill came to my office one day, hopping mad. He complained his surgeon had put in the "wrong lens" during his cataract operation. He was planning to sue that surgeon. I knew and respected his surgeon. I was certain he had done a good job. Solving this case would be a challenge.

As I expected, his operated eye was perfect. He saw 20/20 without correction. His intra-ocular lens was in perfect position. It had no flaws or scratches. Suddenly, I had a hunch about what was wrong. I have an advantage—I am the daughter of an artist and an expert in color vision. "How is your color vision?" I asked. "Terrible!" he roared. "All I can see is blue!"

Bill Draper is the perfect example of the importance of taking a good history. This color information gave me the clue to solve the mystery, enable him to paint again, and prevent a lawsuit.

I knew that the retinal pigments absorb near-ultraviolet light, but humans who have their own natural lens never see this light because the lens blocks it. Now Bill had a plastic lens in his eye, and the intra-ocular lenses at that time did not absorb near-UV light. He was seeing near-UV light for the first time, and it was driving him crazy.

Claude Monet, the Impressionist painter, had the same problem. After cataract surgery, he closed his operated eye to paint and only used his un-operated eye, complaining: "I am drowning in blue!" This and other fascinating stories are told in Patrick Trevor-Roper's book, *The World Through Blunted Sight.*

Bill was especially sensitive to color because he was an artist. A patient who was not an artist might not have been as bothered as he was.

The solution was simple. I ordered Bill lenses in his glasses that block UV light, and *voila!* He could paint again. He was so delighted he painted my portrait for free. Today, this problem no longer exists because all the intra-ocular lenses block near-UV light.

I told my mother repeatedly that her portrait of me was better than Bill's portrait—which I truly believed—but it was no use. This was a declaration of war.

She began to describe my office, then at One East 71st Street, as "–a convenient place for me to go to the toilet when I am in New York getting my portraits framed." One day, she came into my office unannounced and headed straight for the bathroom. I was not suspicious. I did not notice she was carrying three large boxes labeled *Bergdorf Goodman*, *Lord and Taylor*, and *Saks*.

She stayed in the bathroom for a surprisingly long time. She came out wearing a formal evening gown. She sashayed past the gaping patients and nurses, saying: "I need a new dress for Malcolm Forbes's party. This dress is a good color, but I am not sure about the neckline. I will show you the other two, and you can help me decide."

Malcolm Forbes was my parents' neighbor, friend, and bridge partner. He was the greatest media mogul of his time. In addition to motorcycles, yachts, and houses on three continents, he owned a dozen fabulously expensive enamel eggs created by Faberge for the Imperial Family of Russia.

The Forbes annual party was the most important Far Hills social event of the year. Everybody who was anybody came to that party—financial tycoons, movie stars, royalty, and heads of state. The air thundered with helicopters landing on his private heliport. One year at the Forbes party, my father sat next to Imelda Marcos at dinner; the next year, Elizabeth Taylor.

Malcolm was an avid balloonist. At his party, he always stationed a balloon, usually, the one shaped like his *chateau* in Normandy, out front to greet his guests and give them a ride. I was sunbathing near my parents' pool one day when I heard a hiss. I looked up, and there was Malcolm in his hot air balloon, sailing over my head.

I thought my mother's ball gowns in my office were her way of putting me in my place. She was telling me, in no uncertain terms, that her career mattered and mine did not. There wasn't room in our family for more than one celebrity.

My face flamed with anger. The purpose of my office was to save sight. It was not for fashion shows. I had more important things to do than worry about my mother's dress for the Forbes party. I told her—with considerable heat—to get out, fast.

Today, I regret that I was so abrupt. I had no right to judge my mother. She went down one path, and I went down another. In my arrogance, I thought my path was superior to hers.

She needed my help to achieve her maximum sparkle to compete with the other sparkling people at the Forbes party. She did not deserve my anger. She deserved my understanding. If she came back to my office today with her ball gowns, I would not be angry; I would be amused. I would promise to help her pick out the most becoming dress as soon as I finished seeing patients.

A friend asked me who I wanted to meet in Heaven. I did not hesitate. "My parents." I replied. I did not appreciate them while they were alive. I would welcome a chance to make amends.

I would thank my father for being the rock underneath our family. I would sit back and watch my mother sparkle. Those casually inconsiderate remarks of hers would roll right off my back. I would know she means no harm.

My mother and I went through some difficult years after the ball-gowns-in-the-office incident. My guess is that she did not approve of my career because it took me, her mother's substitute, away from her. She wanted a different daughter. I wanted a different mother. We were stuck, like two deer who had locked their horns together in a forest.

I was juggling a lot of balls. My practice was expanding rapidly. I was traveling to scientific meetings all over the world. I had two children and a husband, and they needed me more than she did. I did not want to sympathize with her as she complained, for the thousandth time, that she had married the wrong man—the father I loved. I wanted her to grow up.

I spent my childhood and early adulthood trying to win my mother's approval. I spent my middle age angry at her for not giving me that approval. Everybody else in my life appreciated me and thanked me. Not my mother.

One of Woody Allen's movies shows his mother's immense head as she lectures him from the sky. My parents had the same power over me. They seemed larger than life, even when they were both old and frail. I never stopped trying to impress them, even after they were both dead.

One day, I overheard one of my mother's friends say to my mother: "Cynthia has developed quite good taste in clothes." "Nonsense!" my mother snorted. "Cynthia has no taste in clothes whatsoever." Dressing well was her department, and she didn't want me horning in on it. Remarks like that made me think she didn't love me. My mother loomed so large in my mind that her approval was the only one that mattered.

My strategy of depending on my mother's validation for my self-image was doomed to fail. She never praised anybody, including her children. I was beating her and myself up, trying to get something from her that she could not give. The definition of insanity is to be out of touch with reality. My lifelong quest for her approval was, frankly, insane.

My mother professed great sympathy for the poor. She was, however, unfailingly rude to poor people like taxi drivers and waitresses. She saved her most intense scorn for people who started out poor and then made a lot of money. She was scathing about houses that had flashy, expensive, ostentatious décor—unless they were in Far Hills and had Impressionist paintings on the walls.

I never understood why she was so critical of these people. Most of my ophthalmology friends were in that category. Weren't they admirable for working hard and being successful? Why was her taste superior to theirs? To her, money only had value if it was in the hands of the "right" people?

Today, I think her need to feel superior was a sign that she was fundamentally insecure. She disparaged other people to make herself feel important.

She drew a strict line between necessities and luxuries. "Necessities" allowed—even required—her to spend money. Necessities included two houses, a cook, a cleaning lady, three cars, memberships in two clubs in Edgartown and two in Far Hills (and, for a while, the Cosmopolitan Club in New York), plus six-week trips to Florida in the winter, and Europe in the spring and fall.

She did not allow herself to spend money on "luxuries". The luxuries she scorned included expensive food (she bought cheap *A&P* peanut butter instead of slightly more expensive *Skippy*) and expensive clothes—unless they were on sale. She snapped up sale clothes voraciously, even if they did not fit and were the wrong color. I found a half dozen of these sale items clothes in her closets after she died, the tags still on them. She allowed the candles on her dining room table to burn down so far, her cleaning lady had to scrape them out with a knife.

Did I mention artists are not reasonable?

Then, my mother developed a cataract. I had removed cataracts from three of my uncles, three of my aunts, and my mother-in-law, but I was not about to operate on her, especially since the cataract was in the eye she used for painting (her other eye was blind from macular degeneration). I sent her to one of my friends for surgery.

The day of her operation, I put on scrubs and went into the OR with her. I held her hand while she was under the drapes, while my colleague and the nurses tactfully pretended not to notice. She never thanked me, but after that, she stopped telling people that my office was her favorite New York bathroom.

Something always puzzled me about my parents' wedding—there was almost nobody there. I knew from the wedding photographs the wedding party consisted only of Grandma and Grandpa Johnson, Granny Edey, my mother's brother Mait Edey and his wife Helen, my father's brother Ben Johnson and his wife, and a friend or two.

My mother's explanation for the small number of guests was that she and my father wanted a small wedding because Uncle Coddy had had a huge society wedding a month earlier, so they chose something modest. There was just a hint of moral superiority in her voice.

I got a subtly different slant on my parents' wedding the day I asked my mother—unexpectedly, so she did not have the time to carefully frame her answer—why her guest list was so limited. I caught her off guard. She replied, with some feeling, that her mother would never have been able to "get through"—these were her exact words— "a big wedding".

My antennae shot up. I mulled over her answer for years. Why was my grandmother not able to tolerate a big wedding? I finally put two and two together—long after my mother died, unfortunately.

My mother told me many times that the Granny Edey I loved so much— the woman who was my staunch defender and support—suffered what my mother called a "nervous breakdown" when my mother was nine years old. Granny left her husband and two young children and spent nine months in a mental hospital.

My mother always put a positive spin on this chapter of her life. She lived with Granny's two older sisters—her maiden aunts, Margaret and Helen Armstrong—and they taught her how to draw. Her brother, Mait, went to live with his unmarried Edey aunt, and she fed him delicious food, so he finally gained some weight. Wasn't that lucky for them both?

I do not buy my mother's rosy view of this chapter in her life. She was separated from her mother for nine months—an eternity for a nine-year-old girl. I'm sure she worried for the rest of her life that Granny would have another breakdown. She, like me, spent her childhood on edge, afraid she might set off her high-strung mother.

Granny seemed strong and decisive to me, but I now believe she had a mental illness—most likely the Armstrong family disease, manic depression. No wonder my mother had problems mothering me. She was not well mothered herself. Remember that her father—the pillar of her life, the parent who was predictably loving and kind—died when she was only seventeen.

My mother was a firecracker, fizzing with charm and beauty and talent, and my father was the platform that held her up and allowed her to sparkle. He often said he could not believe she had married him. He persuaded her to come to his fiftieth reunion at Hotchkiss by saying: "You must come because you are my greatest achievement."

He wrote this poem to celebrate their 50th wedding anniversary:

> *"For fifty years, I've lived with her –*
> *   – the best years of my life.*
> *I've never ceased to wonder why she chose to be my wife.*
> *How many opportunities to pick another man!*
> *How easily I could have ended up an "also-ran"!*
> *And I will never cease to think as long as I survive,*
> *Because of her, I'll always be the luckiest man alive."*

Shortly before my 25th reunion from Harvard, I got a questionnaire from a psychologist who was studying my class at ten-year intervals, trying to determine the traits that lead to a successful life. One of her questions was: "Is your father proud of you?" I had no idea what he would say, so I asked him.

His answer poured out of him as if a dam had been swept away. I do not remember his exact words, but it was clear he was proud of me—very proud. I could hardly see through my tears. I had come so close to never hearing him say those words. That was my father—face of stone outside, volcanic feelings inside.

My father kept his good looks and massive strength well into his seventies. In 1992, when he was seventy-nine, he had a stroke. It was the most common type of stroke—a classic left middle cerebral artery infarction.

A guaranteed way to break your heart is to visit your father in an intensive care unit. He could not talk, and he was paralyzed on the right side of his body. He seemed lost, scared, and confused. He held up the cardiac monitor bumping on his chest. His face turned red as he struggled to speak. Finally the word, *"Pourquoi?"* (French for *"Why?"*) exploded out of his mouth. A few French-speaking cells in some remote part of his brain had escaped unharmed.

I sat down on his bed. I took his hand. I told him his speech and his right arm and leg were damaged, but if he worked hard, he could get them back. He listened intently. He seemed relieved. I was a doctor. I knew the truth. Except that I didn't. The speech center on the left side of his brain had been obliterated by the stroke. I wasn't sure he would get his speech back.

His speech therapist was more optimistic. The right side of his brain, the side that contains music, was not damaged. She thought he could relearn a few simple words because he was so musical. She gave him a tape recorder and told him to sing his favorite song all the way through without one mistake.

He chose: "It Had to Be You." He could not play the guitar any more, but—to my surprise and delight—he could still play the piano. I heard him practicing whenever I visited my parents. He would start the recorder, begin to sing, made a mistake, say, "Damn!" in a quiet voice, erase what he had recorded, and start all over again. He worked all day, every day. He only stopped when he had to eat.

My silent father was fighting the battle of his life... to speak to my mother. Painfully, word by word, he recovered almost half his speech…through his music. The therapist was amazed.

My father's stroke transformed my mother in a flash from gad-about coquette into devoted wife. She focused on this man she had criticized all her life like a lioness guarding her cub. She was right there beside him all day, every day, gritting her teeth and saying: "Don't worry, you are going to get better. You are a lot better than you were yesterday."

I believe my father's stroke was a gift to both of my parents. It made my mother realize the man she had been searching for all her life was right there in her own house—her quiet, bald husband. She was able to show him during the five years they had together just how much she loved him.

My father wanted nobody in the house except my mother after his stroke. At the age of eighty, she fired the cook, bought a few cookbooks, and taught herself how to cook. To her surprise, she enjoyed cooking. She even began to watch cooking shows on television.

One day, she called Lynn and asked, "How do I roast a chicken?" "Put it in a pan and shove it into the oven." Lynn said. "I know *that*, but do I put it on its front or its back?" she said.

After his stroke, my father's emotions went up and down without warning—sudden tears, then sudden rages. This is called *emotional liability*, and all stroke victims have this problem. Now, it was my mother's turn to be patient. She had to think for them both. The letters and checks he wrote were illegible, so she had to get to the mailbox before the mailman came, take them out, and re-write them.

My mother's macular degeneration steadily got worse. Slowly, agonizingly, she went blind. An artist who was losing her sight was living with a singer who could not speak or think. She became his brain. He became her eyes, and his powerful limbs took over for her arthritic ones. Together, they made one functional person. They were like two trees that had fallen into each other's branches and were holding each other up.

My parents had five more years together before another stroke in 1997 took him away for good. He leaves behind him a faint sweetness, like one of Granny Edey's magical dissolving peppermints.

My mother lived on for another four years, but there was nothing inside her but misery. She never got back her sparkle, although she put up a good enough front to fool most people.

My mother was easy to love after my father died. All her haughty coldness disappeared, and my resentment went with it. I called her every night, she told me her troubles, and I wove a web of comforting words around her. She always ended by saying, in a surprised tone of voice: "Well, now I feel better."

One day, she suddenly burst into tears. "I always wore such shabby old nightgowns!" she said, between sobs. "I wish I had worn better nightgowns for your father!" This was her way of telling me she wished she had treated him better while he was alive. "Don't worry," I told her. "He loved you madly, especially when you were wearing those old nightgowns."

My mother never praised people, and she hated to hear other people praised. She called this: "gushing". Her anti-gushing rule was suspended only if somebody praised her portraits. This praise she lapped up as a cat laps cream, purring with pleasure.

One night, she said, "I have always preferred men to women, but now I am older, I am getting more attention from my daughters than I am from my son." This was the closest to gushing my mother ever came.

Now that my mother and I finally had a good relationship, she began to disappear before my eyes with shocking speed. Her arthritis got so bad she had to crawl up the stairs on her hands and knees, like a dog, and bump down on her rear end. Her vision got so poor she could only recognize people if they spoke to her.

Of course, she had a car accident. Luckily, she was not hurt, and she did not hurt anybody else. Lynn and I forbade her to drive, but when we were not around, she drove anyway.

Lynn and I called each other every night, trying to figure out how to help her. We offered to move her bedroom downstairs, but she said: "I want to be in my own bed in my own room." We suggested a lift on the stairs and grab rails over the tub. "They will make my house ugly." she said.

She complained all her life about living in Far Hills. Lynn and I offered to move her to New York, where all three of her children and three of her four grandchildren lived. She made this decision in her usual fashion— she asked several people for their opinion and chose the one she wanted to hear. "Grace Terry [one of her Far Hills friends] told me I must never move out of my house." she told me triumphantly.

Lynn took her to several retirement homes. She rejected them all, saying, "The food is bad, the people are not my type, and I hate fluorescent lights."

My mother did not have a strong enough inner life to be happy in a retirement home. She needed external tokens of success to feel complete—her paintings, the adoration of men, her palatial house. She put up with the loneliness, the inconvenience, and the danger of living in her big house because she had a horror of being ordinary. Her house was her identity. It was grand, so it made her feel grand.

I only realized how much that house meant to my parents after they died, and I waded through the chaotic mess of thousands of family photographs and letters they had tossed into drawers and boxes. I discovered dozens and dozens of photographs of the house—in spring, fall, and winter, from close and far away, from every possible angle, from the time it was perched on top of a bald hill to recent times when trees had grown up around it.

The house was a symbol of their love. The letters between my parents always mention it. It was like an idol. Of course, she couldn't leave it.

She was eighty-nine and already planning her ninetieth birthday party and trying to decide what she would wear, when, in 2001, she, too, had a stroke. She could barely speak when I visited her in the ICU.

"Zestril?" she hissed. She wanted to be sure she was getting her blood pressure medicine.

"Don't worry." I told her. "I have already checked. It is in your IV."

"Relafen?" she croaked.

Then she looked at me as if she was really seeing me for the first time in my life.

"Lots of love," she whispered.

The last word I heard from her was: "Love." Her way of expressing love was a confusing jumble of demands, jealousy, expectations, and pride, but those words came from some primitive part of her brain the stroke could not obliterate, and I believed them.

Lynn and Frank wanted to put down a feeding tube. I talked them out of it. I knew my mother did not want to end her life a cripple, turned twice a day, watching TV. An army of her friends called to support me.

We moved her out of the ICU into a private room. We switched her care to her cardiologist, who ordered a morphine drip. She died, quietly and peacefully, a few days later. The last problem I solved for my mother was to give her a pain-free, dignified death.

My relationship with my father was simple. I knew he loved me, and he knew I loved him. I was sad when he died, and I miss him to this day, but I was able to grieve and move on.

My mother's death was another story. I did not see her often. I long ago stopped expecting her to show interest in my life or compassion for my problems. I assumed her death would have only a minor impact on me. Wrong. She did not occupy much space in my life, but she occupied an oversized space in my mind.

I was crushed by her loss. Her death seemed like a catastrophe. I think I was grieving for something that never happened. She died without giving me the one thing I wanted—a full-throated celebration of who I was. Now, I had lost the chance forever.

My mother was not the mother I wanted. I thought she was a party girl. She probably thought I was a grim, prissy drudge. Yet we were connected by an intense, fiery bond. Both of us had a burning ambition to make something of our lives. We were meshed in a never-ending cycle of needs and rejections, expectations and disappointments, admiration, and misunderstanding.

My mother seemed larger than life to many people. As my cousin's husband said: "There was such a lot of her for such a small woman." Men half her age fell in love with her. I talked to one recently. He still speaks of her wistfully. He will never forget her.

Nothing stopped this woman. She took back intimate apparel to stores—bathing suits, underpants—labeled, *"NOT RETURNABLE,"* and the saleslady accepted them meekly and gave her credit. She ate more food than a lumberjack and never gained an ounce.

It was hard to believe all that talent and beauty could just... disappear. Her life had been so glamorous and rich, and her death was so banal and ordinary. I half expected her to make a deal with Death, persuading him to pass her by in return for painting his portrait.

My father was cremated. My mother left his ashes at the funeral parlor for a year and a half until I went down with her to pick them up. When she saw that small white box, about the size of a dictionary but much heavier, her face turned grey, and she seemed to shrink in size. After that, whenever I looked at people, I saw them as small, surprisingly heavy white boxes.

We put him on a shelf in the library. How practical. How lacking in symbol and ritual. My mother was not good at making decisions in general. The decision of where to bury my father was way beyond her capabilities. He sat on the shelf in the library until she, too, died.

After she, too, was cremated, Lynn, Frank, and I took the two white boxes outside our parent's house. We stood over a patch of myrtle and took turns pouring their ashes into an urn made by Lynn. It was strange to feel my parents pouring through my fingers, but this small, intimate ceremony gave me a feeling of pride and completeness. We were the ones who handled our parents' ashes, not some gloomy undertaker. We had managed to make their death personal.

I think our parents would be happy to know their children had tucked them into their final resting place, mingled together as they had been throughout their lives. Some of their ashes fell on the myrtle. My mother would have been pleased. She loved to fertilize her myrtle.

The decision of where to bury the urn was simple—in the plot next to Grandpa and Grandma, which my father had purchased years ago.

After they died, I began the task of looking through my parents' letters. I found many surprises. Some of them left me in tears.

In 1955, when I was thirteen and we were in London, my father wrote a letter to his mother, Grandma Johnson. He tells her I am "–becoming quite a young lady these days." I take more time fixing my hair. I have started to wear silk stockings. I take my glasses off frequently. I am "a curious mixture of child and adult." He had been watching me with interest and love throughout my childhood, while I assumed, from his stone face, that he never saw me.

Several of the letters had been written, but never sent. A postcard to me from my mother says on one side: "Don't just live the length of your life; live the width as well." On the other side, she writes: "You certainly live the width of your life if anyone does." She really did see—and celebrate—the busy complexity of my life.
She starts her letters "Dearest Doctor Cynthia." She ends, "Do take care of your precious self/Lots of love/Can't wait to see you/Much love and congratulations to a wonderful daughter of whom we are enormously and constantly proud."

She was able to gush in a letter, but when we were face to face, she could not. I take these letters to be her true self. I am mortified and sad that I could not feel her love while she was still alive.

Now Lynn and I faced the Herculean job of cleaning out the house where our parents had lived for sixty years. Frank could not help. He had to cope with his mother-in-law's big Far Hills house, which was also crammed with stuff.

We knew this job would not be easy. Our mother's mind was creative, not logical. All the organizational talents she had went into her painting and maintaining her beauty. We expected the worst. The reality was even worse than we expected. The public rooms and guest bedrooms looked as if they belonged in a palace. Her bedroom looked like the residence of a homeless person.

Her bedroom was so disorganized she could never find things she already had, so she bought the same thing over and over—her favorite lipstick, for example—until she had dozens of everything. We could never convince her to throw anything out. One of us would descend periodically on the pandemonium of her dressing room, tidy it up, and throw out all those extra cosmetics. The minute we left, she fished everything out of the wastebasket, and in a few days, her room was back to its usual chaos.

She had kicked my father out of their bedroom because he snored, and his empty bed gave her a spot to store even more useless junk. She covered it a foot high with outdated *S and H* green stamps, recipes clipped from newspapers that were yellow and curled with age, outdated coupons for foods she did not eat, and pots and pans she already had, and unanswered letters dating back years. At the bottom was her birth certificate.

My parents' house had six bedrooms and seventeen closets. Many of these closets were the size of small bedrooms. Each bedroom had at least two bureaus. Every closet, shelf, and bureau was stuffed with a comical mixture of trash and treasure.

We discovered that she dealt with clothes she did not like by throwing them on the floor of her closet. I felt like an archeologist as I excavated this mound. I could date each layer by the presents I gave her for Christmas and her birthday—tasteful, understated clothes that were not remotely sexy enough for her.

At one point, Lynn and I looked at each other and began to laugh. Her clothes were more stylish and risqué than our clothes.

She hung an old shirt of mine within easy reach—a rose-colored blouse with a high neck I gave her to paint in. She almost never took it off. It had magic for her because it had been mine.

Then we found her diaries. I pounced on them eagerly. I was fifty-nine, and I had no idea of who my mother was. Here was my chance to find out. I read several pages, and then I gave up. The diaries contained a recitation of her colds, portraits, and parties. There was not one word about her thoughts or feelings. My elusive mother had evaded me yet again.

My mother often told me she burned all her suitors' love letters. She said this so often she made me suspicious. Sure enough, Lynn and I discovered a stash of love letters hidden between two books in the library. She could not bear to throw them out. They were trophies of her success with men.

After we had cleaned out all the closets and bureaus, I saw something shiny poking out from under one of the beds. It looked like a storage box. It *was* a storage box. My mother had put one under every bed. Oh, no, here we go again, I thought—more junk mixed with priceless family mementos. I was right.

As I gaped at the pathetic piles of useless trash she cherished so fiercely, I said to myself: "This is insane." I suddenly saw her in a new light. She had a hoarding disorder. This master illusionist had re-packaged everything, including herself. She was able to conceal her hoarding because her house was so large.

Hoarders are paralyzed by anxiety when they try to give away possessions—including things that have no value to them. Now I understand why she fished cosmetics from her wastepaper basket and saved expired S and H green stamps.

Many artists are hoarders. They collect junk that appears useless to non-artists. At the time of his death, Picasso had twenty-three rooms crammed with trash he picked up from the dump. El Anatsui, a contemporary Ghanaian artist, creates all his art from trash, usually metal caps from liquor bottles and soft drink cans.

Hoarding is thought to be a form of an obsessive-compulsive disorder. It often develops along with other mental illnesses, such as dementia and schizophrenia. My mother never struck me as suffering from a mental illness, but I now suspect she had a mild form of the Armstrong family disease, manic depression, and I have more sympathy for her.

It took Lynn and me six months to clear out the house. When we were almost finished, we found a box on one of the top shelves of my father's dressing room. It contained awards from his years at Hotchkiss School and Harvard.

Hotchkiss awards a trophy to its most outstanding student each year called the *Treadway Prize*. This prize is a big deal. The name of every winner is engraved on the wall. My father had won the Treadway Prize, and he never told us.

Lynn and I were clearing out the Far Hills house when we heard our mother had died. Lynn left to be with Peter. I lay down on a couch in the living room. I stayed there for hours. I feasted my eyes on every object. I tried to burn it into my memory.

These objects had seen family members come and go. They watched over sixty Thanksgivings, Christmases, and Easters. They saw three children, and five grandchildren, grow up. The clocks had ticked away the lives of three generations.

Every object told me a story. The blue-and-white antique Dutch tiles around the fireplace once surrounded the fireplace of my great-grandfather David Maitland Armstrong's house, *Danskammer*, on the Hudson River. The portraits of three of my ancestors who fought in the Revolutionary War looked down on me with a calm, steady gaze.

Almost all the objects were family pieces. Some came from Ellistan. Others came from Granny's Eel Pond house and her New York apartment. Others came from DMA's house at 58 West 10th Street. Some had been in my family for eight, nine, ten generations. Some would be mine—for a while. Then, they would pass on to my children and grandchildren.

My parents brought me into this house a few days after I was born. I longed to be with them, but they were almost never there. This house was my constant companion, my surrogate parent, a substitute for my parents' love.

Comfortable chairs took the place of comforting arms. The faces of ancestors on the walls looked down on me kindly when the faces of my parents were absent. Nothing ever changed here. This was the rock under my life.

I rejected my childhood life of privilege and high society. Far Hills was an impossible ideal of luxury I did not want and could not afford. I had taken a more realistic and exhilarating path, but this house was always there for me, a refuge of beauty and elegance.

I did not let myself see that my marriage, which began with such high hopes thirty-nine years ago, had steadily deteriorated. The death of my parents revealed the truth. The house I shared with Malcolm was not now, and never would be, my home. My parents' house, with all its thorns, was my only real home.

CHAPTER TWENTY

The Other Woman

Shortly after my parents died, I went to Sarasota, Florida to deliver a paper at the Association of Research in Vision and Ophthalmology (ARVO) meeting. I took a walk on the beach and saw two seagulls mating. They were screaming into the wind with jubilant shrieks. They looked so alive and happy. A thought flashed through my mind that they were free, but I was stuck.

My life was strangely lacking in joy. It was getting harder and harder for me to pry myself out of bed in the morning. Life seemed to be passing before me as if it was a dream. I felt as if I was a spectator of my life instead of living it.

I felt like an imposter while I was working in my office. The testimonials, awards, and diplomas on my office walls, once a source of pride, had lost all their meaning for me. I felt as if I was renting the office from some celebrity.

My mind wasn't working right. I was becoming more and more forgetful. I left my calendar in my OR locker at the hospital and had to go all the way back from Brooklyn to retrieve it. I left my earrings at a swimming pool. I left my purse at a restaurant. I forgot to sign the cleaning lady's check. I did not remember to pack tennis shirts when we went to Long Island for the weekend and had to buy some. This was not usual behavior for a woman who prided herself on being organized and in control.

I could not figure out what was wrong. My parents had died, true, but that was to be expected. Rob and Hope had left home years ago. Both were happily married, and both had a child.

My life must have looked like an unqualified success to the outside world. All my dreams had come true. My practice was booming. My children were happy. Peter Gouras and I were making important discoveries. I was convinced that my thirty-nine-year-old marriage would last for the rest of my life. Malcolm no longer complained about my long hours at work, and I thought the matter was settled. So why wasn't I happy?

I distracted myself by pouring energy into my work. I wrote new ophthalmology teaching programs. I lectured at Grand Rounds at teaching hospitals all around the New York area. I traveled around the world delivering papers about my research with Peter Gouras.

I focused all my energy on my outside world. I left nothing for my inner world. I never allowed myself any quiet time to allow new thoughts to bubble up, to think about who I was and where I was going.

I could solve other people's problems, but I could not solve my own. I could diagnose depression in my patients. I could not diagnose depression in myself.

I did not allow myself to see that life with Malcolm had become a dismal duty. I was afraid to grow old with this man. He refused to recognize weakness in any form, in me or in himself. When I got sick, he got angry and blamed me for not getting proper care.

Today, I realize that Malcolm was also hurting. The culture he grew up in taught him men must be strong and perfect. They cannot show emotions or ask for help. The only emotion Malcolm felt comfortable showing was anger. Malcolm's mother had such high expectations for his career he was bound to fail. He often told me that his education at top-ranked schools gave him an obligation to be a success, and he had failed to live up to this obligation.

I never let myself recognize how incompatible Malcolm and I are. Our conversations were always about practical things, such as planning our week. We were partners in a small business instead of partners in love. I love art, theatre, concerts, novels, poetry, travel, and adventures in the wilderness. Malcolm loves politics, playing tennis and squash, cutting his lawn, and history. I enjoy music. Malcolm is tone-deaf. If I put music on the radio, he snapped it off. The only interest we shared was frequent vigorous exercise.

We had unrealistic expectations of each other from the very beginning of our marriage. I never loved him for who he was, only for what he could do for me. I expected him to take care of me, and he expected me to take care of him. He often complained he had helped me with my career, and now it was my turn to help him with his career, which I could not do.

Malcolm began criticizing me loudly on the tennis court. Some of our friends refused to play with us. Several members of my family told me later they did not say anything about the way Malcolm treated me because they knew I would not listen.

I now realize Malcolm was behaving badly because he no longer loved me. Marriage had brought out the worst in us. Years of small, almost imperceptible, unkind acts had destroyed our love. The offhand critical remark. The stupid, destructive spats over nothing. Saving our best for other people, for unimportant strangers, and saving our worst for each other. The spitefulness. Petty little grudges.

We began to play childish games with each other. We both tried to be last to a meeting, to show the other person we were the busiest and most important. All that accomplished was to make us late for everything. We were stuck in roles. Malcolm played the stern adult. I played the baby, not capable of making decisions—except when they concerned my career.

I let Malcolm control our personal life in return for the social protection of marriage. I thought I could keep him happy by doing what he wanted on the weekends, which was to drive to our house on Long Island, play tennis at the Piping Rock Club, and socialize with friends he grew up with.

During the week, on days I did not have surgery, I began to do things I loved, but Malcolm did not. Increasingly, I felt most alive when I was away from Malcolm. I suspect he felt the same way about me.

I sang chamber music for twenty-five years with two friends who played the violin and piano. I took long bike rides with another friend. I convinced a neurologist, a professional pianist in his earlier life, to play the piano while I sang German *lieder*. When Malcolm came home when George and I were making music together, he stormed into the library, slammed the door, and turned the TV to top volume.

One day, while I was taking out a cataract, I started to sing along with the music. I forgot my patient was an opera singer. He told me later I had a lovely voice. Would I like to sing opera duets with him? Would I! We sang opera duets for a dozen years. He seduced me in Italian, German, and French. This was living.

I resisted going into therapy, but Rob talked me into it. Once I started, I could not remember what I had been so worried about. I expected it to be difficult and agonizing, but it was interesting and comforting. It was not about blaming or judging my parents. It was about understanding how the past persisted in my present life and figuring out how to separate this past from the present.

I tried to use the insights from therapy to reconfigure my relationship with Malcolm, but he would not see my side of the issue. He complained I was picking fights with him.

I became a doctor because I wanted to heal sick eyes. I did not go into medicine to make money, but as I saw more and more patients and did more and more surgery, I started to make a lot of money—more than Malcolm. This money had no meaning to me because I did not own it in my mind. I handed it to Malcolm and let him decide how to spend it.

Most husbands would be delighted if their wives made a lot of money. Malcolm was not one of them. His upbringing made him believe a husband should be the primary bread winner. Earning more money than your wife was what made a man into a man. When I started to make serious money, he thought his role was diminished.

It was so rare in those days for a wife to make more money than her husband that Malcolm and I were interviewed for a magazine article on the subject. Malcolm told the reporter: "We live off the money I make, and we put the money Cynthia makes into savings." This is nonsense, of course, but I thought he was right.

I was a busy surgeon. I was reattaching retinas and removing cataracts for thousands of patients, many of them rich and famous. I was flying around the world to lecture at research meetings. I was teaching hundreds of future ophthalmologists. I was earning real money. Yet I let Malcolm decide what clothes I should wear, where we lived, how we raised our children, how we spent our money, and how I voted.

When I saw the play *A Doll's House* by Henrik Ibsen during that time, I almost jumped out of my seat. The marriage of the characters in the play had a stunning and eerie resemblance to my own marriage. The husband, Torvald, played a role that was uncannily like the role played by Malcolm. I saw myself in Nora, the wife.

When Nora married Torvald, she was a charming child who always did his bidding (Me, back in 1964). Torvald expects Nora to continue to be dependent on him—a doll for him to play with—but Nora becomes a new person, a strong woman who develops her own values and opinions. She wants to control her own life, so she leaves her doll's house. Everybody in the audience cheered when she did so.

It was time for me to leave my doll's house, but I was too afraid. I had never lived alone. I went straight from my parents' house to living with Malcolm. I did not think I could take care of myself. I thought I could not function unless I had a man to take care of me. I gave up my life so completely to Malcolm I was cowed into silence in his presence.

Malcolm did not have warm relationships with his own family, so he did not understand how close I felt to my family. When Hope married Louis Crosier in Edgartown in 1998, I invited all my Johnson and Edey cousins to the wedding. Malcolm did not invite one of his cousins.

When Uncle Ben died, all twelve of the Johnson cousins came to his funeral. I badly wanted Rob and Hope to come. They were both at Princeton, only forty-five minutes away, and it was the reading period between their last class and the beginning of exams, so they didn't have to miss any classes. They were adults, but Malcolm did not allow them to make up their own minds. He flatly refused to let them come—although Ben was my uncle, not his. As usual, I gave in.

Malcolm and I both felt unappreciated. We were becoming more and more frustrated. We were trying our best to please each other, but we did not know how. We never knew what presents to give each other. The adventurous clothes I gave him sat in his closet with their tags on. So did the dowdy, conservative, grey or brown *Brooks Brothers* suits he gave me.

Malcom disliked my charismatic, creative, unconventional Armstrong side. He kept trying to tone me down, to make me sober and respectable. If I wore a skimpy bathing suit at a beach, he would throw a towel over me.

We had an apartment in Brooklyn Heights and a weekend house on the North Shore of Long Island. I tried to make them feel like our home. I bought new rugs, furniture, and curtains. I painted the walls. I arranged and re-arranged the pictures on the wall. Nothing worked.

I felt the way I did when I was a child—always on the outside, looking in at the happiness of others. I gazed through the windows of other people's homes and ached to discover their secret. I fantasized about climbing in through the window and persuading them to adopt me.

In the beginning of our marriage, I always looked forward to the moment Malcolm came home from work. Now, when I heard his step in the hall, I felt a twinge of dread. What new crime was he going to claim I had committed that day?

I stayed in my marriage because I was afraid of living alone, but the truth was I felt less lonely when I was alone in the house than when Malcolm was there with me. We felt uncomfortable when we were together, so we scheduled non-stop social activities. We exercised compulsively. We ate out for every meal, including breakfast. We had fireplaces in both homes, but they stayed cold and dark unless we had guests.

Malcolm and I were grimly enduring each other instead of enjoying each other, but the thought of divorce never crossed my mind. I would like to claim I was a woman with high principles who believed in sticking to commitments, and that was part of it, but the truth was not quite so noble. I did not think I could run my own life. I did not recognize I was already running my own life.

Our marriage had no warmth or joy in it. It was like a *state marriage*, a political alliance between a king and a queen. Our interaction was purely intellectual. We spent all our time together rushing around frantically. We never allowed ourselves any gentle, quiet bonding time.

We both deserved better. We both needed a marriage where we were loved for ourselves. We both needed more fun and laughter in our lives. We both needed to move on and build relationships with more suitable partners.

Malcolm needed a different wife—one who was quieter and more predictable. I needed a different husband—a more adventurous man, a man who wanted to live life creatively.

Only a deep wound could cut open my frozen heart. Before I could make a real home, I had to be shoved out of my marriage. Then, one day, a savior showed up to rescue me. He was the last person I had expected.

The year I turned sixty, Malcolm began to say things that struck me as odd. He said he wished we had spent more time in the kitchen. This came from a man who refused to shop for food, had no concept of how to cook, wolfed down his food without tasting it, and never helped me cook. I should have asked myself where he was enjoying time in the kitchen.

Another day, when we were looking at a bird swimming in a pond, I said: "Look at that hooded merganser." He replied, "If I were with another woman, she would say, "Look at that duck." I never thought to ask him who that other woman might be.

One day, he unexpectedly blurted out: "Pony is my hero." Pony is the man who divorced my sister Lynn and married a younger woman. I was so flabbergasted I could not find the words to answer him.

Then he told me when a woman reaches her sixties, she has lost all her sex appeal, but a man in his sixties is at his peak attractiveness. He mentioned—modestly—that young woman often looked at him seductively on the subway. Seduction was obviously on his mind. I ignored it.

His behavior got stranger and stranger. He began to complain I did not understand men, and neither did my mother. This was bizarre—my mother had thirty-one proposals of marriage—but I did not protest. I did not want to make him angrier than he already was.

He started to get angry over ridiculously small issues. He berated me for not hanging pictures on the wall, and when I hung them, he berated me for not consulting him. His anger was so implacable and irrational I began to worry he was losing his mind.

One day, he told me, in a condescending voice, that I had been a good mother. I felt a flash of anger. Why did he have the right to decide if I was a good mother? Did this imply I was not a good wife?

Shortly after that, he told me he had fallen in love with another woman. He wanted to divorce me and marry her. He said I made him nervous. I "competed" with him because I was a big success. He didn't like my Armstrong unpredictability. I was too emotional. He was sixty-two, and he needed what he called "quiet warmth." He wanted a more restful wife.

He said his girlfriend needed him. He could help her. She activated that wonderful protective nurturing side of him, the side that likes to help people, that wants to fix things. I didn't need him now because I was a powerful surgeon.

I said: "I would have staked my life you would never break up our marriage." He looked at me coldly and replied: "Then you would have died."

A marriage therapist once told me spouses always complain about the same thing. Malcolm made me feel small and squashed. Now Malcolm told me I made him feel small and squashed.

You would think with all the clues that were staring me in the face, I would not have been surprised that Malcolm wanted to divorce me, but I was. Perhaps it was denial. Perhaps I was never able to get inside the head of that man.

I went into a full-blown panic attack. I was riddled with shame. I was a reject, a defective. I tortured myself—why her? What did she have that I did not have? I walked the deserted streets of Brooklyn Heights all hours of the night, just me and the puddles of light under the streetlamps.

My appetite disappeared. I lost twelve pounds. One evening, I went into a supermarket and vowed I would not leave until I found something I could choke down. I rejected ice cream, soup, fruit, and toast. Then I saw a package of pork rinds. I took it home, but it revolted me. I put it away on the shelf.

I was obsessed with keeping Malcolm. I begged. I cried. I reasoned. I read several books about affairs and how marriages can recover from them, underlining key points and taking copious notes. I baked him his favorite dessert every night. I developed cold sores on my tongue from the stress.

I worried breaking up our family would damage our children. I was glad my parents and Malcolm's father were dead. I knew Malcolm's elderly mother, who was our only parent still alive, would be shocked and appalled. I dragged him to three different marriage counselors. They could not fix the unfixable.

I could not concentrate on my research with Peter Gouras and my teaching, so I left both. Peter was understanding. He appreciated the work we did over twenty-five years. We had a good run.

I thought I wanted to keep Malcolm, but what I really wanted to keep was my marriage. My life goal was to be flawless. I was too perfect to get divorced. Divorce was for lesser women. It was a blow to my self-esteem and my identity. It was a failure, and I never had a failure. I had the grandiose idea I was not allowed to make mistakes. Ridiculous. I am human, and that is what humans do.

To keep myself sane, I did what I had done during internship--I began to keep a diary. When I re-read that diary today, I do not recognize those terrified screams.

Then the news came out. All our friends were buzzing about a scandal, and our divorce was the scandal. They must think there was something wrong with me if I could not keep my husband. I was mortified; I was terrified; I was ashamed; I was furious; but… I was not depressed.

My toxic marriage was what had caused my depression. Imagine that.

Malcolm used anger as a battering ram, chipping away the ties that bound me to him, shattering my delusions with his words, pummeling me away from him, and giving me my freedom. He was the savior who showed up when I needed somebody to push me out of a marriage that was killing me.

Malcolm fired me from a job where it was impossible for me to succeed. Marriage to him was a constant hopeless effort. I was always trying to be what he wanted me to be. I was never able to be myself. Malcolm was my identity. I thought divorce was the worst thing that ever happened to me. It turned out to be one of the best. It made me grow up. It proved I could handle anything. It made me compassionate and humble. It taught me how to be a better partner in the future. It gave me a partner who was exactly what I longed for.

Our divorce was chilly and practical. Thirty-nine years of marriage collapsed into two piles of money. One was for me. One was for Malcolm. I got our Brooklyn apartment. He got our house in Center Island.

My children took me in hand as if I were their child and they were my parents. Rob told me to ask a divorce lawyer friend to recommend the best divorce lawyer in New York. He said I would be much happier without Malcolm. He knew how unhappy we were together. Hope opened her big heart wide, cooked me gourmet food, and held me in her arms.

My work saved me. I could forget the mess of my personal life in my office and in the hospital.

Now I was no longer part of a couple, some people whom I thought were my good friends stopped inviting me to parties and returning my phone calls. A married man came to my apartment and tried to have sex with me.

Other people, some of them mere acquaintances, made me feel valuable even though I no longer had a husband. One couple invited me out on their boat on the Fourth of July to watch fireworks. Another couple invited me to Greece. I remember every one of these good-hearted gestures, and I pass them on to other women who are going through a divorce.

A few months went by until the wallpaper-picker re-emerged. My misery turned to fury. I roared through the apartment like a demented whirlwind, purging it of everything that reminded me of Malcolm. I took all the books off the library shelves, laid them on the floor in alphabetical order, put my novels and books of poetry back, and gave Malcolm his political and history books.

I dragged all the drab clothes Malcolm had given me off their hangers and donated them to the local thrift shop. I bought new sexy clothes in bright colors. I saw a street vendor who was selling silver belts and scarves and snapped up one of each. I bought my first car. It was surprisingly easy. I looked up a *Volvo* dealer, picked out a color I liked, paid for it, and drove it home.

The apartment began to feel like a home. My home.

During the least pleasant part of our divorce, I was sitting on a bench in Washington Square Park, watching the pigeons and nannies and students and feeling sorry for myself, when I saw a man about my age sitting opposite me. He was staring straight ahead. He seemed uncommonly alert. He had a bouquet of flowers in one hand and a small box wrapped in silver paper in the other.

An attractive woman breezed up to him. She had a small dog twinkling in front of her. It looked like a lively, fluffy mop. I took in her laughing face and zippy clothes. "Cheerful and good fun." I thought.

The man jumped up and handed her the box and the flowers. The ring flashed in the sun when she opened the box. She started to cry. They walked off together, hand in hand. They were chattering away so intently I thought they would walk straight into a tree.

This vision of joy did not thaw my frozen heart. I vowed I would never marry again. In any event, I thought, all the good men must be taken.

A week later, I read in the *Styles* section of the *New York Times* that one of my patients, a seventy-year-old woman who wrote for the Times, had married, for the first time, a handsome, smart man her age who also worked for the Times. She came to my office a few days later. I asked her how she had found such a catch at her age. "There are good men around at every age," she said. That was encouraging.

When she left, my eyes fell on a copy of *Harvard Magazine* lying on my desk. Misery made me bold. I could not possibly feel worse than I felt right now. I had nothing to lose. I remembered one of my cousins met his wife through a magazine ad. I decided to put a personal ad in the *Crimson Classifieds*. If Malcolm could get a new woman, I could get a new man.

I browsed the ads for inspiration. One ad caught my eye. The man said he was six foot one, fit and handsome. *And conceited,* I thought, but I kept reading. He liked the same things I like—reading, movies, theatre, museums, music, travel, tennis, and nature. When he mentioned motorcycle touring and loafing, I almost stopped, but, somehow, I read on. The last sentence said he was looking for a partner who wanted to live life creatively.

Something about the frank, honest way he expressed himself intrigued me. I called Warren Keegan, and we arranged to meet. Malcolm and I had been separated for only six weeks, and our divorce would not be final for four more years, but I had known about The Other Woman for more than a year. I was through with Malcolm.

Warren was my first date in forty years. The thread that connected us was thinner than a 10-0 nylon suture.

CHAPTER TWENTY-ONE

A Thrice-Divorced Husband

I flipped irritably through the New York Times as I waited, and waited, in the pea-green lounge of a woman's club in New York City. Warren had canceled not just one, but two, previous dates with me at the last minute. Now, he was late. I was getting angrier by the minute.

I cursed myself for agreeing to meet this man. Warren did not look good on paper. I knew he had been married and divorced three times. He lived in Rye, New York. When I checked him out with two friends who live there, they warned me he was a skirt-chaser. "The mothers in Rye don't let their daughters go near him." said one.

"He is a great guy and lots of fun, but he has had hundreds of girlfriends," said the other. "He is bad with women."

The last thing I needed was another skirt-chaser. I had two hours to kill before I was scheduled to meet friends for dinner, or I would have left. This blind date was a massive waste of my time.

A quick step in the hall, and there he was—six foot one, fit and handsome, as advertised. I took in a wide tie splashed with flowers, and a cocky, boyish grin. His short blond hair was lit from behind, so he looked as if light was shining from him. I knew he was sixty-six. He looked twenty years younger.

I'm good at reading body language. I expected to see a depraved lecher. Warren looked alert and confident, relaxed yet full of energy, a happy-go-lucky kid who was ready for a romp, like a stallion sniffing the air for a frolicsome mare.

His snapping blue eyes were sizing me up expertly.

"You are attractive," he said.

And you are late, I wanted to say, but the words stuck in my throat.

He skillfully slipped a hand into the small of my back as we walked towards the elevator. A shock went through me. *He sure is impudent,* I said to myself. I was determined to disapprove of everything he did or said, but—how odd—his hand seemed to know my body better than I did.

He ordered white wine; I ordered peppermint tea. He turned out to be remarkably easy to talk to. Somehow, we began to discuss Wallace Stegner, one of my favorite novelists. He also admired Stegner. We launched into a lively discussion of *The Angle of Repose.* Here was an unusual man, one who enjoyed novels.

We were only together for an hour, but he seemed strangely familiar. I felt as if I had known him all my life. I could have talked to him all night long. I caught myself looking at his mouth and wondering what it would feel like if he kissed me.

I don't know how we got on the subject, but I told him I loved to ride, and I had fox hunted. This idle piece of trivia turned out to be invaluable.

Then we parted. I had to admit he was engaging, but I did not want to see him again. A man with three divorces was the last man on earth I needed in my life. I shoved him out of my mind.

I didn't remember who he was when he called me two weeks later and invited me to join him for a week at Darwin Ranch, a dude ranch in Wyoming. He knew I liked to ride, and he wanted company.

I hesitated. I have always wanted to go to a dude ranch. I had already canceled my patients that week because I was planning to visit Lynn and Peter in Edgartown… but I turned him down. I did not want to let him know I was available at such short notice.

That afternoon, Hope and I climbed a mountain. I mentioned Warren's invitation, and she sized up the situation with lightning speed. "Call him back and tell him *yes,*" she said. "You love nature and riding. You can visit Lynn and Peter any time. Just make sure you have separate bedrooms."

We agreed to meet at the airport. I had met him only once and briefly. There were three or four men sitting in the waiting area who were possible candidates. I could not decide which one was Warren. I felt like an idiot. Then Warren looked up, and that happy smile lit up his face, and I knew exactly who he was.

Our second date was nine days long. We spent seven of those days in a one-room cabin a day's drive from civilization. It had one bed. Not king. Not a queen. A double.

I woke up to the clean, sharp scent of sagebrush. I watched a red sun rise over a mountain meadow dotted with horses. I had not felt this happy in years. *There is nothing like clear mountain air and majestic views of nature to lift the spirits,* I told myself. By the end of the week, I realized it was not the crisp air, or the breathtaking vistas, or the horses that were lifting my spirits. It was Warren.

Warren bubbled over with an incurable and infectious optimism and curiosity. He had a rare ability to put unpleasant things behind him and enjoy life. Most men would have given up trying to find the right woman after three divorces. Not Warren. He knew she was out there. All he had to do was locate her.

Warren grew up in Junction City, Kansas, a small town located in the exact geographic center of the US. The only reading material in his childhood home was an encyclopedia, a Bible, and a few copies of *Life* magazine (My home was crammed with books, many written by relatives).

Except for his schoolbooks, he had only read comics and Boy Scout manuals until he went to Kansas State College of Agriculture and Applied Sciences, now called Kansas State University (I went to Harvard). Once Warren started to read, he never stopped. He gobbled books down like peanuts. He loved any and every type of book—novels, histories, plays, poetry, political books, philosophy. He brought thirteen books with him to the ranch and read interesting sections aloud to me.

He had a lot to boast about, but he was modest and comfortable in his own skin. He was Professor of International Business and Marketing at Pace University, and he had written thirty books. I was never bored when I was with Warren.

Warren did not have the superficial upper-class manners that impressed me in Malcolm. He did not pull out my chair, open my door, or help me on with my coat. He had no idea how to set a table. He scattered food all over the table when he ate. Instead, he was a natural gentleman, kind and generous to everybody he met.

Warren's father left school after eighth grade to work on the family farm (My father graduated from Harvard). His mother's parents were immigrants from Sweden: his father's parents came from Ireland. (Some of my ancestors came to America in the 1630s). Warren earned three advanced degrees, two of them from Harvard. Here was a man who had made his own way, like Grandpa Johnson.

Warren and I grew up in very different worlds, but we had remarkably similar childhoods in one important aspect—we were both forced to function as adults when we were very young. When I was eleven, I was guiding my younger sister and brother around London. When Warren was eleven, he was driving a tractor on his father's farm. He had his first car accident when he was twelve, when he ran the only red light in Junction City.

Our childhoods were alike in an even more fundamental way—neither of us had experienced consistent, dependable love from our mothers. Through no fault of their own, our mothers blew hot, then cold. We could never predict how they would treat us.

Warren never knew if his mother would hit him or hug him. She would praise him, then suddenly turn on a dime and punish him severely for some minor offense. No wonder he could not build a healthy relationship with his three wives and hundreds of girlfriends.

I never knew whether my mother would ignore me or smother me with love. No wonder I had difficulties with intimacy during my marriage to Malcolm.

In a novel, we would have fallen in love, married, and lived happily ever after, but we were both gun-shy after our previous romantic fiascos. I was not jumping up and down to commit to a philanderer. Warren was not eager to risk a fourth divorce. We were like two wary dogs, sniffing each other over carefully. Neither of us was ready to move in together and become a couple.

We took it slow when we got back from the ranch. I lived in Brooklyn Heights during the week, and he lived in Rye, and we got together on weekends. My gut told me I could trust this man, but I got a queasy feeling when I remembered his checkered record with women.

I was reminded of his lurid past frequently. There were memorabilia of his other romances all over his house—cosmetics; condoms, a wedding ring; personal lubricants; photos of previous weddings, and stationery inscribed *"Mrs. Warren Keegan"*.

I spent my first weekends with Warren catching up on the sleep I had missed when my marriage was falling apart. One Saturday, Rob called me at 10 AM. Warren told him that I was still in bed. Rob did not believe him. He told Warren I must have risen at 5 AM, taken a run, gone for a bike ride, and was now swimming. Wrong. I was still in the sack.

I was a sober, workaholic child, and I became a sober, workaholic adult. This lighthearted kid from Kansas showed me how to relax and enjoy life. When I tried to over-schedule, he reminded me life is no fun if you pack too much in. Finding Warren added years to my life.

We didn't allow ourselves to recognize it at first, but we fell in love at first sight. There was a chemistry between us that was unstoppable. This irresistible attraction was locked in a stalemate with immovable distrust. Only a magician could bring these two commitment-wary people together. As if on cue, two talented magicians took up the challenge: our two therapists.

Our therapists were like two puppeteers, skillfully maneuvering us together. After Warren and I had a weekend together, I went back to New York to talk to my therapist about him, and Warren went to his therapist to talk about me. Slowly, painfully, with the help of our therapists, Warren and I worked out a healthy relationship with a member of the opposite sex for the first time in our lives.

Warren had been in Jungian analysis for years, trying to understand and break his life-long habit of loving and leaving women. His relationship with his mother taught him women cannot be trusted. He believed emotional intimacy with a woman would mean he would be suffocated and lose his independence, so he unconsciously developed a fool-proof method to sabotage a relationship as soon as it became close.

He played out the same script over and over. He would meet a woman, fall for her, and decide she was a goddess of perfection who could read his mind, meet his every wish and solve all his problems. After he got to know her, and he realized she was just a human being with flaws, he became disenchanted, and he ditched her. His therapist called this his *Eden Project*—he was looking for perfection, so he could not love a real flesh-and-blood woman.

I was also trying to cure my problems with intimacy with the opposite sex, which, like Warren's, came from my relationship with my mother. She got cold and angry when I told her my feelings, so I thought a man would stop loving me if I said what I really thought. In my marriage to Malcolm, I was a dependent doormat who always gave in to him on everything—except my career.

My therapist said a relationship with a man would never work if I did everything for him and never expected anything back. When I asked a man to do something for me, I was telling him he was important to me. I had finally learned how to tell people what I needed forcefully and clearly in the operating room. Now, I had to learn how to do this with a male partner.

She gave me a tough assignment—speak my mind to Warren. The first time I did, I thought the ceiling would fall down on my head. To my surprise, he did not love me less; he loved me more. I became a human being, instead of a stiff, grinning robot.

A big plus in our relationship was Warren did not want to control me or tell me what to do. I could put as much time and energy into my work as I wanted, and he didn't mind. He put lots of energy and time into his teaching and consulting. Another plus was neither of us insisted on being right all the time. We didn't compete, or jockey for position. We were equals.

Warren did not court me like a lover. He made me pay for all my travel and food. When I came to Rye on weekends, he left the house on Saturday mornings to play tennis and shop, leaving me alone for hours. When he came back, he went into his office and shut the door.

I had to prove—to myself and to him—that I could take care of myself when he wasn't around. This gave me the option of leaving him if he mistreated me.

One evening, we went out for dinner and a movie. Warren got in a bad mood. He started to complain about the food and the film. Then he started to criticize me.
He was blaming me for something that was not my fault. This has been a trigger for me ever since my mother did it to me in London.

If I had been with Malcolm, I would have either apologized abjectly, or burst into tears. Thanks to therapy, I had a chance for a new kind of relationship. I did not have to orbit around a mean man who was treating me badly, no matter how smart and charming he was. I had learned how to say what I wanted, simply and clearly.

I told Warren I did not like the way he was treating me, and I was going back to Brooklyn the next morning. I meant it, and he knew I meant it. I moved out of our bedroom and into one of the guest rooms.

An hour went by. Then the door opened, and a naked, pink, wrinkled, remorseful man walked in. "I love you, and I don't want to lose you," he said. "I'm sorry." I had found a man who knew how to apologize.

In retrospect, I grabbed onto Warren too hard at first. I should have stepped back and let this woman-wounded man come to me. Instead, I tried to make him into my replacement man, and his house into my replacement home. I started to move things into his house—clothes, my kayak, and my bicycle. When I asked if I could move in my grand piano, Warren balked. He got grumpier and grumpier.

My experience with Malcolm had taught me that grumpy men have secrets. I asked Warren if he was in love with another woman. He told me he could not stop thinking about another woman who had also answered his Crimson Classifieds ad. He wanted to spend time with her without seeing me. He wanted a separation.

He could not have devised a better method to find out if I really loved him. He had thrown down a gauntlet: did I love him enough to give him the freedom to spend several months with another woman?

Our separation did not begin well. I told him I felt humiliated, betrayed, and angry. A chorus of advice came from my friends and family: dump this two-timing jerk and forget about him. Only two people urged me to give him his freedom and wait him out. "He is just doing his homework," said my Harvard roommate, Lisa Stokes-Taylor. "If he commits to you, you will have a man worth having," said my brother-in-law, Peter Bienstock.

I turned down a joyous free spirit from a simple background, my MIT boyfriend, when I was a student at Harvard. I did not want to let this one get away. I did my own homework. I went out with several other men during our three months apart. They all seemed pathetic compared to Warren.

I found out later Warren did not spend much time with the other woman during those three months. Instead, he spent a lot of time with his therapist. Slowly, steadily, his therapist convinced him to have faith in me. He told me about the good news in typical Warren fashion—honest, blunt, and without varnish: "I couldn't find enough things wrong with you to justify dumping you."

Warren realized I was his last and best chance to have a good relationship with a woman. I was the only woman who could end his Eden Project. He trusted me as he had never trusted a woman. He gave me his whole heart without any reservations. He proved it by letting me move my grand piano into his living room.

I helped Warren struggle out of his shell, and he helped me struggle out of mine. We showed each other all our flaws, but we could not shake the other's devotion. We gave each other the unshakable, unconditional love we did not get from our mothers. We healed each other.

Thanks to his years of therapy, Warren understood the hidden drives that lurked inside my mind, and I understood his. He saw me without illusions or delusions. Only my closest women friends understood me as well as Warren did. I had not felt this close to a man since my MIT boyfriend at Harvard.

I had no doubt this serial lady-killer would be faithful to me. Warren had researched hundreds of other women. I was the only one who understood him and loved him the way he needed to be loved. If he was stupid enough to bolt, I didn't want him.

Warren was an addition to my life, not an essential part of who I was. He made me happy just by being himself. I did not orbit around him, and he did not orbit around me. We orbited around each other, moving away, then coming back, as if there was an invisible leash between us.

The same traits that make a person likeable have a downside. I loved Warren's ability to relax and enjoy life, but his enjoyment of loafing made him casual about details. My absent-minded professor left books and clothes scattered all over the house. The only way I could get him to clean up was to invite people over. When he visited me in Brooklyn, I could not trust him to unplug the toaster, turn off the coffee warmer and the computer and close the windows. If I left him a checklist, he forgot to look at it.

One weekend, we went to Far Hills to attend my niece's wedding. I was working on Friday, so I asked Warren to bring my suitcase while he drove out in his car, and I went out by train. He forgot to put my suitcase in his car, so he left it back in Rye. I had no clothes to wear for the wedding.

If I had exploded in anger, I could have ended our relationship right then and there, but he looked so contrite I did not have the heart to berate him. He offered to drive back to Rye to get my suitcase, but instead, we went to Lynn's house in Princeton, and she lent me some of her clothes.

Warren's forgetfulness did not stop me from loving him. It showed me he was human. It made me believe he would forgive my annoying habits.

We learned how to curb each other's destructive tendencies. One day, I took a hot cooking dish from the oven and ran cold water over it. It shattered into pieces. He began to yell at me. I could hear his mother's uncontrollable fury in his voice. I told him it was only a dish, and he had no right to berate me. He got the point and stopped. He thanked me for helping him to escape his temper.

After we got together after our three-month separation, Warren began to tell me we would get married someday. I had zero interest in marrying anybody. Marriage to Malcolm was like being in prison. It taught me that a devoted suitor can transform into a man with a temper once that ring was on my left hand. I liked things the way they were.

I married Malcolm because I needed him to complete me, give my life direction, and tell me what to do. I was complete in myself now. I knew who I was. I had a life that suited me. I didn't need to be dependent on a man. I didn't need a husband.

After three years went by, my dislike of marriage began to wane. I knew the best husband for me was one who would let me be myself. That was Warren. He had no interest in changing me or controlling me. I knew he would be happy with anything I wanted to do.

I had one reservation—Warren was six years older than I was. Before I committed to him, I wanted to make sure he was healthy. The advantage of being a retina specialist was I could find out by taking a good hard look at his retinal blood vessels. I talked him into coming in for an eye exam. When I saw his arteries were as open as pipes, I was reassured I would not be saddled with a frail old man. I decided to spend the rest of my life with him.

My heart told me Malcolm and I were not a good match, but my head overruled my heart. My head told me Warren was a bad bet, but my heart knew we were perfect together. This time, my heart overruled my head. He was seventy. I was sixty-four. We did not have all the time in the world. When he proposed, I said *yes*.

Warren's third wife insisted on an expensive engagement ring. She also demanded he put her name on the deed to his house. She took a million dollars of his money with her when she left him.

I introduced Warren to his first pre-nuptial agreement. His money and his house in Rye were his. My money and my Brooklyn apartment were mine. I told him I did not want an engagement ring.

We strolled down the aisle on our wedding day holding hands and wearing *leis* around our necks sent by a Hawaiian friend of Warren's. My granddaughters, seven, six, and four, were our flower girls. Warren's two grandsons, eight and five, and my five-year-old grandson were our ring and Bible bearers. The grandchildren fell all over each other in heaps after the ceremony. I did not take Warren's surname.

Pictured: Me and Warren on our wedding day, September 15, 2007, with our three children, their spouses, and our eight grandchildren.

We went to Hawaii for our honeymoon. When I asked Warren where he found our superb resort, he told me he had stayed there with a previous girlfriend. For a moment, I felt offended. Then I started to laugh. He was honest with me. That was all that mattered.

Many of Warren's friends told me how happy he was after we met. "He has a twinkle in his eye now," one friend said. Warren told his sister: "I never thought I would see the day when I would experience this kind of joy. If I die tomorrow, I will have loved and been loved."

I was so happy now that all the worried, tense frown lines on my face disappeared. A few of my friends asked if I had had a face lift.

Warren and I skied in Alta, Utah, for a week every winter. One year, I fell and sprained both thumbs. Four days later, I was back in the operating room doing surgery.

As you know, surgeons disinfect their hands with Betadine sponges before they operate. These sponges come sealed in sterile plastic pouches.

My injured thumbs were too weak to pull open the Betadine pouch. I had to ask the scrub nurse to pull it open for me. I had no problems manipulating the light surgical instruments, but this was a wake-up call. I either had to stop skiing or stop performing operating room surgery.

The decision wasn't even close. Warren was my chance to live life creatively. The time had come for me to leave the operating room and stop doing knife surgery and restrict my surgery to non-LASIK laser surgery.

I was sixty-four. I had been in the operating room for thirty years. I had seen surgeons who stayed too long. I wanted to leave when I was at the top of my game, before I had a complication that I could have handled better when I was younger.

I retired from the operating room in 2006. Warren came to watch on my last day. He took the only photograph I have of me as a surgeon. It is on the cover of this book.
I did not tell anybody I was leaving. A goodbye party would have made me too sad. I just snuck away, feeling sad and guilty.

On summer evenings, Warren took his wine and honey-roasted peanuts, and I took my herbal tea, and we went down to his dock to watch the sunset. As the sparks that wink on the waves turned from diamonds to rubies, and the sun dissolved into a fiery sky, we settled down to enjoy the show.

We surprise a flock of mallards. They leap up, instantly aloft, wings whirring so fast they are almost invisible. One of them leaves behind a white splat rocking on the waves.

We watch a great blue heron stalk a snack in the shallows. It makes a sound like a rusty door hinge when it flaps majestically away. A black-capped night heron touches down on a neighboring dock. It greets us with a sociable *"Quork"*.

We admire a half dozen terns with natty black skull caps as they plunge, headfirst, into the waves, getting dinner the hard way. Angular black shapes flash by us, snapping up gnats, so acrobatic, barn swallows. Red-tailed hawks circle up, up on the wind, higher, and higher, calm and dignified. Cormorants, better swimmers than flyers, are all business as they zip briskly past, their wings almost touching the water.

We hear a *plip*. A tiny, shiny fish just jumped out of the water, escaping a bigger fish below. An iridescent blue dragonfly hovers in front of us for a second. It scrutinizes us carefully with eyes that are bigger than its head. Then, it is off before I can blink.

In the spring, mallard, Canada goose, and swan families steam by, the hatchlings mid-convoy, the mother and father fore and aft, each bird precisely the same distance from the other. In the fall, monarch butterflies zig and zag erratically past, haphazard orange scraps seemingly without purpose or direction, making their way down to Mexico.

A sudden squall hits. Tiny jets of water, miniature fountains, leap up around the dock. We grab our gear and dash for home.

"I can't believe we are married," says Warren. "Neither can I," I reply. "We are having too much fun."

When I get into bed, Warren is worried I might feel cold. He floats a blanket over me, soft as a baby's hair, a cloud of warmth. I close my eyes. I drift off to sleep. I am home.

CHAPTER TWENTY-TWO

The Doctor Becomes a Patient: 2012

I bet you have never heard of *Chronic Pain Syndrome.* I did not know it existed until I developed it myself when I was seventy. Few doctors know how to diagnose and treat this downward spiral of depression and pain, although researchers discovered years ago what causes it and how to treat it.

After you finish reading this chapter, you will know more about this little-known, yet surprisingly common, illness than most doctors do. You will learn about the latest research in Chronic Pain, and the new drugs that are on the horizon.

I dreamed of living life creatively when I was married to Malcolm. When I was a little old lady in her sixties, I started to live a life with Warren that was creative beyond my wildest dreams.

Warren was not kidding when he said he liked motorcycle touring. He had not just one, but two *BMW* motorcycles. He took me for a ride on one of them the weekend after we came back from Wyoming.

I hopped up behind my six-foot-one hunk and slid my arms around his waist. He put a Mozart opera on the CD player, fed it into our helmets, and we blasted off with the strains of *Don Giovanni* echoing in our brains. The great dome of the sky arched above us, and the whole world was waiting for us.

Riding on a motorcycle is not like riding in a car. A car is a box of stale air that takes you from Point A to Point B. When you are on a motorcycle, you are right in the middle of the landscape. You smell hot asphalt, new-mown hay, the strong sharp scent of rotting leaves, fresh-baked bread. You hear the cries of children, the yip of dogs, the clear calls of birds. You feel every nuance of the road as you lean into turns.

We rode a motorcycle along Australia's Great Ocean Road, waves pounding exotic rock formations and surfers to the left of us, parasailers gliding over our heads, my heart singing with happiness. We rode all the way around New Zealand's South Island, where the Roaring Forties winds almost blew us off the bike. We dodged wallabies in Tasmania, road runners in the California desert, and longhorn cattle in the Texas hill country.

We blasted over the canyon land of Utah, across the Wyoming prairies, up and down the hills of Vermont, and along the shores of New York's glacial Finger Lakes. We crept down rust-colored cliffs, steep as a wall, in West Texas. We sailed through New Zealand forests filled with giant tree ferns, so dense they turned midday to dusk. We rode a boat through caverns lit by glowworms.

We soared up Utah's Giant Staircase, flying over black, orange, yellow, and white clay eighty million years old, vaulting centuries with every foot. We swam naked in the Virgin River in Zion National Park, with the giant stone visages and the white fluff of the cottonwood trees our only witnesses. We saw the Grand Canyon by moonlight, the High Desert of San Diego at sunset, and Colorado's Mesa Verde in the snow.

Pictured:CJM, Warren, and his BMW touring motorcycle, 2009.

Motorcycle touring had a downside. I shook with cold in the winter despite my heated jacket and seat, and sweated waterfalls in the summer. I had to pack all my clothes in a box the size of a toaster oven. I changed for dinner by swapping my white socks for black and throwing a silver scarf around my neck.

Part of the reason I went on motorcycle trips with Warren was he was at his best then, engaged, happy, and fully alive. I did difficult things to connect to this complicated man, just as I did difficult things to connect to my complicated father—getting up early to watch him shave, running long distances in London—and to Grandpa Johnson—fox hunting on a lethal idiot of a horse.

We went on motorcycle trips for eight years. In 2011, while we were on what turned out to be our last motorcycle trip, through Yellowstone National Park, I noticed a pain in my left buttock after I had sat on the motorcycle for several hours. The pain got so bad we had to cut our trip short.

Even though I stopped going on motorcycle trips, my buttock pain kept getting worse. I went to one doctor after another. I saw fourteen different physical therapists and six different acupuncturists. I had injections of cod liver oil in my muscles and injections of steroids in my spine. I tried biofeedback, laser treatment, and electric stimulation of my brain. Nothing helped.

I went to a "pain management" doctor. All he did was to give me a series of different opiates. I had bad reactions to all of them. I ended up on *Klonopin* and morphine.

I once felt sorry for the little old ladies who were creeping up the subway stairs as I bounded cheerfully past them. By early 2012, I was just as slow as they were. Then I was even slower. Then, I could not climb the stairs at all. The pain got so bad I could not pick up one crumb from the floor or pull one weed from my garden.

I barely kept my practice going. I took a limo to my office, dozed during the trip in, saw patients, then collapsed in the back and dozed until I got home. I am reasonably certain I provided good care—nobody complained, and all the patients I saw during this period came back.

I went to a neurosurgeon. He told me my pain was caused by excess movement between two vertebrae in my lower spine. He promised the pain would go away completely if he fused those two vertebrae. He was supremely confident in his diagnosis, even though I kept telling him the pain was nowhere near my spine, it was in my left buttock. I was desperate. I jumped for the operation.

That neurosurgeon made a stunningly inaccurate diagnosis. The worst pain of my life started after that spinal fusion surgery. I since learned that spinal fusion for back pain was on the top of the list of unnecessary surgeries performed on Medicare patients in 2010.

I have been a resilient, optimistic woman all my life, but the pain was so bad it made me feel hopeless and helpless. I prowled around the house at 1 AM, 2 AM, 3 AM, sleeping in fits and starts on one bed after another, one couch after another. When the sun rose, it brought no relief, just another day to endure. I began to consider which of the kitchen knives was sharpest if I decided to slit my wrists.

My world got smaller and smaller, until there was nothing else in it but pain. Pain crouched on top of my brain like a black demon. Everything else in my life faded away. When I was not in the office, I was lying in bed at Warren's house with the shades down.

I felt lonely, but when the people I loved most—my sister, daughter, son, and best friends—came to visit, I could not wait for them to leave. Their worried faces seemed like blurred dots, chattering away in a language I could not understand.

Nine months after the pain began, my luck changed. I went to a pain specialist, who referred me to another pain specialist, who referred me to Dr. Norman Marcus. Dr. Marcus injected lidocaine into my muscles. When that did not help, he suggested I go to a pain center at a major teaching hospital. I cannot reveal the name because of privacy rules. Warren left the decision up to me.

While I was trying to decide whether to go to the pain center, I visited Hope in New Hampshire. This is usually my favorite week of the year, but when I got there, all I could do was lie on the floor and cry.

Hope lay down beside me and put her arms around me. She told me I was depleted, and fragile, and in despair. I was putting up a front and giving too much energy to other people. I would not get back on track until I began to put energy into myself. My confused mind needed a structured environment where I could sleep and get stronger. I had to go to the pain center.

I listened to my perceptive, wise, empathetic daughter, and I went. Before they let me come, I had to sign a form promising I would stay at least three weeks. During the three weeks I was an inpatient at the pain center, I kept myself sane with my usual technique – I kept a diary. Here it is.

DAY 1

Today, Warren drove me to the Pain Center. He hugged me goodbye. I went in, and the heavy door slammed shut behind me and locked with an ominous clunk. A sign on the door says: "DANGER! ELOPEMENT RISK!" I cannot go out of that door until the doctors give me permission.

The minute I walked in, a nurse grabbed my suitcase and purse and went through everything inside. He took away my medications, sewing kit, nail clippers, tweezers, and everything that has a cord, i.e., my cell phone charger and hair dryer, and locked them away. I cannot use them until my doctors give me permission.

I am not allowed to take a bath, only a shower. The bulletin board over my bed does not have any thumbtacks. I can only use scotch tape.

I get the picture. This place must be severe because chronic pain patients are depressed, and depressed people kill themselves.

I am one of nine patients with chronic pain. There are also nine geriatric patients here with psychological problems.

The center is run by psychiatrists. It is crawling with nurses at three different levels (I have not figured out the distinctions yet); social workers; "coordinators" (no idea); and medical and nursing students. I have yet to see a doctor. Everyone is perky, upbeat, and concerned.

This place looks like a kindergarten. Lavender linoleum covers the floor. The walls are purple, and they are plastered with signs saying: "Shhh! Patients healing!", Partnership Pledges (whatever they are), and suggestions about deep breathing and "mindfulness". Every windowsill is packed with dried-up dead bodies of geraniums.

The food is unappetizing, and—surprising for a hospital— unhealthy. I will subsist on bananas and peanut butter, as I did during medical school. Fortunately, both are available in abundance.

My nurse took samples of my blood and urine. He checks my blood pressure several times a day. Each time he does, he questions me about my mood, and asks me if I am planning to hurt myself. Then he tells me to rate my pain on a scale of one to ten, ten being the worst and one the least. I say: "Nine point five".

We have group therapy three times a day. I went to my first session this afternoon. The stories of my fellow pain patients made me want to cry. All spoke of the loneliness of chronic pain, and how it has stolen their life. Several of them have tried to commit suicide.

Most of them are in the middle of difficult drug withdrawals, either from opiates (like oxycodone), or tranquilizers (such as Klonopin), or both. I will join them as the doctors begin to withdraw me from Morphine and Klonopin.

I did not want a roommate. I wanted to hibernate in my own cave, licking my wounds in private. To my surprise, I am glad there is a body in the bed next to me. I am locked away from all the people who care about me. Now I have somebody to care for, somebody who understands what I am going through because she also suffers from chronic pain.

I am not sure whether this place will drive me crazy or save my life.

DAY 2

They treat me like a baby here. I am only allowed to take medicines if they have been ordered by a doctor. When it is time to take a pill, the nurse asks me every time: "What is your name and date of birth?" Then he takes Morphine and Klonopin from a locked cabinet in a locked room, hands me the pills and a glass of water, and watches me swallow them.

I feel more and more depleted. I cannot relax. My pain is even worse than it was yesterday. I cannot begin to think of reading anything—even a newspaper.

My life is totally out of my control. I have been infantilized. I cannot cut my own toenails, sew my own clothes, prepare my own food, take my own medications, or leave the floor to take a walk. Last night, I begged the nurse for Tylenol. Not ordered. No dice. My nurse will not give me any medicine for diarrhea unless he personally sees a loose stool in the toilet.

My bed is narrow, hard, and short. My roommate has set the temperature in our room to ninety degrees, and she complains if I try to lower it. She is heavily sedated, so she snores like a freight train.

Sleep is not possible. The nurses come into our room several times during the night to give her medication and take her blood pressure. They turn on the light, which wakes her—and me—up.

Last night, one of the geriatric patients down the hall got disoriented in the middle of the night. He turned on his alarm, which was as loud as a fire engine. Then he did it again. And again. After a half dozen of these alarms, I asked for an extra Klonopin. Not ordered. No dice.

The biofeedback and physical therapy here are inferior to what I had outside, and I cannot get acupuncture and treatment by Dr Marcus. The only thing I cannot get outside is group therapy, but there must be pain support groups back home I could go to.

I enjoy talking to the other pain patients. I learn from them. I admire the different ways they have coped with the pain that destroyed their lives, but I feel I am taking up a bed that could better be used by somebody else. I will wait to hear what the psychiatrists have to say tomorrow, but my plan is to go home, as soon as possible.

DAY 3

Yesterday, I almost signed out a dozen times, but each time I remembered I had nowhere to go. I have been everywhere, I have tried everything, and nothing has worked. The buck stops here in this lavender clinic crammed with mummified geraniums. I am a member of the Last Chance Club. There are no quick fixes here. All nine of us have suffered debilitating, life-destroying pain for at least six months. Almost all of us have gone through surgical procedures that left us in even more pain than before.

I finally met my psychiatrist today. Dr. Z is a tall, thin, intense, bald man in his forties. He has a military bearing, and he exudes confidence and competence. He was wearing a white coat, orange shoes, and socks with black-and-yellow stripes.

"You will take 50 mg of a new medication called Pristiq, an antidepressant, in the morning and Lithium at night. Pristiq is especially good for pain, and it is not likely to affect your weight or your sex drive." he said. "We will gradually taper you off Morphine and Klonopin."

"I have heard antidepressants are no more effective than placebos." I said. "They do not work well for mild to moderate depression, but they are fifty to sixty percent effective in severe depression." Dr. Z said. He added, looking straight into my eyes: "You are severely depressed."

My jaw dropped. I was shocked. True, I was spending most of my days in bed, crying, and I was thinking of committing suicide, but the great Dr. Cynthia MacKay could not be depressed.

I have been trained to recognize signs of depression in my patients, but the thought I might be depressed myself never crossed my mind—just as I hadn't recognized I was depressed when my marriage to Malcolm was falling apart. I put up such a good front trying to fool the rest of the world I managed to fool myself.

Today, in group therapy, one of the patients told me I would not get better until I stopped fighting the doctors. "Get in the back seat and put a muzzle on." were his exact words. He also told me I had to start taking care of myself and stop taking care of other people.

By coming to the Pain Center, I have finally admitted I am in bad shape. I am the one who needs help. I need to drop the pretense of being a powerful, invulnerable doctor. I need to focus on helping Cynthia.

DAY 4

I took my first dose of Pristiq yesterday afternoon. A few hours later, I felt hopeful, full of energy, mind in control, no crying. I almost forgot the pain in my left buttock.

By early evening I had a full-blown drug reaction—aches all over my body, knots of pain in my forehead, jaws, hands, and knees, and a nasty feeling of restlessness in my legs. This is what a bad case of Lyme Disease must feel like. These side effects got even worse after I took my first Lithium pill. I spent the night trotting back and forth to the nursing station, getting ice packs, and begging for Tylenol. I did not sleep at all last night.

When I told Dr. Z my tale of woe this morning, he said, "Go right on taking your medications. Drug reactions are always the worst during the first 24 hours. The first dose is the biggest hurdle. These side effects will go away during the next days to weeks."

I must have looked skeptical because he added: "We cure people here. They walk in, severely depressed and in great pain, and they walk out smiling. Doctors are the worst patients of all. I have cured three in the past month. Trust me. We have a 98% cure rate."

I must trust my mind to...a total stranger. Dr. Z has made me worse. I must have faith he will eventually make me better.

I feel as if I am crawling on my hands and knees over burning coals and razor blades. I can barely move. I hurt all over. I am so exhausted I cannot think straight. My second dose of Pristiq is coming up. I'm curled up in a ball on my bed, like a grub, waiting for group therapy to begin.

DAY 5

When I talked to Warren last night, he told me the psychiatry resident called him and asked how functional I was at home. Did I have support—-children, friends, siblings? Was I able to work? I was impressed. These people really care.

Psychiatric residents, nurses, and social workers lead our group therapy sessions. They tell us how to deal with pain and stress, how to relax, and how to talk to ourselves in positive, optimistic ways. I am beginning to realize these sessions are the most helpful part of the program.

During one of our group therapy sessions today, we played a card game called "Apples to Apples". We could not remember what cards we had put down, because our brains are so scrambled from the side effects of our new medications and/or withdrawal from our old medications. We just looked at each other, shrugged, and laughed.

I have had pain everywhere in my body since I started Pristiq and Lithium, not just in my buttocks. I must believe this, too, shall pass. There is no alternative. I lay awake all night last night in my narrow, hard bed, stared at the ceiling, and listened to my roommate snore.

DAY 6

A few hours after I take Lithium, I start to feel feverish and nauseated, as if I have the worst case of flu of my life. I have turned into a rag doll stuffed full of aches.

Last night, I defied the Mind Gods: I refused to take Lithium. The head nurse came to talk to me right away. She seemed upset. "We will make you better, but you have to do what we say," she said. I did not budge.

The psychiatry resident was in my room in half an hour, which is a miracle because they usually take three hours to wander down. She knelt on the floor beside my bed and preached me the gospel: "These side effects will go away. You must continue your meds."

I gave up. My Mind Gods won. I swallowed my Lithium and went through another night, in pain, without sleep.

When Dr. Z tripped into my room this morning, he rewarded me for my good behavior by giving me privileges to leave the Pain Center, alone, for 20-minute periods to visit the rest of the hospital. Now I can buy my own food!

Today, during one of our group sessions, we were supposed to watch a movie, but our brains were too scrambled to concentrate. We all snuck out, one by one.

DAY 7

I have taken Lithium for five nights, and the side effects are not going away, they are getting worse. Last night, I wrote down what I was feeling, hour by hour:

12 AM: Took Lithium.
1 AM: Starting to itch all over my body, especially legs and scalp; legs are twitching.
2 AM: Severe nausea; severe pain in hands, elbows, knees, and shoulders.
3 AM: Aching all over. Feverish. Pain is so bad I cannot sleep.
4 AM: I feel as if I have a roaring case of flu. Forget trying to sleep.
5 AM: No sleep.

When my Mind God read this, he relented, and took me off Lithium. To compensate, he gave me a second dose of Pristiq at night.

When I told the other patients in group therapy today about my Great Lithium Victory, I immediately took flak from all sides. X said: "You must stop fighting the doctors if you want to get well. You doctors are the worst patients of all." X is a large, gentle, twenty-five-year-old man with soft brown eyes. He has had severe abdominal pain since he was a child. He has been at the Pain Center for three months.

"Am I just as difficult as all the other doctors? "I asked.
"You are pretty standard," X said.

A, a thirty-one-year-old woman who has had debilitating migraines her entire life, lifted her head off the table, pulled off her dark glasses, and said, "Your standards for yourself are too high. You must surrender and stop trying to be the best. Yesterday, you were even trying to win at Bingo".

"I was joking." I replied.
"Ninety percent joke, Ten percent no joke." said A.
"They cure people here," added X. "Three months ago, a woman came in who had a plane ticket to Switzerland in her purse. She was planning to fly there to die a dignified, painless death. She had the consent and support of her entire family, including her nine-year-old daughter. She cancelled her ticket and went home."

"I have wanted to die every day of my life." said A.

I am learning more from my fellow pain patients than from all the doctors, nurses, and social workers put together. We are fellow soldiers on a battlefield of pain, trudging down a road towards a distant goal we cannot see, side by side, just trying to catch our next breath.

DAY 8

My concentration has improved since I started taking Pristiq. I am beginning to tolerate this medicine better—aches slightly less, a bit more energy. I still can't choke down much food except bananas and peanut butter.

Everybody here warns me I will get worse before I get better. I am still worse than when I arrived, but I'm less worse.

We go to physical therapy every day except Saturday and Sunday. Before I arrived, my body was as limp as overcooked spaghetti. I thought I was so fragile I would fall apart with the slightest exertion. I had not exercised in months.

A physical therapist assessed me on the day I arrived and gave me some stretches and exercises. I have done more and more as time has passed. Today, I climbed on an elliptical machine and became out of breath for the first time since my back surgery nine months ago.

Today, in group therapy, a social worker told us to describe the most stressful time of our lives. Everybody except for me said: "Going to the Pain Center." I said: "Internship," but it was a close call.

When the nurse took away the medications from my luggage eight days ago, he missed a small bottle in the bottom of my purse that contained a few Tylenol pills. I woke up at 3 AM in severe pain. I staggered to the nursing station and pleaded for some Tylenol. The nurse refused to give me any until my scheduled dose at 6 AM.

I went back to my room. I took out the bottle. I shook two Tylenol pills into my hand. I looked at them for a few minutes. I remembered I must not fight my doctors. I put them back again.

DAY 9

Yesterday I heard a strange sound as I was walking down the hall. I stopped to see where it was coming from. I finally realized it was coming from me. I was whistling.

Today, we had no physical or group therapy because it is the weekend. I picked up some watercolors and painted a picture of my grandchildren in a sailboat on Dublin Lake. The wind was whipping the sail, their hair was flying, the sun was setting, and Monadnock Mountain was looming over them.

One of the nurses saw the painting and said: "I would like to go there!"

Me, too.

DAY 10

I could never have tolerated Pristiq without the support and encouragement I have had in the pain clinic. The side effects are too horrific—aches all over, wild mood swings, itching, twitching, no energy, anxiety, and no sleep. If I were back home, I would have flung this drug into the wastebasket after the first dose.

A new patient arrived today, a sparkler of a nurse my age. She hails from Dallas. She started to complain right away, the words tumbling out of her, a waterfall of words. She grumbled about her hard bed, the noise at night, the depressing geriatric patients, her meds, and her nurse, H (H is gay, and he is one of the most compassionate and involved nurses here).

"This place looks like something out of a movie." she said, accurately.

I saw the "me" of ten days ago—terrified, angry, at the end of my rope. I took a deep breath and tried to talk her into staying.

I told her how I came to trust Dr. Z and his Mind God Team. I am better in so many ways. My buttock pain is beginning to go away. I am more cheerful. I have hope now. I did not mention I am also worse. I ache in every limb. Again, I did not sleep last night.

Today in group therapy, the social worker asked us to describe our childhoods.

After a short silence, R said: "My mother went insane when I was four years old. She was locked up in a mental institution for the rest of her life."

My roommate, J, said: "When I was young, my father lost his job. My mother had to work at a job she hated. She was angry and resentful. She ruthlessly drove me to succeed."

"My mother made me into her mother. She forced me to come to her house every day and shop and cook for her," the firecracker nurse from Dallas said. "When I was in the hospital with pneumonia, she called me every day to complain she needed food."

"My parents are so difficult and demanding I have forbidden them to call or visit while I am here," said a woman anthropologist in her twenties.

"When my father left my mother for another woman, he sent me an email to tell me he had cut me out of his will," said S. S has put a sign on her door that says: "Are you feeling sad today? Get the fuck up."

When I began to describe my childhood and my relationship with my mother, S interrupted me and said: "What is your relationship with your daughter?"

"I–I." I stopped to collect my thoughts. Then I said simply, "We are best friends. She comes to me when she has a problem, and I come to her when I need help. She was the one who persuaded me to come here."

"You broke the chain." she said.

"What do you mean?" I asked.

"You do not have the same relationship with your daughter your mother had with you." she said.

All of us were forced to act as parents to our needy, clueless parents when we were children. We spent our childhoods on high alert, muscles clenched with anxiety, desperately trying to help parents who could not be helped. We became perfectionists, driven by internal pressure we imposed on ourselves, obsessed with success, struggling to take control of our chaotic lives.

The social worker did not seem surprised.

DAY 11

Warren comes today! I cannot spend the night with him, but we will have the afternoon and evening together.

I have not had a good night's sleep since I got here. Last night, my Mind Gods gave me a small dose (7.5 mg) of Remeron, an antidepressant that acts as a sedative at low doses.

I looked at that pill, crossed my fingers, closed my eyes, and gulped it down. I felt like Alice in Wonderland. I had no idea what it would *do. I was on a trip into the unknown. Aches all over? Twitches? Itches? Feeling as if I was burning up? Hallucinations?*

The next thing I knew, it was 8 AM. A miracle. I am dopey as a drunk skunk this morning, but my Mind Gods have promised me the lethargy will diminish with time.

Picasso's last self-portrait, painted when he was in his 90s, has a look of sheer terror as he stares into the face of Death. He painted his eyes as red circles with black circles inside. They look like the eyes of a trapped animal.

When I looked into my eyes in the mirror during drug withdrawal, haunted red circles looked back at me. During the last few days, my eyes look like question marks--exhausted, sick, but no longer haunted.

DAY 12

I spent the whole day with Warren yesterday. We even went to a museum. But I was preoccupied. It was hard for me to concentrate. Instead of staying with Warren the entire time I was allowed, I went back to the hospital early. I did not feel at home with my own husband. My home is now the Pain Center.

I felt anxious and restless and dizzy and tremulous because the doctors are weaning me off Klonopin. I was also worried about my blood pressure. High blood pressure is one of the side effects of Pristiq. My systolic blood pressure was one hundred and seventy-seven yesterday morning, when it usually runs ninety to one hundred.

I cannot believe my neurosurgeon gave me Klonopin to help the pain. I now know Klonopin is not effective against pain. I have taken it for six months, and even though it is a small dose, I have become addicted.

Today, my blood pressure is almost back to normal. My cousin Cynthia McClintock will visit in a few hours. I look forward to spending time with this sensible, smart, warm-hearted woman.

I have come to appreciate ophthalmology during my pain journey. The diagnosis is clear, and the surgery is instantly gratifying. A patient has a dense cataract, I take it out, the bandage comes off the next day, the patient is deliriously happy, and he or she goes off to a joyous new life of sight.

In pain management, finding the right medication is trial and error. Each brain has its own unique chemistry, and nobody reacts to these pain drugs in the same way. The diagnosis is murky, and the road to success takes many twists and turns. Everybody gets worse before they get better.

There will be no instant gratification for me, or for anybody with chronic pain. I am on a precarious journey, with only a promise from the doctors to keep me going.

DAY 13

This place is astounding--tough but astounding. My pain today is less than half what it was two weeks ago. I feel optimistic for the first time in a year.

My nurse called Warren yesterday and asked him to describe our day together. How much was I able to I do? Did I seem strong? They must be trying to decide if I am well enough to go home!

Today in group therapy, I learned Chronic Pain Syndrome can develop in susceptible people if they have severe pain that lasts for more than three months. The pain causes anxiety, insomnia, lack of activity, isolation, and depression, which lowers the pain threshold, which makes the patient feel more pain. A vicious feed-back loop is set up.

I am lucky to be here, and lucky to have insurance to cover my stay. I thank all my friends and family who encouraged me to come here from the bottom of my heart.

DAY 14

Warren brought me a CD player when he visited last weekend. It has been a lifesaver. Now I can listen to books at night when I cannot sleep.

I spent most of last night wandering around the streets of Bath with Captain Wentworth and Anne Elliot in Jane Austen's "Persuasion". The last disc ended as the sun started to peek through the curtains. Which of you sent me the CD of Jane Austen's Emma? It arrived in the nick of time.

Last night was my first night off Klonopin, so my sleep was interrupted, light and crammed with vivid dreams. Klonopin suppresses REM, i.e., dreaming, sleep, so I will be catching up on my dreams for the next few weeks.

This place feels as comforting as a nursery now. I am surrounded by people who care about me, want to help me, and – most important--know how to help me.

My day begins when a cheerful nurse's aide, clanking with exotic Jamaican jewelry, bustles in at 7 AM. She takes my blood pressure and temperature, and she weighs me once a week. My medications make me so nauseated I have no interest in food, so I have lost several pounds.

The next to arrive is my nurse. He--at least half are male--asks me to rate my pain and mood. When I arrived at the pain center, I rated my pain at nine point five (ten being the worst) and my mood at one (ten being the best). Today, I rated my pain four, and my mood eight.

He gives me my medications, and then he does a MiniMental test: I must remember three objects, write a sentence, and identify two forms. Did I eat? Did I have a bowel movement? If not, there is prune juice at the nursing station.

After breakfast, the psychiatrist, resident, and medical student file in. I write down my questions beforehand, and they patiently answer all of them.

We go to the gym for physical therapy in the late morning. Three group therapy sessions fill our afternoon and evening. They say only an alcoholic can help another alcoholic. Only a chronic pain patient can help another chronic pain patient.

I am doing a job that must be done, and I will not leave until it is finished.

DAY 15

Still coming off Klonopin, so very little sleep last night, in short bursts, with intense dreams. Luckily, morphine and Klonopin made me so sick I took low doses, so I will not have to go through a prolonged withdrawal. This means I will get out of here sooner than most of the other patients.

Last night, I listened to the first CD of "Emma" over and over. I would go to sleep, wake up, realize I had missed several minutes, go back to the beginning, and start all over again. It was a wild night, with Emma and Mr. Knightly scampering through my dreams.

I was dead tired this morning. After the nurses' aide left the room, I tried to go back to sleep instead of going to breakfast. Not possible. The nurse was in my room in a flash, telling me it was time to eat.

This place runs on a strict protocol. If you stick to the program, you get better.

Doctors often believe they are invincible and immortal, but we are only too human. I took care of my patients, but – like too many other doctors—I did not take care of myself. I will leave this place humbled.

DAY 16

The last two days were the best I have had in years. I told the nurse my pain was "four," half of what it was when I arrived. I felt happy and hopeful. I still wasn't sleeping, but I figured that was because I had been off Klonopin for two nights.

Then, yesterday evening, the pain came back—fiery demons shooting down the backs of my legs, aches all over my body, stomach cramps, and no sleep last night. My mind began to spin like a crazy top. My miraculous new life was slipping away. I could not figure out what had gone wrong. A late Remuron reaction, I decided, must be the problem.

I was in tears when my psychiatrist came around this morning. He reassured me that this was Klonopin withdrawal, and the pain would go away. Then, one of the NURSES—yes, nurses—explained to me what was going on.

I have never been in a hospital where the nurses are full partners with the doctors. I always thought it was the job of doctors to explain the side effects of medications. The nurses here know just as much about chronic pain as the doctors do.

My nurse told me Klonopin takes 72 hours to leave the body, so the full force of withdrawal had not hit me until last night. She also said that breakdown products of Klonopin are stored in fat, so heavy people with many fat cells can have relapses that go on for as long as three months.

Since I am slim, I should be finished with almost all my withdrawal from Klonopin in a few weeks. The more I exercise, the quicker my withdrawal will be over.

DAY 17

A week from today, Warren and I will have been together for nine years and married for five. Our wedding vows stipulated in sickness and in health, but they did not mention Warren would have to drive back and forth between Rye and the pain center three times in three weeks, which he has done without complaint.

Yesterday, in group therapy, a nurse gave us a talk about sleep hygiene. Sleep is always a problem for chronic pain patients because it is the last to improve. She told us we needed an uncluttered bedroom, a comfortable mattress, an early light supper, and nothing in bed except sleep and sex. If sleep does not come *within half an hour, she told us, get up, sit in a chair, and eat a light snack.*

Last night, I felt as if two halves of my brain were locked in combat. One half was so tired I wanted to go to sleep on any flat surface that came into my sight. The other half was so wired no sleep could pry its way in. At 2 AM, after I tossed about in my baking hot room on my hard, skinny bed for several hours in time to my roommate's snoring, I remembered the nurse's words. One banana, and one chapter of "The House of Mirth", sent to me by Warren's sister Marian Fuller, and I was asleep.

Today, Dr. Z told me depression is a combination of biological vulnerability and environmental stress. Once the switch is flipped, it is flipped permanently. Anybody who has had two episodes of depression is 98 percent likely to have a third one. I should take antidepressants for the rest of my life.

I have had two episodes of depression. The first was caused by my toxic marriage. The second was caused by buttock pain. I must take Pristiq for the rest of my life.

My Armstrong-Edey ancestors passed me genes that gave me a capacity for joy and an adventurous spirit, but they have a dark side. I am grateful for the invention of antidepressants, and for the pain center that brought them to me.

DAY 18

Today I go home!

I am so upbeat now the nurses have taken to calling me Sunshine. My fellow patients seemed sad and jealous to see me go, but I hope I will be an inspiration to them. Some of them have been here for months.

Coming here has been the most stressful, difficult, and traumatic experience of my life, and that includes internship. At least my Pain Center experience didn't last as long.

And that is my last entry. As my good husband drove me back to Rye, I felt as if I had spent the last three weeks in a vast Siberia of the Mind, watching helplessly as battling armies struggled to take control of my brain.

First came the Battle of the Antidepressants. Benign invaders marched in. For two weeks, I lay in bed, sleepless, sweating, and aching, as my brain adjusted to its new rulers. Just when I started to feel the best I have in years, the Battle of Klonopin and Morphine Withdrawal began. I spent another week tossing and aching in bed without sleep.

The first thing I did when I got home was cut off my hospital wristband. I felt a sense of dread when the nurse put it on. Now, I feel nothing but gratitude. I am lucky that brilliant scientists have worked for years to identify chronic pain, understand the mechanism, and figure out how to treat it.

The first researcher to realize that chronic pain syndrome comes from the mind instead of the body was Dr. John Sarno, Professor of Rehabilitation Medicine at NYU, in the 1980s. Sarno realized that pain is a conversation between your brain and your body. All pain is real, but because pain is felt in the brain, the brain can interpret it as more intense, or less intense. Fear and catastrophizing make pain worse. Feeling safe, happy, and calm does not eliminate pain, but it makes it less strong.

Sarno was also the first physician to realize all chronic pain patients have suffered psychological trauma as children. His peers laughed at his theory. Now we know he was right. All the patients at the Pain Center, including me, had difficult childhoods.

My father told me once everybody in our family loved each other very much. I do believe my parents loved me, but they had such challenging childhoods themselves they had no idea how to nurture their children in the way we needed to be nurtured.

Sarno also recognized that women are more susceptible to chronic pain syndrome than men. Several dozen patients passed through the Pain Clinic during the three weeks I was there. Only two were men.

Chronic pain syndrome begins with damaged, inflamed nerves. Any nerve injury can trigger chronic pain, including fibromyalgia, migraine headaches, irritable bowel syndrome, arthritis, and LASIK. Inflammation in corneal nerves is what causes chronic pain in LASIK patients. This is easily visible on scans.

I learned at the Pain Center the central nervous system—the brain and the spinal cord—are *neuroplastic*, which means they change their structure in response to outside stimuli. Your brain remodels every time you form a new memory or learn a new skill.

If severe nerve inflammation lasts for more than three months, your brain starts to "turn up the volume" of pain messages coming into the brain from the peripheral nerves. Frantic pain signals start to whirl around inside your brain, running around and around in hard-wired, well-worn pathways. This process is called *central sensitization.*

Once your brain and spinal cord are re-wired by severe, long-lasting pain, a terrifying downward spiral begins. Everything in life starts to feel like torture, including things that once gave you joy. There is no easy escape from this.

The doctors I went to before I came to the Pain Center believed an obsolete and dead wrong theory of pain. They assumed my pain was caused by some mechanical problem in my spine. They deluged me with tests – MRIs, X-rays, CT scans, ultrasounds, and tests of nerve and muscle activity. They injected drugs into my spine. They even fused two of my lumbar vertebrae.

They were grievously ignorant about the latest findings in chronic pain research. Chronic pain is never caused by gross spine problems. Instead, it is caused by microscopic changes in the brain and spine that are not visible on scans. One of these microscopic changes is the death of *gating neurons* in the spine. Gating neurons act as "nursemaids" to the other nerves in your body. They feed the nerves, take away waste, and help them to communicate with other nerves.

Gating neurons sit right over the spot in your spine where pain nerves coming up from the body connect with the spinal nerves that carry signals up to the brain. Gating neurons act as watchmen in the spine. They decide how much pain to allow up to the brain. Once the gating neurons are destroyed by chronic pain, any signal coming up from the body—pain, touch, heat, cold, or pressure—roars straight up to the brain without any modulation.

In addition to receiving signals from sensory nerves, the gating neurons receive signals coming down from several brain centers, including the ones for fear, frustration, anger, and sadness. If you stub your toe, the amount of pain you feel depends partly on your emotional state at the time—happy or sad, optimistic, or pessimistic, anxious, or calm.

The severe pain in my left buttock made me anxious and lonely, which boosted my stress hormones, which made my pain worse, which made me lonelier and more anxious. A story started to race through my brain—my pain would never go away, and my life was over.

The pain must have destroyed most of my gating neurons. My spine surgery must have knocked off the few that remained. I imagine I did not have one gating neuron in my spine when I came to the Pain Center. Without any gating neurons to protect it, the pain centers in my brain went crazy. My *limbic* system—the "reptile brain" that processes emotions—took over and flooded my brain with fear and negative thoughts.

The pain center has flipped back the switch. My gating neurons have grown back. They will continue to protect me from chronic pain—but only as long as I continue to take Pristiq and stay away from opioids.

Diabetic patients need to take insulin every day. Patients with high blood pressure need to take diuretics. I need to take Pristiq. If I stop taking it, the gating neurons in my spine will disappear again, and my pain will return.

I learned at the Pain Center opioids are seductive quick fixes that end up backfiring. They work well for acute pain, but they make chronic pain worse. If opioids are taken every day for a long time, they enhance sensitivity to pain, instead of decreasing it. Patients get habituated, the opiates stop working, the pain and anxiety come back stronger, and the dose must be increased. Now they are hooked. The first thing the Pain Center does is to withdraw patients from opioids.

One of the pain management doctors I saw before I came to the Pain Center prescribed all his patients the same medicines, regardless of how long the pain had been there and how severe the pain was. He gave all of them opiates—such as morphine, *Fentanyl,* and *Oxycontin*—and tranquilizers, such as *Klonopin, Xanax,* and *Valium.* He was woefully ignorant about the evidence that opioids, in addition to being dangerous, are not effective for treating chronic pain.

Pristiq, and *Cymbalta,* a cousin of Pristiq, are the two drugs that are currently used to treat chronic pain. They are both antidepressants, which makes sense. Chronic pain runs through the same pathways in the brain as depression. These two drugs are the opposite of the quick fix opiates. The side effects are harrowing at the beginning. It takes time before the side effects fade, and the pain relief kicks in.

It is easy to feel sympathetic when somebody has obvious signs of injury—bruises, a cast, and bandages. When somebody has pain that is not visible, people often suspect they are malingering.

There were no tests available to diagnose chronic pain at the time I went to the Pain Center in 2012. The doctors had to take my word I was in pain. Today, it is easy to definitively diagnose chronic pain because all chronic pain patients have typical changes in their brain when they are tested with functional magnetic resonance imaging (fMRI).

Chronic pain affects approximately one-fifth of the world's population, so there is a huge market for new drugs that treat it. Pristiq and Cymbalta are the gold standard right now, but even more effective drugs are in the pipeline. They will be the biggest advance in pain management since the Sumerians discovered the opium-rich seeds of the poppy four thousand years ago.

In 2017, I had to take a compulsory New York State examination that was designed to teach doctors about chronic pain. It stated, repeatedly, doctors should use opiates at the smallest possible dose, for the shortest possible time. I passed easily. Finally, the word is getting out.

The only pain medication I take today is Pristiq. As that small square pink pill slides down my throat twice a day, I send a prayer of thanks to the scientists who invented it, and the doctors who gave it to me. When I see a flight of stairs, I remember how I once crept up and down, wincing with every step. Now, I float up and down easily. I am so proud of myself that I invent excuses to make extra trips up and down.

The doctors at the Pain Center warned me that if I get too tired, my pain will come back. They are right. I can no longer give way to euphoria and shove my body beyond its limits. I listen to my body now. When I start to feel stressed, and that familiar twinge starts up in my left buttock, this is an early warning signal that I must stop rushing around and pushing myself to be the best.

Very few pain stories have a happy ending, especially at my age. I feel the way cancer patients must feel when they go into remission. I am grateful for every day I am free of pain. I don't have time to be critical of myself or others. If I burn my hand, stub my toe, or cut myself, I ignore the pain.

My mind took over my brain, and almost killed me. I have, finally, learned how to control my mind. It is surprisingly simple. If an angry, anxious, negative, self-pitying thought creeps into my mind, I tell it to leave. If you want to find out how to do this, read *The Power of Now,* by Eckhart Tolle.

I was the perfect candidate to develop chronic pain. I have a family history of depression and manic depression. I spent my childhood obsessively trying to mother my mother. The injury I suffered during fox hunting was exacerbated by sitting on a motorcycle for long periods.

I learned as a child to put up a cheerful front, and never admit I had a problem. I got to the point where I could no longer function that way. I was burning myself up. The pain center turned off my perpetual motion machine and took the pressure off my stressed-out body and mind.

I discovered what caused my chronic pain when I went to my first yoga class a few weeks after I got home from the Pain Center. Everything went well until I tried to stretch my left hip across my body towards my right shoulder. That hip would not budge—not a quarter of an inch. It was frozen in place. It felt as if it was encased in cement.

I was mystified. What could have caused this curious restriction, and why was it only on one side of my body? Suddenly, I knew the answer. The source of my chronic pain must have been the accident I had when I was fox hunting, and my crazy horse, Briar Time, fell on my left hip and ripped it apart. Layers of scar tissue must have formed as the hip healed, although it was too thin to show up in the X-rays and MRIs.

The scar tissue prevented my left hip from moving normally, so some of the muscles in my hip and lower back became weak. Other muscles compensated by overacting and becoming stiff. Instead of having a balanced gait, with all the muscles working together, I was using a few over-strong muscles, while my over-weak muscles did nothing. My entire lower body was unbalanced.

I went after my left hip with determination. I stretched it twice a day, every day. Slowly, slowly, it began to move—half an inch, one inch, two inches. I also strengthened the weak muscles. After six months of stretching and exercising, the pain in my left buttock has vanished— hopefully forever.

I could have avoided all those injections, acupuncture treatments, physical therapy, and that horrible operation—by doing yoga. The irony is Hope had been telling me for years I should take up yoga.

Warren was everything I could have asked for, and more, during my year of chronic pain. He stayed right by my side. He did not blame me or tell me I was faking the pain. He helped me not only by supporting me, but also by being self-sufficient. He didn't go under when I went under.

The news was so bad before I went to the Pain Center my friends stopped asking about my pain. Now I am cured, they cannot hear enough about it. "How are you doing?" they say, as a slight smile of anticipation flickers around their lips. "My pain is almost completely gone." I tell them. "Today, I went kayaking for an hour. Yesterday, I took a two-hour bike ride."

Friends tell me I am brave and strong to have survived chronic pain. I do not think of myself as a hero. I am merely persistent. I kept smashing my head against doors until one door opened.

My goal now is to help other people with chronic pain. Please share this chapter with anybody who might have this syndrome. And remember this: If you have long-lasting pain, *do not take opioids*. Take *Pristiq* or *Cymbalta*. If you have severe reactions to Pristiq or Cymbalta, you may need to be an inpatient at a Pain Center.

CHAPTER TWENTY-THREE

Six Months to Live: 2014

A divorce lawyer told me divorce improves the life of both spouses when a marriage goes bad, and both will be happier afterwards, but the spouse who does not get the idea first is always mad. That was me. I was *much* happier after I was divorced from Malcolm, but I was angry at him for leaving me. I avoided him at family events. I refused to have any contact with him.

Then, one night, I had a dream. Malcolm sold our Brooklyn apartment and bought another one. He took me over to see it. It was a wreck. Plaster was falling off the ceiling, the walls were full of holes, it was filled with garbage, and the floor was flooded with a foul-smelling black liquid. "I need to buy a garbage can," I said. That woke me up.

I thought and thought about that dream. Suddenly, I knew what it was saying. I was holding a grudge against Malcolm for abandoning me. I could not let go of the false story I was a wronged woman. My anger was festering inside me like that putrid black liquid.

I re-read my diaries. They showed me how we built our marriage together. We were equally responsible for why it lasted thirty-nine years, and why it failed. Malcolm deserves fifty percent of the credit for our two extraordinary children. He had the guts and honesty to bust up a marriage that was destroying both of us. Divorce added years to both our lives.

I had not spoken to Malcolm in years. I called him up a few months after I came home from the Pain Center, and we met for dinner. We chatted away like the best of friends. He made a big effort. He had prepared a few jokes. He was nervous. He told one of them twice.

He was wearing a wedding ring. That was a surprise. He refused to wear a ring when he was married to me. When I commented on the ring, he said: "You have to compromise to have a good marriage." I suspect Malcolm feels married for the first time in his life.

I am grateful for the happy years we had together. Over the years, I changed, and he changed. For reasons beyond our control, Malcolm needed a different wife, and I needed a different husband. There is no blame in that.

Shortly after my dinner with Malcolm, on January 2, 2014, Warren called me into the bathroom and pointed to the toilet bowl. It was filled with red blotches that looked like cranberry jelly. Blood! My heart began to pound. When a man Warren's age has blood in his urine, he has cancer—either kidney, or bladder.

I rushed him to a urologist the next day. A scan showed he had bladder cancer that extended into his pelvis. I rushed into the ladies' room and vomited into the toilet.

As I sat trembling on the toilet seat, soaked in sweat, the wallpaper-remover began to emerge. I was Wonder Woman, a powerful surgeon. I knew the medical system. I would get Warren the best care in the world. I would save him.

I called an old friend who is the Chairman of Ophthalmology at Memorial-Sloane Kettering and asked for his help. Thirty minutes later, he called me back and told me the Chairman of Urology at MSK would see Warren the next morning. The doctor told us Warren had six months to live.

Our life became a blur of blood tests, scans, chemo sessions, transfusions, bad news, good news, and, finally, news so bad it was beyond comprehension.

I saw the full measure of Warren when he got cancer. He stayed upbeat and stoic. Unless I asked, he never complained about his debilitating fatigue and neuropathy. He did not want to be a burden to me, so he took charge of his problems as much as possible. When he had to wear a catheter in his penis, he invented a device to hang it up so he could sleep. The minute he began to feel better, he wanted to help me.

I continued to work during Warren's battle with cancer. While I was working, I was able to push Warren's problems to the back of my mind and focus on my patients' problems.

When I found Warren, I found the caring community I had dreamed of. I made many good friends in Rye, and they have big hearts. Every other day, the doorbell rang at 5 PM, and a friend brought us home-cooked food for two days. One of the husbands came over and cooked us pecan pancakes for breakfast.

I was so grateful for their thoughtfulness I almost cried. I was at the end of my rope. I was barely keeping my practice going. I was doing all the shopping, cooking, and washing up, but Warren had no appetite to eat the food I cooked. The new food stimulated his appetite. He was even more stimulated by the interest and concern of our friends.

Warren became weaker and weaker as the year dragged along. Eventually, he spent his days lying on a couch downstairs. One day, he looked up at me with that dazzling smile of his and said, "If this is as good as it gets, I'm enjoying life. I can read and watch TV and talk to my friends." He was telling me not to feel sorry for him.

During his last three months of life, this brilliant intellectual lost his ability to read. It broke my heart, but he wasn't fazed. He devised a project to keep his spirits up—he took all his books off the shelves, and organized them into categories: fiction, history, biography, spiritual, travel. He loved books so much he felt happy just holding them.

He was accepted into two promising drug trials. We kept our hopes up. Then, he began to go downhill with shocking speed. A scan showed he had cancer in his brain. Both drugs failed. He was dying. He never put his books back on the shelves.

He was admitted to Memorial Hospital. More scans. More IVs. More catheters. Surgery to put in a sieve in his leg vein to trap blood clots. Even more scans. How cruel to do all this to a dying man. I called his oncologist. I was so upset I was screaming. "Stop torturing him! You'll have him on the autopsy table in a week!" The oncologist hung up. He went to visit Warren and asked him if he wanted further heroic treatment. Warren said no.

Memorial Hospital knows how to tailor a perfect death. The nurses took out the catheters. They started a morphine drip and checked it every hour. If he complained of pain, they increased the dose. If he got agitated, they gave him medicine to calm him down. If he couldn't sleep, they gave him a sleeping pill. He died one week later, peaceful, and pain-free.

He could not speak when I visited him on his last conscious day. His face was a mask of despair. He knew exactly what was happening. I will remember his expression to my dying day.

I did not know what to do. How could I comfort him? I stroked his face. I hugged him. I told him I loved him. Nothing wiped that grief off his face. So, I did what Johnsons do at times of emotion—I climbed into his bed, put my arms around him, and, with tears streaming down my face, I began to sing.

I sang folk songs, gospel, popular songs, calypso. I sang "You Are My Sunshine", "Jamaica Farewell", "Clementine", "This Is My Island in the Sun", "Red River Valley", "Row, Row, Row Your Boat". His deep, resonant voice joined in from time to time.

Then it was time to go. His face was calm and peaceful. With his last ounce of strength, he whispered: "I love you so much." He slipped into a coma that night. He died two days later, on New Year's Eve, 2014. All my efforts to save him gave him only an extra six months of life.

I had always dreaded being with a dying person. My last day with Warren cured me of my fear. What he wanted was so simple—he needed to hear my voice one more time, so he could let go and die in peace.

When Warren was diagnosed with cancer, a friend told me I was lucky I was a doctor, so I could bear it more easily. She was wrong. If Warren had been my patient, I could have detached, but he was my husband. In the OR, I could pull myself together and function during stress. I could not do this when Warren died.

Part of me died when Warren died. I lost Warren, and I also lost the person I was when I was with Warren. I was inconsolable. All I could think about was Warren. Everything else was a blur. My grief was so all-consuming it frightened me. My brain did not work. I could not think. I could not plan. I felt crazy, frozen, numb, empty. When I tried to read, I could not remember a word after I put the book down. I was lucky Pristiq kept my chronic pain from coming back.

Then, the guilt began. I hadn't snuggled him enough. I wished he would die because he was suffering so much. I was angry at him for smoking, which caused his cancer. I felt relief when he died because I no longer had to take care of a desperately sick man. I was mad at him for dying and abandoning me. I did not bring him home to die—although I knew I could not have managed his pain as well as the hospital. I did not think I would ever enjoy life again.

I was lonely, but I did not do well in company. I wanted to talk about Warren, but most people changed the subject when I mentioned his name.

My friends invited me over too soon, and, once they did their duty, they stopped inviting me. I went to a dinner party a month after Warren died. Everybody was laughing. I was not in a fit state to enjoy this. I felt the way I felt at the Ellistan Sunday lunches—alienated from the merriment.

When one of my friends loses a loved one, I don't invite them to a big party during those first bad months. I call them, come to visit, talk to them. Mostly, I just listen.

I discovered how grief can scramble a brain a few months after Warren died, and I took a trip to Iceland with my daughter and two grandchildren. We walked off the plane in Keflavik airport well after midnight… and nobody came to meet us. I had not completed our tour booking. We had no reservations for hotels, no car, and no activities scheduled. Iceland has 370,000 residents. Two million tourists swarm the island during peak season.

Lucky for us, Icelanders are intelligent and good-hearted, 100% are literate, and everybody speaks English. We were saved by a kind taxi driver, who found us lodgings in Reykjavik. Hope hired a travel agent the next day, and he scrounged up a rental car for us and made bookings at the major sights.

Despite the agent's best efforts, he could not find a place for us to spend the night before we were scheduled to drive from the Golden Triangle to Vannajokull, the largest glacier in Europe. I told Hope we would buy camping gear and sleep outside for the night.

My twelve-year-old grandson Wilder heard us. He hauled out his computer, and his fingers began to fly. In ten minutes, he found us a place to stay. There was only one problem. It was on an island.

We barely made the last ferry to Heimaey, one of the volcanic Vestmannaeyjar Islands. We crossed a wild bay, then slipped past towering cliffs skimmed by puffins and topped with sheep lifted to the grassy tops by resourceful Icelanders to fatten up during the summer, into a harbor filled with fishing boats.

We had the trip of our lives. We stayed in places most tourists never see. We saved thousands of dollars… and I learned women who have recently lost their husbands cannot be trusted with travel arrangements.

I felt a strange clarity after Warren died, His life had been so precious everything else in my life seemed trivial. If my sister began to bicker with her husband, I wanted to scream at them, "Stop! One of you could die tomorrow!"

Tolstoy describes this peculiar lucidity in his novel *War and Peace*. Prince Andrei falls, mortally wounded, at the Battle of Borodino. He looks up at the sky, immense, calm, and beautiful, and he thinks if people just lay on their backs and looked up at the sky, all war would end.

The mental clarity I felt after Warren's death lasted one year. After that, the common details of everyday life gradually replaced it. It was too poignant and painful to sustain.

The only time I could function—and function well—during the year after Warren died was when I was at work. My work buoyed me up through the year he was sick, and it sustained me after he died. As I helped other people with their problems, I felt my own problems less.

Warren and I had a prenuptial agreement. His will said I could live for one year in the house we shared for eleven years. After that, I had to move. I could either go back to Brooklyn Heights or find another house in Rye. I never hesitated. My home was Rye.

I bought a house in nearby Rye Brook. My friends did not wait for me to ask them for help; they just came over and helped. One friend helped me pack up Warren's house and helped unpack the new house a week later.

Each time, she brought lunch. Another friend designed my garden. Another, an architect, drew up plans for my master bathroom. Another decorated my house. Another was my lawyer for the purchase.

Clearing out Warren's house was a series of painful goodbyes. Everything in the house reminded me of him. I had to go through all his clothes, his books, his favorite chair, all those photographs; cry; and then decide what to do with them.

I discovered my absent-minded professor husband was almost as much of a hoarder as my mother. I unearthed four turkey roasting pans, fifty-six champagne flutes (most in their original boxes), six cans of WD40, enough drinking glasses to stock a small army, three coffee makers, and several dozen fine quality wool suits, thickly spattered with mold.

This project was a blessing in disguise. Busy hands kept my mind from brooding. I gave away and gave away. Slowly and steadily, I dismantled our life together. Item by item, I said goodbye to Warren.

Then I had to decide how long to wear Warren's wedding ring. Some of my friends took off their rings as soon as their husbands died. Others kept theirs on until the day they died. I wore Warren's ring for a year. Then I realized his death did not mean he was no longer with me.

I took off his ring, and put it in my jewelry box. It fits perfectly inside Warren's ring. When I open the box, I see them gleaming, tucked around each other, and I shake my head and smile.

I will miss this effervescent man with his big laugh for the rest of my life, but I have not lost him. Closeness does not go away after a physical body is gone. He will always be right there, deep down inside my heart.

Most people never have what Warren and I had. We had enough joy and fun and adventure and excitement for a lifetime. If I die tomorrow, I will have loved, and been loved. Nothing can take that away from me.

Warren's death dominated my life for a year. Then, I realized I could not let it dominate the rest of my life. I did not want to define myself as a widow. I had to be me, not the wife of a dead man. I didn't want to give up on life, growth, and new experiences. I wanted to celebrate him, not mourn him. I had to stop moping, move on from his loss, and make the rest of my life mean something. If I was going to live, I would have to let go of my grief.

I tackled widowhood the way I tackle all problems—as something I could solve with hard work and determination. I read several books on grief. *A Grief Observed,* by C. S Lewis, was especially helpful. I reached out to other widows. I joined a bereavement group. Slowly, I built a patchwork quilt of friends and family to replace the comforter of Warren's love.

If somebody tells me their spouse has died, I tell them I understand grief. I recommend the things that helped me.

And I listen.

CHAPTER TWENTY-FOUR

An Autumn Romance

Warren and I socialized for years with Arthur Stampleman, a classmate of Warren's at Harvard Business School, and his wife, Nancy. Arthur visited Warren often after he got cancer. I was impressed by his generosity and thoughtfulness.

Nancy died five weeks after Warren died. When I invited Arthur over for dinner two weeks later, romance was the last thing on my mind. I would have laughed out loud if somebody suggested I might marry him. I thought he was a friend I could help—period.

When Warren was alive, I had someone who listened, understood, and cared. If we were apart during the day, we stored up news we would tell each other over dinner. After he died, I lost the one person who was interested in what had happened to me during each day—all the little moments that make up a life. I did not come first with anybody anymore.

I suggested Arthur and I call each other every night, to check in. As we talked week after week, I began to realize Arthur was sensitive, super smart, and—most important—kind.

Arthur grew up in Montreal. His parents immigrated to the U.S. from Vilna, Lithuania in the early 1900s. He worked at Citibank for thirty-six years. After he retired, he became a docent at the Bruce Museum in Greenwich. He is not shy, exactly, but he is formal. He wears a coat and tie, when other men wear sweaters. I did not know him well.

A new Arthur emerged when we began to go to concerts, art exhibits, theatre, and opera. Under that formal exterior lay an original mind. Bubbling curiosity. An impish sense of humor. Zest for life. Optimism. Flexibility. Generosity. Steadiness. Common sense mixed with fierce intelligence. An excellent listener. I admired his scheduling talents, his persistence, and his loyalty. I even—most of the time—enjoyed his puns.

I forgot my hearing aids when we were at a cocktail party one evening. Arthur gave me one of his. This was a better present than diamonds or mink.

I unconsciously absorbed my mother's belief that bankers are boring. Arthur showed me that was just as silly as believing surgeons are not creative. He likes to schedule something every hour of the day. For the first time in my life, I had to rein in an overly enthusiastic man.

I was impressed when I watched Arthur run a meeting. He reminded me of an expert conductor coaxing a superb performance from a bunch of balky musicians. He made a list of topics to discuss ahead of time and gave everybody a copy. He was calm, and succinct, and he never raised his voice, but, somehow, we discussed every topic, everyone had a chance to speak, and the meeting ended right on time.

Arthur had a happy, uncomplicated childhood, so he turned into a happy, uncomplicated man. His family had dinner together every night. His parents were warm and involved. He said his relationship with them was so natural he never thought about it. Now, that is a novel idea. My parents were so distant it that was hard to believe they cared about me.

It was not love at first sight, or second sight, but after a year's worth of sights, I was thoroughly in love with Arthur. He made me feel happy and safe. He brought joy into my life when I thought I would never feel it again. I liked the person I was when I was with him—comfortable and relaxed. Like Warren, he was delighted I had a life of my own without him.

He proposed marriage after we dated for six months. I said *no*. I vowed I would never marry again. It was heart-wrenching to lose Warren. I did not want to be a widow again. I thought I could never love anybody as much as I loved Warren. I also felt we did not know each other well enough. I knew from personal experience marriages can fail. Arthur did not. He fell in love with Nancy, married her, and they lived happily until she died.

My resistance to marrying Arthur began to crumble in August of 2016, when I visited Lynn and Peter in Martha's Vineyard. I ran into rough surf, and injured my knee so badly I could not drive myself home. I knew if I asked Arthur to fly up and drive me back to Rye, he would come. He did.

I looked at marriage to Arthur full in the face. I knew we would face serious problems in the near future. One of us—probably me—would end up taking care of the other. I wanted a companion with a level head, a sense of humor, and high principles—a man I could trust and respect. That is Arthur. I decided to live whatever life I had left fiercely, passionately, and with Arthur. When I was seventy-four, and he was eighty-one, I said *yes*.

My first wedding was Episcopalian. My second was Presbyterian. Arthur and I had a Jewish ceremony. Rabbi Robert Rothman married us under a chuppah at Wainwright House in Rye on December 29, 2016— the one date that fit the schedules of our six grandchildren. Arthur smashed a glass with his foot. We drank kosher wine from a silver cup that Arthur's father had brought from Lithuania.

Our granddaughters were our bridesmaids. My grandson Wilder walked me down the aisle. Arthur's grandson, Sam, carried my ring. Our grandchildren became friends on Instagram before they met.

Pictured: Marriage of Cynthia Johnson MacKay and Arthur Stampleman, December 29, 2016, with assorted grandchildren.

Then Arthur moved into my house, bringing his art collection with him. My mother taught me to appreciate artists of the late nineteenth and early twentieth century. Now, I live with modern art.

One of the things that made me nervous about marrying Arthur was he is so different from Warren, and I am so different from Nancy, yet it has worked. We have an affectionate, fun, easygoing relationship that is the rock under our lives. We feel comfortable in our own skins, so we feel comfortable with each other. We talk over every decision. We compromise. We sort out disagreements quickly.

I thought my marriage to Arthur would be only a pleasant friendship and companionship. It is much more. We have a real romance. We know we will not have much time together, so we relish every minute. He makes me feel young again. Our relationship is so natural we never think about it. You cannot ask for more.

Arthur keeps his brain tuned to Cynthia. He is reasonable and fair. He listens. He remembers my likes, dislikes, and schedule better than I do—although, for other matters, his short-term memory is not great. That is devotion.

We have not forgotten our previous spouses. He often calls me "Nancy." I often call him "Warren." They showed us how to build a good marriage. We used those skills to build another good marriage.

We overlapped at Harvard for one year, 1960-1961, when I was a freshman at the college, and he was a second-year student at the Business School. We never met, but we agree we would not have married if we had. We were each looking for somebody different. Arthur's parents might not have been happy if he married a gentile. My parents might not have approved of Arthur—*or* Warren, for that matter.

When we go to bed at night, Arthur falls asleep the minute his head hits the pillow. I toss, turn, read, and toss some more. Finally, I wriggle over to him. He doesn't wake up, but one arm shoots out and hauls me in close. I grunt with happiness. I tailor my breathing to his. My muscles relax. I go to sleep.

One night, we are sleeping wound up together when he wakes me to tell me he needs to turn over because he has pain in one of his legs. "How about you?" he asks. "I have pain in my left hip and my right knee," I reply. "That's a pain in the ass," he says. I start to shake with laughter. He joins in. Here we are, two creaky octogenarians, laughing uncontrollably in the middle of the night in the pitch dark.

On August 16, 2018, after two years of marriage to Arthur, I retired, after forty years of ophthalmology. I was one month shy of seventy-six. I dreaded retirement. I kept going as long as I could. I could not think of anything I would love as much as my medical career.

Retirement was like a small death in the beginning. I was rudely ejected from an intensely satisfying world. I thought I would never find anything as exhilarating as sailing through a case in the OR, or shooting bursts of laser light into an eye, healing it with my own hands. I had to leave my colleagues, who were shaping the world of ophthalmology. I left my patients and the one-sided intimacy that bound us together. We enjoyed an ever-changing celebration that rolled along for forty years.

During the years I practiced medicine, I never had to worry about what I was going to do each day. Now, Dr. Cynthia MacKay was gone. I had to re-invent myself as plain old Cynthia MacKay.

All my ophthalmology friends are men, because so few women during my era were ophthalmologists. It is more difficult for a woman to keep up a friendship with a man compared to a woman. Now, I have had a chance to build friendships with some amazing women.

My life is more playful since I retired. I can follow my curiosity instead of plugging along dutifully solving problems for other people. I even enjoy some of the feminine pursuits I scorned when I was a child – such as cooking and shopping for clothes.

Arthur and I go to the theatre, art exhibits, chamber music and orchestra concerts, opera, and lectures. Of course, I still sing. We take courses online from *One Day University* and the *Smithsonian*. And I wrote this memoir. I do not have enough hours in the day to do all the things I want to do.

I miss my practice and my patients, but my dreams tell me it was time to leave.

In one dream, I am at a huge party at one of New York's most prestigious private clubs. All the best people are there. I overhear one waiter saying to another that one thousand guests are present. The host is my patient. I have removed both of his cataracts. When he greets me, I scan his eyes anxiously, worried that his pupils are not equal.

In another dream, I have operated on the eyes of two children, but I have not yet sutured the incisions. They jump off the operating table and start to run around. I finally persuade one to lie down, and—without a microscope—begin to sew. My suture falls on dirty ground. In yet another, I am in the middle of an operation when a fly lands on the eye.

I am glad I am no longer in the operating room.

My therapist disapproved of the way I snuck out of the OR without saying goodbye, trying to avoid a farewell party. She gave me an assignment: enjoy my last days with my patients and accept their thanks graciously. I always feel uncomfortable when people praise me—I think I am only doing my job—but I obeyed.

Some patients hugged me. Others cried. Others sent letters, cards, emails, flowers, chocolates, champagne. Some said I made a big difference in their lives. One said they do not make doctors like me these days. Another told me I was more than her doctor; I was her psychologist. Another wrote I was the light at the end of his dark journey of sight. Several came to the office without any reason except to wish me goodbye.

I felt touched, embarrassed, guilty for leaving—and grateful.

I did manage to survive in a man's world, against all odds. I fought my way out of a world of leisure and privilege, and into a world of high-stakes, top-flight medicine. I had the privilege of restoring vision, and preventing blindness, for tens of thousands of patients. I have taught hundreds of eye residents—all so eager to learn, so diligent, so determined to do their best. They remind me of me when I was their age.

I have mentored other women. I invited several women, including Harvard undergraduates who were thinking of going to medical school, to stay with me and shadow me in the OR and office. When I was on the Admissions Committee of the Harkness Eye Institute, I pushed to admit women, including a friend of Hope who is a respected surgeon at Massachusetts Eye and Ear Infirmary. I have led a useful life.

Hope told me I have lived multiple lifetimes in my life. She is right.

I recently had a dream I was back at Ellistan giving a talk about glaucoma to a dozen children. Despite much chaos, it goes well. Most of them get the point. One girl writes an excellent, clear, summary. My parents and grandparents are sitting near the wall with a dozen other Far Hills grandees. They seem pleased. I have used my medical credentials to get the approval I longed for as a child.

I did not look forward to my seventies, but to my surprise this decade has turned out to be the happiest of my life. I spent my first six decades striving to become something—a college graduate, a wife, a mother, an eye surgeon. I worried constantly whether I was doing enough. I heard praise in a whisper, and criticism in a loudspeaker. I was so critical of myself, and so driven to be perfect, that if somebody got angry at me, I was paralyzed by guilt.

The door has not closed in my old age, it has opened to new friends and interests. I no longer need to prove myself. I am who I am. I can do what I want, instead of single-mindedly doing what I think I ought to do.

I am starting to look like my mother when she was my age. She hated those loose folds of skin under her chin I am beginning to develop. She called them her "wattles". I suspect she disliked her wattles because she thought they prevented her from attracting men. I do not resent my wattles. They sometimes get me a seat in the subway. If a man does not want me because of my wattles, I have no interest in him.

I regret the harsh view I had of my parents. I was immature, petty, judgmental, and wrong. I now believe they were neither gods, nor devils, but decent, well-intentioned people who did their best. They were clueless, but they were not malicious. They had no choice but to raise me the way they themselves were raised.

I often dream about my mother. My dreams are always the same. She has decorated herself, her room, or her house in an explosion of flamboyant colors—shocking pink, flame red, mustard yellow, sizzling scarlet, passionate purple, and, always, her favorite color, bluish-green, or greenish blue. She sits in the middle of the delirious riot she has created, smiling her pussy smile. She dares me to criticize her.

I cannot find a single fault in her. I cheer her on. Her indominable, fiery, unstoppable spirit lives on in me, my children, and my grandchildren. Do I regret how cross I was with her, back in the days when I longed for a different mother? You bet.

An avid fox hunter bought my grandparents' house in Far Hills. The stables are running full tilt again, and the Essex Fox Hounds still meets there on Thanksgiving Day. The "stirrup cup" Tom the butler brought with him from England is still served hot, but they make it with a lot less alcohol and a lot more fruit juice.

The couple who bought my family's house appreciates its fine bones. They have restored it with so much love and attention that it looks even better than when we lived there. They have converted my mother's studio into a library and office. The wife is a poet, so the great room with the high ceiling is still used to create art.

I made peace with my mother, but I think most often of my father. There he is—the center of all eyes at a beach picnic. The black sky is studded with stars. Red sparks dance in the bonfire. The sea breeze is gentle now. The only sounds are the soft hiss of the waves, and an occasional pop from the fire.

My father begins to sing one of his favorite songs.

It is: "Who Could Ask for Anything More?"

EPILOGUE

When I started to think seriously about going to medical school, I did not know how I would survive four years of medical school, a year of internship, three years of surgical training, and a fellowship—while caring for two young children.

I succeeded because I had a clear goal, I took one day at a time, and I worked hard. My children were healthy, and I made a big effort to spend quality time with them. My husband was on board, and I never gave up.

I am fortunate I had role models within my own family who showed me success comes with determination and hard work. I am also lucky my parents were able to send me to good schools, thanks to the dogged toil of my father, who commuted without complaint five hours every weekday for years.

I had a suspicion it would not be easy to survive in a man's world. This turned out to be true. However, I got there eventually, and my practice was successful because many people prefer a woman doctor.

Women earned fifty-nine cents for every dollar made by a man doing the same work when I was a child. In 1963, when I was twenty, the Equal Pay Act was passed, which mandated women must get equal pay for equal work.

In 2023, women working full time year-round were paid roughly eighty-four percent of what men were paid. If Stanley Bosworth tried to pay a woman less than half the salary of a man with the same credentials today, he would be slapped with a gender discrimination suit before he could blink.

Women have made gains in many fields where they were underrepresented. This is especially true of the man's world of medicine I had to deal with.

- US medicine is on track to become a female-dominated profession. Women outnumber men in medical school today. In

2021-2022, fifty-seven percent of applicants to US medical schools, and fifty-three percent of enrollments, were women.

- One-third of current graduates in STEM fields, and forty percent of students in business schools, are women.
- Women are now the majority in law schools.

When I was trying to decide whether to apply to medical school, I could not find any research that would tell me if women had the talent to be surgeons. Two studies published in *JAMA Surgery* online in August 2023 give the answer.

One study, *Surgeon Sex and Long-Term Postoperative Outcomes*, was done at Mount Sinai Hospital and affiliates in Toronto. The researchers studied the outcomes, at ninety days and one year after surgery, of over a million Canadian patients who had one of twenty-five common operations between 2007 and 2019. One hundred and fifty-one thousand, or roughly fifteen percent of these procedures, were done by women.

The study clearly showed patients operated on by female surgeons were *significantly less likely* to experience death, hospital readmission, or major medical complications.

Another study, done in Sweden, looked at more than one hundred and fifty thousand patients who had their gall bladders removed between 2006 and 2019. Again, the women did better than the men. The researchers found female surgeons converted to open surgery less frequently and had significantly fewer surgical complications, and their patients had shorter hospital stays.

The reason for the sex discrepancy found in these two studies is not entirely clear. The Swedish study noted the female surgeons operated more slowly. Since the women took more time to complete operations, the team speculated the women surgeons might be more methodical and less likely to take risks. I quote: "Being accurate and careful … beats risk-taking and speed when it comes to consistently achieving good outcomes."

I hope many more young female medical students will decide to be surgeons.

Thank you for reading this book. I have been lucky to have the job of my dreams. I encourage you to achieve your own dreams. All it takes is persistence, persistence, and more persistence.

APPENDIX A: *The Structure of The Eye*

In this appendix you'll find a brief description of the eye and many of its parts, to help you better appreciate the various procedures and conditions described in this book.

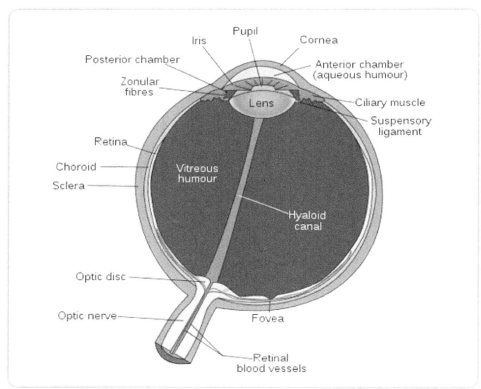

Pictured: The eye and its associated parts.

What is my:–

1. CORNEA?

Your CORNEA is the transparent, curved window in the front of your eye. All the light that enters your eye comes through your cornea. Your cornea has three layers: the EPITHELIUM, the part that is exposed to the air; the ENDOTHELIUM, the innermost layer; and the STROMA, the layer in the middle. Like every part of your body, your cornea needs nourishment, but it must be free of blood vessels to maintain its clarity, so, instead of blood, the epithelium is nourished by your tears, and the stroma and endothelium by your AQUEOUS HUMOR, the clear liquid that fills the front compartment of your eye. Your cornea provides roughly 70% of the focusing power of the eye, the rest being provided by your LENS.

2. LENS?

Your lens is a transparent structure the size and shape of an *M&M* candy. It is suspended by thin strands, called ZONULES, from a structure called the CILIARY MUSCLE, which runs around your eye immediately behind your IRIS. Your lens has an inner, tougher center, called the NUCLEUS; a softer outer layer, called the CORTEX; and a skin, called the CAPSULE. When you focus up close, your ciliary muscle contracts, and your lens gets fatter. When this muscle relaxes, your lens gets thinner, and your eye focuses at distance. Your lens grows all through your life, adding one layer each year. As your lens gets larger, it gets stiffer, and harder to focus. By the time you are in your forties you will no longer be able to change the focus of your lens, so you will need magnifying glasses to read. A cloudy lens is called a CATARACT.

3. IRIS?

Your IRIS is the part of your eye that gives it color. It is a muscle that is the shape of a lifesaver. Your iris acts like a window shade, opening and closing automatically to change the size of your PUPIL, the black opening in its center. This regulates the amount of light admitted into your eye. The color of your iris—brown, blue, or green—is determined by the amount and distribution of a pigment, MELANIN. Brown eyes have more melanin than blue eyes, so they are less sensitive to bright light.

4. SCLERA?

Your SCLERA is the tough white outer covering of your eye.

5. CONJUNCTIVA?

Your conjunctiva is the flexible, clear mucous membrane that covers the inside of your lids, and the outside of your sclera. Hair-thin arteries and veins run through it. If these blood vessels become inflamed, you have CONJUNCTIVITIS. Your conjunctiva keeps your eye moist. It is studded with GOBLET CELLS, which produce mucous, an important part of your tears.

6. TEAR FILM?

Tears protect, clean and lubricate your eye. Normal tears have three layers: an outer layer of OIL, which prevents your tears from evaporating; an inner layer of MUCOUS, which keeps your tears attached to your eye; and a middle watery layer, which is complex and fascinating. This middle layer is like your blood, but without cells. It contains most of the substances found in blood, including salts, sugar, hormones, and antibodies that protect against invading organisms. It is especially high in Vitamin C. Most of your middle layer is produced by your LACRIMAL GLANDS, bean-sized glands which lie just above each upper eyelid. The oil in your tears is made by little bottle-shaped glands, called MEIBOMIAN GLANDS, which are found along the margins of all four eye lids.

7. AQUEOUS?

AQUEOUS is a clear fluid that circulates steadily through the ANTERIOR CHAMBER of your eye, night and day, bringing oxygen and sugar to your cornea and lens, and taking away wastes. This fluid is produced by your CILIARY BODY, which runs around the eye just behind the iris, near the ciliary muscle. Aqueous drains out of your eye through the TRABECULAR MESHWORK, into SCHLEMM'S CANAL and then into the veins around your eye. Normally, inflow equals outflow, so the pressure inside your eye is maintained between 8 and 22 millimeters of mercury. If your eye has a drain that is not working properly, the pressure inside your eye will rise. This high pressure will eventually damage your OPTIC NERVE, and you will start to go blind. This is *GLAUCOMA*.

8. VITREOUS?

The VITREOUS is the transparent jelly that fills the POSTERIOR CHAMBER of your eye. The vitreous is firm and clear when you are young. As you get older, it gets less firm, and more watery. It eventually collapses on itself, like a tent folding, or a balloon that has lost its air. Because this process detaches the vitreous from the RETINA, it is called a VITREOUS DETACHMENT. After your vitreous detaches you will notice strands called FLOATERS.

9. RETINA?

Your RETINA is an extension of your brain. It is the light-sensitive nerve tissue that lines the inside of your eye, like the film inside a camera. It has twelve layers. When light is focused by the cornea and lens onto your retina, millions of tiny PHOTORECEPTORS give off electrical signals. These signals feed into 1.2 million OPTIC NERVE fibers. The optic nerve acts as a cable, carrying this information up to the VISUAL CORTEX, which is in the OCCIPITAL LOBE, in the back of your brain. Most human blindness is caused by diseases of the retina: in infants, amblyopia, or lazy eye; in adults, diabetic retinopathy; in the elderly, macular degeneration.

10. RODS AND CONES?

Photoreceptors come in two different types, 120 million RODS, and 6 5 million CONES. Your rods, mainly located in the periphery of your retina, are super sensitive. They operate only when the light is dim. They can only detect large forms and shapes, in black, white, and shades of gray. Cones, located mainly in the center of the retina, operate in bright light. The ones in your MACULA enable your eye to see details. There are three different types of cones: red, green, and blue. This allows you to have color vision.

11. RETINAL PIGMENT EPITHELIUM?

The retina sits on top of a layer of darkly pigmented cells called the RETINAL PIGMENT EPITHELIUM, or RPE. The RPE is packed with melanin, which absorbs scattered and reflected light. The RPE acts as a nurse for the retina, trimming off the aging tops of the photoreceptors every day, and bringing the retina the chemicals it needs for vision.

12. MACULA?

The MACULA is a tiny area right in the center of your retina. Although it is only the size of the head of a pin, it is responsible for all your detailed sight. 90% of the signals that go to your occipital lobe come from your macula. If your macula is damaged, you will no longer be able to read, drive, or recognize faces. You will, in fact, be legally blind, although you will still retain your peripheral vision. The little indentation in the very center of your macula is called your FOVEA. The fovea provides your most detailed sight. There are no blood vessels, and no rods, in the fovea.

13. THE BLOOD SUPPLY OF YOUR RETINA?
The inner third of your retina is nourished by your CENTRAL RETINAL ARTERY (CRA) and CENTRAL RETINAL VEIN (CRV). These enter and leave your eye at the OPTIC DISK, the place where the optic nerve originates. They fork, like the branches of a tree, as they run out to the periphery of the retina. The outer two thirds of your retina is nourished by your CHOROID, a thick layer of blood vessels sandwiched between your RPE and your sclera. The retina and the conjunctiva are the only parts of your body where your doctor can see your blood vessels. When a doctor looks at these blood vessels, he gets information about the health of your body.

14. THE EYE MUSCLE SYSTEM?
There are six tiny muscles connected to each of your eyes. They are the size of thick rubber bands. They pull the eye up and down, left and right, and clockwise and counterclockwise. These muscles are commanded and coordinated by three nerves, located in the brain stem.

Made in the USA
Columbia, SC
04 September 2024

41504009R00183